MW00624567

Mafia Made

A True Story of Murder, Racketeering, and Drug Trafficking

By Anthony Caucci & Rebecca Caucci

dragon
*tree*books

1620 SW 5th Avenue
Pompano Beach, Florida 33060
(954)788-4775
editors@editingforauthors.com
dragontreebooks.com

Acknowledgments

All credit goes to the love of my life, Rebecca Caucci. Without her, this book would have never been written. From the beginning to the end, she spent countless hours writing and interviewing me. This book was Rebecca's dream, and she has made her dream a reality.

To my daughter, Sabella. Because of you, I see the world in a whole new way. You are my life.

I would like to thank my mother Suzanne Caucci for showing me how to get through some of the toughest times in my life. She is a true inspiration and has never left my side. I love you always and forever.

And thanks to Jon VanZile for his wisdom and professionalism during the editing and book formatting process. He's an absolute expert in every way.

Disclaimer

In order for the reader to get the best experience out of this book, we wrote this book to reflect the facts and events as they actually took place. To stay true to the story, we used language that may offend people, including racial terms. We made the decision to include this language to stay authentic to the time and place covered in this book. We believe that all races are perfectly equal and emphatically oppose racism at every level.

Prologue: They Tried to Cut His Head Off

The way I grew up, I learned my most important lessons outside of school—usually at a bar, where my dad did most of his business.

I remember one lesson real well. I was five years old, and it was the mid-1970s. I was with my dad, in one of his regular bars where all the South Florida Mobsters did business. There was a guy there named George Byrum who went by the name of Dick Byrum. He was a close family friend who often took my parents to the Bahamas on his boat and came around a lot for dinner. He was like an uncle to me and my older brother Marc.

On this particular day, I went to the restroom to take a leak. I was using the urinal when I heard the door slam open and a guy screaming. Two big guys were beating the shit outta someone. I just stood facing the wall, afraid to turn around to see what was happening. It was Dick screaming.

One of the two men doing the beating was Tony Plate, nicknamed Pit Bull or TP. Tony was also a close family friend. He earned his nickname because he was known to be a vicious Mafia hit man. One time he threatened to bite a chunk out of someone's face if the guy didn't pay back his loan. People were so afraid of him that even some of his own crew were scared to get in a car with him. Tony was a "made man," in charge of overseeing operations in Florida for the Gambino family. He reported to the underboss Neil Dellacroce.

Not only was Plate notorious for being a cold-blooded killer, he had a look in his eyes that projected pure evil and scared the shit out of most grown men—and he also gave a hell of a piggyback ride. I liked him because he was always very nice to me and always good for a $20.

I was scared. I had never heard a grown man beg for his life, especially a man I knew and loved—and the man doing the work on him was also someone I loved. I watched them just pulverize my friend Dick until they got tired. Dick kept screaming, "I'll have the money on Wednesday, I promise!"

When they were done beating him, Plate said, "You're lucky I don't kill you."

Plate looked at me, gave me a wink, and said, "Hey son, bring me a drink. I'm sweating like a whore in church here."

"Okay, Tony." As I went to open the door, I noticed there was blood on the brand-new shoes my mother had just bought me. "Damn. My mom's gonna kill me. I just got these."

"What's wrong, kiddo?" Plate replied.

I showed him my shoes. Then he looked at bloody Dick on the floor and screamed, "Look what you did to the kid's shoes, you fucking piece of shit!" They beat the shit out of him some more, then Plate looked down at me, panting, and said, "Don't worry. I'll talk to your mom." Then he said to Dick, "You better have two new pairs for him tomorrow, you prick, or I'll break your fucking legs."

"Okay! Okay! Okay!" Dick barely got the words out.

"What size shoe, kid?" Plate asked me.

"I don't know, Tony," I replied nervously.

Plate washed the blood off his hands at the sink, kneeled down to look inside my shoe, and said, "You're a twelve, kid."

"Okay thanks, Tony."

I got out of there and told my dad what had happened to Dick. He looked me in the eyes and said, "Listen, Dick did a bad thing and he's paying the price for it. But the story is, he fell and hit his head on the sink, got it?"

"Yeah, I got it, Pop. But Dick's in real bad shape, there's blood everywhere."

"Okay, go in the kitchen, get some towels, and clean up the mess. But don't run…act like everything is normal."

"Pop, Tony wants a drink too. What should I bring him?"

"He just had a workout…bring him a beer." He chuckled.

I got Tony's beer and as many towels as I could find, then I went back to the restroom and handed Tony the beer on his way out the door. He quickly drank the whole bottle and said, "You're a life-saver, kid. You see that pathetic mutt lying on the floor in a pool of his own blood? Grab his wallet and take $50 for having to clean his mess up."

"Okay, Tony."

"And be careful. Make sure you don't slip and hit your head. I'll never hear the end of it from your mother."

I slowly walked over to Dick, trying not to slip, and put my hands into his pockets to find some cash.

"Whaddya doing, kid? Reading him a bedtime story?" Tony said.

"I got it, Tony."

Dick winked at me, as if to say, "It's okay." Tony and his goon walked out, and the goon guarded the door from the other side. Dick was lying on the floor with his head propped up on the wall. The place was covered with his blood, like the inside of a slaughterhouse. I didn't know where to begin.

I turned the faucet on and cleaned as fast as I could. I could see Dick from the corner of my eye and could tell he was breathing okay. He was bleeding from his nose, mouth, and ears, and missing a tooth or two. What did he do to deserve this? He always seemed like a real good guy. Why would they beat him so badly over money? There had to be something else to it, but I couldn't figure it out. One minute he's at the bar drinking with his friends, and the next minute the same guys are beating the living shit outta him.

As I cleaned, Dick grabbed my hand. I stopped and looked at him. Hardly able to talk, he said, "Sorry, pal."

"For what?" I asked, feeling sorry for him.

"For getting blood on your new shoes. You shouldn't have had to see any of this. I'll get you some new ones tomorrow." Then he spit a tooth onto the floor.

"Okay, Dick." I put a hand on his shoulder and said, "Are you gonna be okay?" He just closed his eyes and let out a big sigh.

I opened the door and told the goon waiting outside that I was done. He rubbed my head and pinched me on the cheek. "You're a good kid," he said and smiled.

I took a seat next to my dad at the bar and gave him a soft elbow to his ribs to get his attention. He looked down at me with a curious look. I gave him a nod, as if to say follow me, then I jumped off the stool and stood near the juke box, pretending to pick a song. My dad came over to stand next to me. "Why did that happen to Dick?" I asked quietly.

He reached into his pocket to get a dollar for the machine and said, "Listen, never, ever steal from your friends and always pay your debts. Do you remember that house we went to last weekend that needed a few walls painted?"

"Yeah...that guy Anthony...what the fuck's his last name?"

"Hey, you watch your mouth!"

"Sorry, Pop."

"His name is Anthony Gaggi, and he's a capo with the Gambino family. Dick told a couple of scumbag thieves they could make an easy score robbing Gaggi's house. The problem was, nobody was supposed to be there, and they didn't realize who Gaggi was. The thieves pulled a gun on Gaggi and threw him a beating while his wife watched. So they had to teach Dick a lesson. Dick did a very bad thing, son. He was trusted with something from a very important man, and he thought he could make a couple of bucks by organizing a robbery. Poor Dick thinks he's taking a beating because of a gambling debt, but little does he know this is just the beginning. The word got out that Dick organized the whole thing and he will have to pay the price. He just doesn't know it yet."

"Is this how you teach an adult a lesson?" I thought, "I'll never complain again when Mom punishes me."

A few weeks later after school, I heard my mom crying in her room. The door was cracked open, so I peeked in to see what was going on. She was talking on the phone. "Did you hear about what happened to Dick? He's dead. They killed him! They cut off both his arms and legs and tried to cut his head off. They pulled his pants down to his knees and left him in a bathtub in a Miami hotel, where a maid found him."

I quietly backed away from the door and tip-toed to my room. Sitting on my bed, I remembered the sadness in Dick's eyes, like he knew exactly what was coming. I liked Dick, he was my friend. Even in a pool of his own blood, he still tried to make me feel better. But the truth was, I knew he did the wrong thing. I remembered my dad saying, "This is just the beginning." It all came together. This was the real punishment my dad was talking about. I didn't think it could get any worse than what I had seen in the bathroom, but I was only five…what did I know? This lesson would follow me through my entire life: this is what happens when you steal from friends. I made a promise to myself then and there: I'll never steal from my friends.

I looked down at my new pair of sneakers and thought of Dick. I knew I'd miss him…and his big tips.

I tried to go to sleep, but I could hear my mom sobbing. I couldn't even tell her what had really happened to Dick or what I had seen in the bathroom. It kept playing over and over in my mind, all that blood. Silent tears dripped down my face.

A phrase I often heard around the bars suddenly became clear: "Whaddya gonna do?" Now I understood what it meant. Things happen you have no control over, and there's nothing you can do about it, so you just move on. You don't learn that in kindergarten.

1 | "My First Mob Lesson"

By the time I saw my friend Dick get beat in the bathroom, I was already getting used to a new life. My parents had gotten divorced the year before, when I was four, so every weekend I went to my dad's house and into a whole different world. He wasn't like other dads—my mom had caught him cheating and chased him around with a knife before throwing him out.

When I was with him, he took me with him everywhere he went. Most of the time we went to upscale bars and restaurants, where all the Mobsters hung out and did business. Our daily rounds included the famous Joe Sonken's Gold Coast in Hollywood, Florida, the Diplomat Hotel in Hallandale, Manero's in Hallandale, Tiffany's Gardens on Hollywood Circle, Oceans 11 in Hollywood, Shark 'N Tarpon in North Miami Beach, The Moose Club, and the Lamp Post.

We'd go to each place once, sometimes twice a day. When football season was on, I got to pass out football cards or gambling sheets to whoever wanted to bet. The cards listed all the college games played on Saturday and all the NFL games on Sunday. Each guy had a code he would write on the betting sheet—no names—along with their picks. Money never changed hands. Just a code name, the picks, and the amount of the bet. The bets had codes also. One dollar really meant $100; fifty cents meant $50; a nickel was $500; and a dime was $1,000. One time I asked my dad why anyone would bet only one dollar. He said, "Nothing is what it is, son. A dollar really means he's betting $100."

"Ohh," I said, but I still didn't understand. Why not just put in the real amount? As I grew up, those words stuck with me: "Nothing is what it is." As I went around the bar handing out the football betting cards and picking them up, I sometimes got nice tips. There were times I went home with $100 or more…a lot of money for a little kid.

Sunday football was the most fun. The cigarette smoke was so thick you could barely tell who was sitting on the other side of the bar, and it was sometimes hard to breath because I suffered from what turned out to be severe asthma. People got more drunk and rowdy as the day went on. They yelled at the TV screen as if they were the coach and the players were listening to them. My dad's voice could be heard above them all, screaming at players as they raced to make touchdowns. "Come on, you motherfucker," he'd scream, "You should have stayed in school, you slow prick," or, "This fucking bum couldn't hit an elephant from two yards."

Many of the guys who were connected to the five main Mafia families—Bonanno, Gambino, Genovese, Luchese, and Colombo—came into the bar and handed me a $20 when they saw me. When they needed a refill, they'd say, "Hey, son!" or, "Hey, kid!" and hold up their empty glass. I knew what that meant: another tip. Everywhere we went, I was making money. Going to the bars was how it was back then—no bars, no money—and I didn't question it. I was just happy to be with my father and a part of the action. I knew almost everyone who was connected, and they all treated me like a son.

After experiencing the Mob's bar scenes and making all that money, school seemed very boring. I hated school! Getting up when it was still dark outside, listening to damn nursery rhymes and "nap time" like all the other five-year-olds. How's anyone supposed to get ahead like that? I was making damn good money for someone who hadn't even turned five yet.

Who needed school?

2 | I Want to Stick a Pencil in His Fucking Eye

When I was about eight years old, I was walking down the hall one day between classes and a kid I didn't know tripped me. I fell and dropped my books. At first I thought it was an accident, until I heard a group of kids laughing at me and the one who tripped me saying, "Pussy-ass cracker white piece of shit!"

Then, as I gathered all my shit on the ground, this mother-fucker kicked me right in the ribs. When I looked up I saw a big, fat nigger looking down at me, giving me the middle finger. His name was Dwight Johnson, and he was known to pick on white kids smaller and younger than him. The school knew about this kid but never did anything about it.

I remembered Dick getting the shit kicked out of him in the bathroom. As I picked up all my books and pencils, there was one pencil laying just out of reach. As I reached for it, I thought, "I want to stick this pencil right through this coon's eye." But I didn't want to get kicked out of school, no matter how much I hated school. My mom would have put a whooping on me with the flat side of a big hairbrush.

As the day went on, I grew more furious and wanted revenge. But I was in a pinch. I figured it was just another one of those things. "Whaddya gonna do?" I had to let it go.

It was a Friday, and my dad was picking me up from school so I could spend the weekend with him. He always waited in the same spot in his long black Lincoln Continental. As we pulled away from the school, he asked me what was wrong, as he could see I was upset about something. I began to tell him the story, but before I could finish, he pulled a fast U-turn over the median and said, "That motherfucker."

I wasn't sure what was going on as we pulled back into the school parking lot.

"Where the fuck is he?" my dad screamed. There were so many kids getting out of school, it was hard to know. Then I remembered that Dwight usually waited in the playground after school for his parents to pick him up. I told my Dad where he should be. We drove around to the other side of the school. There Dwight was, playing basketball with other kids. My dad parked, lit a cigarette, and just sat quietly while I sat there nervously, not knowing what he was thinking.

Finally he asked me, "So what did you do after he tripped you?"

I kept silent as I knew he did not want to hear that I didn't do anything.

"You let that coon trip you, and you didn't do nothin'?" he said.

"I didn't want to get in trouble, pop."

"Trouble? you have no idea what trouble is, boy. The next time someone touches you, you split their fucking head open. Listen, you'll never get in trouble for defending yourself. As a matter of fact, I will take you for an ice cream. But if you don't stand up for yourself, I will straighten you out real fast, do I make myself clear?"

"Yes, pop."

"Don't 'Yes, pop' me. You're an Italian, so act like one. You *always* stand up for yourself, your family, and your friends! Got it?"

"Yes, I understand."

We waited there for about two hours, watching Dwight play ball. I had no idea what was going on, but I knew we weren't sitting there waiting for it to rain women. As Pops liked to say when he was having a lousy day, "If it was raining women I'd get hit in the head with a fag."

My dad never took his eyes off Dwight. Finally, an old beat-up van pulled up, and Dwight grabbed his books and ran to the van.

"Got ya, motherfucker," my dad said. He told me to grab a piece of paper and pencil. As Dwight got in the van my Dad drove by it very slowly and said, "Write this down. HWZ173."

"I got it," I said, puzzled. "But what's this for?"

"Ehh, nothing," came his reply.

That weekend it was business as usual, and Dwight was the last thing on my mind. We went to the bars, watched the football games, and I made a few bucks doing my usual thing. On Sunday afternoon, while people were screaming at the games on TV, I heard the bartender yell, "Caucci!" My father and I looked up. At the other end of the bar stood three guys in black leather jackets and dark sunglasses; they looked like wise guys. My dad looked down at me and said, "You stay here."

He walked over and everyone greeted each other with a kiss on the cheek. Then they all walked outside. I could see them through the glass talking with their hands, like Italians do when they get excited or angry. After a few minutes they all came back into the bar and stood behind me and my Dad. My Dad ordered us a round of drinks: three Johnny Walkers on the rocks and one Coke, my usual.

They hung out with us for the rest of that day, telling jokes and yelling across the bar to other guys they knew, making fun of their friends, just good old ball-breaking and having fun. By now I knew that Italians would say the most horrible things to each other and just laugh it off. But the funny thing about it was that whatever they said was true most of the time. Like, "Hey, Paulie, your ex-wife still banging the mail man?" Paulie would reply, "No, he got tired of her so he's banging your grandmother now!" And the whole bar would burst out laughing. This went on all day and really made time fly.

When it was almost time to go home, one of the guys said to me, " Tell me what happened at school with the nigger kid."

I was surprised he knew, but I told him the story.

"Did you ever have a problem with him before?"

"Nope," I said, "never even spoke to him. I don't know much about him except he likes to pick on younger white kids at school."

"That's okay, we know a few things, kid."

"Really? Like what?"

But he just told me to forget about it and changed the subject. A few minutes later, Coast Guard John—a federal agent for the U.S. Coast Guard and a personal friend of the family—walked in and sat next to my Dad, handing him a piece of paper. Pop gave it a quick glance and put it into his pocket. I had no idea what was going on.

At the end of the day, everyone said their good-byes and I went back to my dad's house. My mom usually picked me up at seven on Sunday nights, but this week my dad said he would take me to school Monday morning. That was unusual, but she said okay.

On Monday morning, I woke up around 9 a.m. and walked into the kitchen. My dad was eating eggs on toast with an Irish coffee. Nothing like starting the day with a little alcohol.

"Pops, it's nine o'clock, I'm late for school."

"No, you're not," he said. "You're sick today so go take a shower."

"Oh yeah!" No school!

Instead, we went around to all the bars…but there wasn't a lot of action on weekdays. No football, and all the regulars were working. Instead, my dad took a lot of phone calls and we spent time checking up on his workers. Back then, my dad had a very successful painting and remodeling company. It was an easy business for him, since the Mob had its hands in almost the whole construction industry. Getting contracts was almost a guarantee. If my dad submitted a bid to paint a high-rise condo, all he had to do was make a couple of phone calls and the job was his. He just had to make sure that the right people got their end.

Everyone in town was on the take, even the city officials and some of the cops. Sometimes outside contractors would bid against my dad or other connected guys at a much lower price. Whenever that happened, we would get word from a city official. My dad would make a quick phone call to Tony Plate, and the other guy would withdraw his bid and never bid against us again. Back then, making money was easy if you were connected.

At about three o'clock that afternoon, we were sitting at the bar in Maneros in Hallandale. My dad looked at his watch and said, "Show time." He looked at me and said, "Let's go, we got something to take care of, Twinkle Toes."

"Twinkle Toes? What the hell did I do?" I replied, wondering if he was just breaking my balls.

"Nothin', absolutely NOTHING. That's the fuckin' problem," he mumbled under his breath.

We jumped in his car and drove to a strange neighborhood with run-down houses and shit in all the yards. It didn't take me long to figure out I was in nigger town, but I wasn't sure why we were there. Maybe he had a job nearby? He pulled into a parking lot in front of an old convenience store with a few black men shooting dice out front.

As customers went in and out of the store, we got a lot of dirty looks. A few guys mumbled under their breath, but the only thing I remembered hearing was, "I would love to kill me a cracker today."

My dad told me to never get offended when someone called me a cracker. "It's a compliment, and the niggers don't even realize it," he said.

A few minutes later, a car pulled up next to us. It was another long black Lincoln Continental, just like my dad's. The windows were tinted dark, so it was hard to see who was driving. The window rolled down, and I saw the three wise guys from the bar. The driver said to my dad in a thick New York accent, "Hey, Caucci, you ready to do this thing?"

"Goddamn right I am, follow me." My dad pulled out a piece of paper from his pocket. It was the same paper he'd received from Coast Guard John. He read the address, then drove down the street very slowly, trying to find a house. Finally, he said, "Got ya, motherfucker!"

He drove to the end of the street with the other car following and then pulled a U-turn. We both pulled over to the side of the road. We were maybe five houses away from the house he was scoping. He put the car in park, lit a cigarette, reclined his seat, and said, "Now we wait."

"Wait for what, pop?" I still didn't know what was going on.

"Nothing," he answered through his cigarette smoke. "We just have to talk to somebody about a thing, that's all."

He put the AM radio on and listened to the sports station. I looked around the neighborhood. We didn't belong here. We stuck out like a white man on a basketball team. People were giving us dirty looks, but nobody had the balls to say anything because two black Lincoln Continentals full of Italians only meant one thing...

I closed my eyes to take a nap, but then suddenly my dad gave me a hard slap on the thigh. "There he is, we got him!" he said.

"Got who?" I thought.

Dad rolled down the window and signaled the car behind us to come around. I looked at the house and saw a familiar beat-up old van with the side door open. Three people were unloading groceries and taking them into the house. Then it hit me...it was Dwight, the nigger kid that tripped me at school, with his mother and father. His father was one big son of a bitch, dressed in a blue jumpsuit and had what looked like dried cement on his clothes and boots. He had to be at least 6'5" and weighed close to

300 lbs. That's when I knew the shit was gonna hit the fan, and I couldn't wait to see the look on Dwight's face when he saw us.

After they went inside, we waited another ten minutes then slowly pulled up to his front yard. Dad, me, and the three guys all got out. One of the three knocked on the door. A well-dressed black woman who looked worn down opened the door. The fear on her face was obvious when she saw us. "How may I help you gentlemen?" she asked in a scared voice.

"Look, lady, you got a big fucking problem here and we've come to fix it," my dad said in a deadly voice.

"Oh, I see," she says nervously. "Hold on, let me get my husband."

As she went to shut the door, one of the guys forced it open and made his way in, while the second guy held it open. The third guy stayed outside with my dad and me so we could see what was going on.

"Don't you fucking move, lady, just call your husband," my dad said.

"Carl? Carl!" she yelled nervously. There was no response, so she yelled louder. "Carl!"

"What the fuck you want, woman?" came an angry, deep voice from the back room.

"You have visitors, Carl."

"Bitch, I don't wanna talk to nobody!" he screamed. "If I gotta get outta this bed, your ass is gonna be sorry."

"Carl, please, it's important, you need to come out here," she screamed.

A door somewhere in the back of the house slammed and heavy footsteps sounded as Carl walked to the front room. He came around the corner into the living room and saw us. "What the fuck you crackers want?" he demanded.

Without hesitating, the guy holding the door open cracked him right in the forehead with a blackjack. Then the other two forced their way inside and joined in on the beating. Suddenly the big tough guy was screaming, "Help me, help me, please stop!"

But they didn't stop. They kicked him in the ribs and stomped on his head until he started crying. I couldn't believe it. The big, tough guy was actually crying like a little girl. My friend Dick was half dead when he took his beating and didn't shed a tear. In fact, he even managed to smile at me.

I took a quick glance at the woman and noticed her smiling, like she was enjoying the show.

Then my Dad said, "Wait, stop! Do you hear that? I think I hear a baby crying."

The guys chuckled. "Not so tough now, eh nigger?"

Then I heard a noise and saw Dwight come out of the bathroom with a towel wrapped around. He saw his father lying bloody on the floor and looked like he'd seen a ghost. Dad took one look at him and said, "Get your little black ass over here."

Shaking, he walked over very slowly.

"Did you trip my son at school?" my dad asked, nodding toward me.

"Uh...uh...nope..." Dwight was shaking in fear.

"Don't you fucking lie to me, you little shit. Look at your father."

Dwight's eyes darted from his father to me to the guys behind me. He swallowed nervously. "Well...yes, sir, I did," Dwight said softly. That's when I saw a stream of piss running down his leg. I guess he wasn't so tough either.

"Good, good," my dad said. "That's a good boy for telling the truth." Then my dad said, "I just want to thank you for tripping my son in school." Dwight stood frozen in shock. "You're probably wondering why I'm thanking you," my dad went on. "Ya see, today two valuable lessons were learned that I can pass on to my son. The first lesson is what happens to people who fuck with us. The second lesson is you never know who you're fucking with. So thank you for helping me teach these important life lesson to my son." Looking at the man on the floor, my dad said, "Did your dad here teach you to pick on people smaller and younger than you?"

"No, sir" Dwight replied softly, staring at the ground.

"Well somebody taught you to act like this. If you wanna prove you're a tough guy, try fucking with someone bigger than you. Picking on kids smaller than you just shows you're weak."

Then, in a very low voice the black woman said, "Sir, that's not his father."

My dad shrugged. "That may not be his father, but he's the man of the house and the message has been delivered! Do you understand?"

"Yes, sir, I sure do."

My dad put a gentle arm around Dwight's shoulder and pointed to me. "You better make sure he never trips again, not even by accident, you hear me? You make sure to tell all your friends at school what happens when you fuck with him."

Dwight nodded.

On the way out the door, my Dad looked Dwight's mother straight in the eyes and said, "No cops, you hear?"

"Yes, sir," she replied with a big smile on her face.

As we walked back to the car, the lady opened the door and ran outside.

"Excuse me, sir, excuse me!" She ran over to the crew. They circled around her and she said very quietly, "That's not Dwight's daddy, but you didn't get the wrong man. That man beats me at least four times a week. Vengeance is mine, says the Lord," she said. "And thank you, thank you, Mr. Anthony." A tear rolled down her face.

My dad put his arm around her and said, "Vengeance is the Lord's, but the pleasure is all ours. I guess he works in mysterious ways." He then reached into his pocket and counted out $1,000. "This is for you, because your husband won't be able to work for a while. And here is my phone number. If he touches you again, just give me a call and we'll be glad to come back. When we're done with him, he'll have a lot more cement on him than just his boots, you make sure you tell him that."

She started to cry and wrapped her arms around my dad and said "God bless you! My prayers were answered on this day. Thank you, and God bless your son as well." Then she grabbed both my hands and said, "I am truly sorry Dwight did that to you, I am so ashamed." I could see by the look on her face that she was not the same broken woman who had answered the door. I thought about what she had said. She believed God had sent four tough Italians to do his work. I felt good and I could tell my dad did too.

When we got back to the car, one of the guys started laughing and said to my dad, "Hey Caucci, what's it feel like having a black broad's arms around you?"

My Dad laughed and said, "I'd take her over your old lady any day. At least she smells good and doesn't have a crooked eye."

"Caucci, you dirty motherfucker!" They all laughed.

I thought about this in the car on the way home. We beat the shit out of the wrong man and got a thank you. Go figure.

The next few days in school were very different. Even the teachers were different. Nobody got in my way, and nobody talked to me. Just the way I liked it.

But that was when the whispering started: "Caucci's dad's in the Mafia."

The mafia! What a bunch of morons…

The next weekend, while we're eating lunch at the Diplomate Hotel in Hallandale, I asked my dad, "Pop, are you in the Mafia?"

He nearly choked on his martini and said with a frown, "The Mafia? There's no such thing as the Mafia. You watch too many movies. I'm gonna tell your mother to keep you away from that TV, it's poisoning your mind. We're Italians…we just do things a little differently, that's all."

A few more days went by, and I could not stop thinking about everything that had happened. How did my dad track down Dwight? The feeling of revenge was very fulfilling, against Dwight and against the man teaching him to be a bully. Also, helping that poor woman who had been praying for help felt really good too…probably the best part of the whole day. I could not imagine my mom being treated like that. The message was loud and clear, and my entire school knew it.

One day at lunchtime, the cafeteria was crowded because It was raining outside so nobody was playing basketball or shooting the shit. As I looked for a place to sit, I saw Dwight just sitting there having a good old time, bullshitting and laughing with his friends like nothing had even happened. I remembered him tripping me and laughing. I remembered wanting to stab him in the eye with the pencil and wondering why someone so big would pick on someone so much smaller and younger. Since he was such a big kid and most kids were scared of him, there were a lot of kids that wanted to be his friend—or at least they pretended they were his friend for protection. It pissed me off, seeing him have a good time knowing that someone else had taken a beating because of what he had done to me. He had actually gotten away with it and someone else took his punishment.

I decided I was going to make it very clear that he had gotten away with nothing. I was going to show him and his "friends" how things really were. I was taking his fucking seat.

I calmly walked to the table, never taking my eyes off him. The closer I got, the more anger I felt. I knew what I was going to do, and I was praying he would say or do something stupid because I was going to slam my tray right across his face and stomp on his fucking head. When I got to his table, it got very quiet, except he was still running his loud fucking mouth and telling some stupid story. I stood there, waiting for him to acknowledge me. When he finally did look up, I looked him in the eyes and said in a very calm voice, "Get up, nigger, you're in my seat."

All the kids around him said, "Ohh!" or covered their mouths in disbelief, waiting for a fight. Here was someone calling Dwight out. We made eye contact for about three seconds, but then he put his head down, picked up his tray, threw it in the trash, and walked away. When I sat down, the other kids stared at me in disbelief. I took a bite of my pizza, wiped my face with a napkin, and said to the other three kids still sitting there, "You's three can get the fuck out of here too!" They grabbed their shit and ran like little girls.

There I was, sitting at the table all alone, with nobody to bother me or tell me some stupid fucking story and at that moment it all sank in: I was untouchable, and it felt great.

3 | My First Score with The Mob

By age eleven, I was really starting to get into the swing of things. Except for school. I knew what was important—I had to know my math, especially during football season—but I hated the rest, maybe except for writing. Math and writing were things my dad did every day for his legit business. When he would put in a bid for a paint job, he needed square footage, man hours, material to complete a job. And it had to be in English. If you couldn't speak English and you were born in the United States, I thought your parents should have been slapped.

One day, my school wanted "the students" to raise money. Another fucking scam…first it was a car wash, then a bake sale, and now they wanted us to sell chocolate bars. One box of chocolate had twenty-four bars in it. We were to sell each bar for two dollars each so the school would get $48 per box. They wanted us to knock on people's doors. The student who sold the most chocolate got an award. Hold on, didn't they just teach me chocolate is unhealthy? Anyway…

On Friday, Mrs. Johnson, my teacher, called our names and asked how many boxes each of us had committed to sell. Committed to sell? It sounded like the school was putting the squeeze on me! The school manipulated the students by making it a competition and they actually fell for it. You should have heard the kids trying to outdo each other. "I'll take 10!" "I'll take 20!" I couldn't fucking believe it. Then it was my turn. "Anthony," she said, "how may boxes are you going to commit to?"

"I will commit to one, and only if I can return it if I don't sell it."

The kids laughed, but Mrs. Johnson shook her head and mumbled, "Why aren't I surprised? Okay, one it is, Anthony."

At the end of the day, the chocolate was piled up in bags with our names on the bags. I walked in, grabbed my single box of chocolate, threw it in my book bag, and off I went, wondering how the other kids were going to carry all those boxes home in their bags.

Since it was Friday, I was going to my Dad's, so he picked me up 6 p.m. I bolted out of the house when he honked, yelling to my mom, "See you on Sunday!"

"So," he said, once we were driving, "how was school?"

"Ehh, you know."

"You want to stop by Manero's and grab something to eat?" What he actually meant was, "Let's stop by Manero's to get you a steak and I'll have a couple of cocktails to finish off the night."

"Sounds good to me, Pop." We drove for a while, then I said, "Do you believe the school wants us to sell chocolate bars?"

He frowned at me. "Chocolate bars?"

I reached down and pulled the box of chocolate from my bag. "They want two dollars per bar, and there are twenty-four bars per box. I can get a Snickers for fifty cents, but they want two bucks. The school is robbing us."

"And what's your end?"

"Nothin'."

He frowned deeper in disbelief and said, "*Nothing*? You mean you have to sell it for them, and you don't get a piece of the action?"

"Yep."

"Are they good?" he asked. "The bars, I mean. They better be the best chocolate bars I ever had."

"I don't know. I haven't tried one."

"How you supposed to sell something if you don't know if it's any good or not? Open it up and let's try 'em out."

I handed one to him and took one for myself while he took a bite. His eyes opened wide like a goldfish as he said, "*Marone!*"

"Really, Pop? Are they that good?"

"What kind of fucking chocolate is this" he says while I took a bite. Wow, he was right. To hell with the steak…I decided I was eating chocolate for dinner. I had three bars, and he stuck with one.

When we were done, I said, "We ate four bars, so I'm into the school for eight dollars!"

"Ehh, don't worry," he said. "We'll make it up on the back end."

When we arrived at Manero's, he told me to grab some chocolate, so I got one bar, thinking he wanted another.

"How you gonna make a score with one chocolate bar? Grab the whole box."

"Okay," I said, wondering how we were going to score with a box of chocolate.

Inside, we sat at the bar in our usual spot. My Dad ordered his usual martini and got a Coke for me.

He took a sip from his drink, then said, "Take your chocolate and ask everyone you know if they would like to buy one. But now they're three dollars apiece. You never do nothing for free. You work, you get paid. Slave days are over."

"Okay, pop." I walked around the bar, asking the people I knew if they would like to buy one. I could not believe how many people liked chocolate (or at least that's what I thought). Only one guy said, "No thanks, kid." I sold out in under ten minutes. I went back to the bar with a smile from ear to ear. "Pop, you won't believe it."

"Let me guess…you sold out."

"How'd you know?"

"Son, that's how this thing works. These are our friends, and friends of friends. Everyone knows you, and none of our friends or friends of friends are going to say no to you. If it was one of their kids, we would do the same." He smiled. "Now count your money. You had twenty bars at three bucks apiece. How much should you have?"

"Sixty dollars."

"And you owe the school forty-eight dollars, correct?"

"Yep."

"Okay, what's your end?"

"Twelve dollars."

"Right! We ate four bars and still made twelve dollars. It may not seem like a lot a of money, but not bad for ten minutes of work, hey?"

"Yeah, not bad at all, Pop." I sat for a few minutes, trying to figure out where he was going. Then I figured, what if I had taken ten or twenty boxes? I could have made $480 dollars in one night. Now *that* would have been a hell of a score.

Then my Dad leaned over and whispered in my ear, "Did anyone not buy from you?"

"Yeah, just the one guy over there."

"Who?" he said, sounding surprised and slightly pissed off

"The fat guy at the corner of the bar. The one you call Earache because he never stops talking."

Dad sat back and yelled across the bar, "Hey, Earache, bring your fat ass over here and let me buy you a drink."

Earache walked over with a big smile on his face.

"Let me have a Scotch on the rocks for my good friend Earache here," Dad said to the bartender. "I'll take one for the road and another Coke for my kid."

The drinks arrived, and my Dad lifted his glass toward Earache. "Salute!" The two men tapped glasses. They made some small talk and it looked like everyone was having a lot of fun, especially Earache. Then my Dad waved the bartender over and asked for the check. The bartender looked at him confused, shaking his head to signal that my dad didn't need to pay. He never paid a bar tab. But my dad wouldn't hear it. "No no no," he said, "this time I insist, the check please."

The bartender slid the check to my Dad and gave him a thank-you nod.

"Thank you so much for the drink, Tony," Earache said.

"My pleasure," my Dad replied, holding Earache's fat head in his hands and squishing his cheeks together. Then he gave him a kiss on the forehead.

Then, just as Earache turned around and was about to walk back to his seat, my Dad grabbed him by the shoulder and turned him back around. "Hey, there's one thing I forgot to ask you."

"Yeah, what's that, Tony?" Earache said with a drunk, happy look.

Dad put an arm around Earache's neck and pulled him real close, so he could talk directly into his ear. "Did my son ask you if you wanted to buy a chocolate bar, you mutt?" he said.

Earache stuttered, "Uh...uh...well..."

"Shut up, you fat rodent. My son asks you to do him a favor and you treat him like a fucking bum."

"I'm...uh...I'm well..."

"I said shut the fuck up! How about I do everyone here a big favor and cut your fucking tongue out? Then you can talk as much as you want."

"Please, Tony, I'm sorry. I didn't mean any disrespect. I'm just low on money!" Beads of sweat were starting to form on his forehead.

"You sit here drinking all day, you fat fuck, but you don't got no money? Get the fuck outta here. Next week you're gonna buy two boxes from my son. That'll be $144. And if you don't show up, I'm going to buy them for you, then you'll pay me five points a week until we are even. Got it?"

"Yeah, I got it, Tony..." He was already backing away.

But my dad wasn't done with him yet. "Hey, ain't you forgetting something?"

Earache stopped, looking scared and confused.

"Don't be rude," my dad said. "Pay the fucking bar tab and put a fifty dollar tip on it for this nice gentleman." He pointed at the bartender. Then my Dad looked at me with a smile and said, "Some people just don't know how to act. Let's go home."

I got it. "A frickin' three dollar chocolate bar ended up costing Earache over two hundred. He obviously wasn't schooled very well, hey Pop?"

"Once in a while people have to be reminded how things work!" he said, laughing.

The weekend passed quickly. On Sunday night, my mom showed up outside, honking the horn as usual. I gave my dad a hug and said, "See you next week, Pop."

"You bet, kiddo." Then he said, "You want to make a nice score?"

My eyes opened with excitement. "Would love to...what you have in mind?"

"Tell me, what's the deal with selling this chocolate?"

I explained it and told him that at the end of the month, whoever sold the most chocolate got some kind of award.

"Okay," he said, "this is what I want you to do. Tell your teacher on Monday that you'll buy 150 boxes, but you're only going to pay $1.50 per bar."

"A hundred fifty boxes? Who's gonna buy 150 boxes?" I asked.

"Don't you worry about that...just tell them we'll pay for them up front in cash, okay?"

"Got it, Pop."

He went on, "If we can pull this off, there are a few conditions. First, don't tell your mother, and second you tell your teacher that none of the other kids are to know about this. This has to be kept under wraps. Also, you tell them you don't want no award for selling the most chocolate. They gotta give it to another kid."

"Sure, that's fine with me, I don't care about no award anyway." I wasn't quite sure why he wanted to keep it so quiet, but I wasn't going to argue.

When Monday came, I waited until school let out before I asked Mrs. Johnson if I could talk to her privately.

She looked at me suspiciously and said rudely, "Sure, Anthony what can I help you with?

"Listen," I said, "I have a business proposition for the school. I need 150 boxes of chocolate."

"A hundred fifty? Don't be silly." She laughed sarcastically and rolled her eyes.

But I didn't let her get to me and said, "A hundred fifty boxes. On Friday, I'll bring the cash. But the deal is that I'm only paying $1.50 per bar since I'm buying so many."

"Anthony, you know they're two dollars each," she said. "Why should you get them for less?"

"I know how much they are, but do the math. The school still makes a fifty cent profit per bar at a minimum...that's $1,800 for the school."

"Rules are the rules, Anthony," she said with a smirk. "I cannot agree to that."

"If you say so, Mrs. Johnson." I started to walk away, then stopped and turned around. "If you don't want to do it, I'll go ask the principal myself to see if he'll make this one-time exception. But don't worry, I'll be sure to tell him you said absolutely not."

She frowned. "Before you do that, let me see what I can do." She said it like she was doing me a favor, but I could see I had her by the balls.

The next day, the principal called me into his office and asked me if what I was requesting was true.

"Absolutely, Mr. Rothstein," I said. "If you'd like, you can call my father and ask him yourself."

So the principal picked up the phone and called my dad's house while I sat thinking of what to say next.

"Looks like your dad's not home, Anthony," he said, hanging up.

"Oh, he doesn't get home until around 6 p.m." I figured my dad was probably on his third martini by now.

"I see," he said. "Is it alright if I call him at work?"

I had some quick thinking to do. "Well, he's a contractor and has a few different jobs going on. He'll be at one of three restaurants right now. Try this number. It's the number to Joe Sonken's Gold Coast Restaurant. Just ask to be transferred to the bar. He's remodeling it, so he should be there."

That was the first time I had to lie about my dad, but I had no clue what to say.

As usual, my dad was there. When he picked up the phone, the principal said, "Hello, Mr. Caucci this is Principal Rothstein. I'm sitting here with your son, Anthony. He tells me that he needs 150 boxes of chocolate on Friday and will pay cash."

"That's correct."

"You want them at $1.50 per bar? Do you mind me asking, what are you going to do with all that chocolate?"

"We are going to sell it for the church and donate the profit. This way the school gets to make some money and we help the church out at the same time."

"Oh, in that case absolutely! I'll have the boxes here Friday waiting for you."

"Sounds good…and do me a favor. Tell my son I'll pick him up Friday afternoon after school, not his mom's house. I'll bring you the cash then."

"Okay, Mr. Caucci, thank you and God bless you." The principal hung up the phone and looked at me with a sly smile. "Why didn't you tell me you are raising money for the church?"

It was news to me, but without skipping a beat I said, "Well, Mr. Rothstein, you know how it seems like the Catholic Church always tries to make you feel guilty about something when you go to service?"

"Uh…I'm not too familiar with the Catholic Church. I'm Jewish."

"Oh…what a shame! But whaddya gonna do? Nobody's perfect!" I said, breaking his balls. "You know how the Jews are always trying to squeeze money out of people? Well, the Catholic Church does the same thing, just in a different way."

With a very perplexed look on his face he said, "Please explain."

"It's simple…my dad is good friends with the priest at our church, and this Sunday when everyone is at Mass, the priest is going to try to persuade them to buy the chocolate to raise money for the church, if you know what I mean."

"Sorry, Anthony, I don't quite understand."

"This Sunday at Mass, the sermon is going to be about giving money to the church and how God blesses those who do. The priest is going to push this message real hard. He'll ask everyone to contribute by buying chocolate bars, and most people will feel guilty if they don't. The best part is, when someone buys a box, the priest is going to write their name on a board with the amount they donated so everyone can see. This puts the squeeze on other members to donate. It's the exact same thing the school is doing to the students with this chocolate racket, but just in a different way. The priest is going to let everyone know that all the profits are being donated to the church from your school. So not only will the school make money, but it will also get the credit for donating to the church. It's a win/win Mr. Rothstein, we can't go wrong."

"That is very, uh…very creative, Anthony."

"Yeah, it's a nice racket isn't it, Mr. Rothstein?"

"I don't know what to say." He was completely flabbergasted.

"One more thing," I said. "I don't want the award. It's very important that the other students don't know anything about this because I have a huge advantage on them, so it's just not fair. If the other students find out, it will take all the fun out of the competition and they won't try very hard to raise money. Then the school will end up losing a lot of money. And if you don't hit your goal, you won't get your bonus, isn't that right?"

He fumbled for words. "Uh…yeah, I guess that's kind of accurate. I never thought of it in that way."

"That's okay, most people usually don't."

"Anthony, you are doing a very good deed, and I am pleasantly surprised. And thank you for including the school's name when you donate to the church."

"My pleasure, Mr. Rothstein. But ain't that ironic?"

"What's ironic?"

"The Jews whack Jesus and blame it on the Italians, and here you are, a Jew helping Italians raise money for the Church. It's almost like you're doing your penance!"

After his shock wore off, he laughed so damned hard I couldn't believe it. The guy had a personality after all.

On Friday, I waited for my dad inside my classroom. He had said he would wait for the school to empty out before he came in. When he walked in, he had two not-so-friendly looking guys with him. Each guy had a dolly for chocolates boxes. Mrs. Johnson's face fell in shock.

My Dad went to meet her. "Ah...so you're Mrs Johnson? Anthony talks about you all the time. I just wanna thank you for always being so nice and, ya know, helpful to Anthony. I'm looking forward to seeing you again. So are my friends here," he said with a big smile, except that his eyes made it very clear he was not happy. "Anthony told me he is doing real good in your class and should be getting As all year. That really makes me happy!"

The look on her face told me she got the message as he gave her the $5,400 in $100 bills, counting it out so quickly she could barely keep up. After several trips, we loaded all 150 boxes and off we went.

"Where to, Pop?" I asked.

"It's Friday, and everyone will be going out tonight since they just got paid. We'll see all of our good friends too. Let's move this damn chocolate."

First we stopped at Manero's in Hallandale. As we walked in, my dad said, "First, go to everyone you know. Start with the guys you see all the time and tell them you're raising money for the church. You sell the entire box for $60...that's cheaper than three dollars each, like you sold last week, correct?"

"Yep."

"If anyone gives you any shit, you look them in the face and say politely but loud enough for others around to hear, 'I'm trying to raise money for the church.' Your first target is Paulie, a local bookmaker with the Gambino family."

Paulie was in the middle of a conversation with a Bonanno crew member, so I waited patiently for him to acknowledge me and give me the signal to approach.

"What you got there, kid?" he said with a smile.

"I'm selling chocolate for the church."

"Oh really? For the church?" He could see the scam from a mile away, but went along with it. "What's a box going for these days?"

"Sixty dollars."

"Okay, kid, here's $120 for two boxes and tell your old man he still owes me $500 from last week's football."

"Okay, let me get the other box for you."

"Get da fuck outta hear with dat chocolate," he said, chuckling. "You trying to fucking kill me? Give the money and the chocolate to the church." He winked and looked over at my Dad, who was sitting at the bar. They raised glasses to each other. "Salute, Caucci!" "Salute, Paulie!"

Then there was Tennessee Frankie, who drove semi-trucks across country. He was a great guy and a close family friend. He always had a truckload of stuff for sale—and I always wondered how he got so lucky finding shit that fell out of people's trucks. The strange thing was, the items never seemed to get damaged. As a matter of fact, all of the furniture in our house had fallen off the back of someone's truck. There must have been some very unlucky truck drivers out there.

Frankie also said he'd take two boxes, and he also told me to keep the chocolate. I thought, "What the hell is going on here?"

Everywhere we went that weekend, people bought chocolate but most of them didn't even take it. Sunday afternoon came quickly, and I knew my mom was coming to pick me up in a few hours from my dad's house. My dad was sitting at the bar watching the football game.

"Hey, Pop, Mom's supposed to be picking me up in couple of hours… we gotta go home."

"Call your mother and tell her I'll take you to school in the morning," he said. "We have to see how we made out."

"Okay, sounds good."

Then my Dad leaned over and whispered, "You see that guy sitting over there with the hat and the cigar? Go give him $500 from the money you earned, but do it discreetly and don't let anyone see you. His name is Jerry Chilli."

I nodded and walked over to the man my Dad pointed out. Jerry was in the middle of telling a story that I just caught the end of. "Then they put him in the trunk and drove him into the canal. And guess what happened next? Your never gonna believe this…THE COCKSUCKER COULDN'T SWIM!" Everyone around Jerry laughed their balls off.

Then he looked down at me and said "Hey, you're Caucci's kid?"

"Yes, sir."

"What's doin'?"

I waved him to come closer because I didn't want the others to hear, so he leaned in and said, "What's up, kid?"

"Well…I got a little something for ya."

"Is that right?" he said in the growl of someone who has been smoking cigars a long time. "You got something for me? I like that, but I like it better when I hear I gotta *lot* of something for ya." He laughed at his own joke.

I gave him a handshake with the $500 folded between my fingers so nobody could see. He counted it discreetly and said, "Not bad, kid. This come from you?"

"Yes, sir."

"How'd you make it?"

"I sold boxes of chocolate to everyone around town."

"You sold chocolate?" he said, leaning closer with eyebrows raised and looking surprised.

"Yeah, for the church."

"Oh, I see. You got a racket going on. Good job, kid!"

He gave me a pinch on the cheek and ruffled my hair and said, "Okay, now get outta here, kid!" Then he raised his drink and yelled across the bar to my dad, "Hey, Caucci! You're somethin' else."

I went home that evening with my dad and we laid out all the money on the table.

"Okay," he said, "how much did we put in, how much did we get back, and what's our end?"

"Well, we have all these boxes of chocolate left over."

"Don't worry about what's left, just do the math."

"Okay, give me a pencil. We had 150 boxes, each with 24 bars. So, multiply 150 times 24 to get 3,600 bars, and 3,600 bars cost $1.50 each so that's 3,600 times $1.50 for $5,400. So it cost us $5,400 to start."

"Excellent. Now count the money. Separate the bills into $1, $5, $10, $20, $50, and $100s."

I spread it out on the table and started counting.

"We put in $5,400 and got back $10,560 plus most of the chocolate." I did some more figuring. "Holy shit, Pop, our end is $5,160."

"Okay, since we're partners, I'll take $2,500 you take $2,500 and we'll give the church $160 for now."

"But what are we gonna do with all this chocolate?" I asked.

"What the fuck's da matter with you? You got a head made of brick? We're gonna sell it back to the school."

"But why would the school buy their own chocolate back?" I was confused and couldn't figure out his angle. Pop was always pulling a rabbit outta his ass at the last second.

"Because Mr. Rothstein doesn't have a choice," he said. "We made a side deal…any chocolate left over would be returned to the school and the money refunded. Then Rothstein and the priest will whack it up."

"How did you get Mr. Rothstein to agree to that?"

My dad just smiled at me and took a sip of his martini. "Sound fair?"

"More than fair, Pop."

"Good. Now you can buy that dirt bike you wanted. You earned it. Just make sure that nobody knows about this. I'll tell your mother you hit a trifecta at the track. Whatever you do, you never want to attract attention to yourself. Keep your head down, mouth shut, and eyes open. Never let people know what you are capable of. The kid who sold the most boxes of chocolate in your school was you! What would you rather have? A certificate of achievement from your school with everyone applauding you or $2,500 cash that nobody knows about?"

"I think I'm starting to see how this thing works. You can wipe your ass with that certificate, I'll take the cash," I said with a smile.

"We can do what we do because of that guy you gave the $500 to. He is the capo of the Bonanno family and good friends with your grandpa."

"Is grandpa in the Mafia?"

"No, he's not 'in' the Mafia, but he has very strong connections with the Five Families. See, your grandpa is very clever…because once you become a member of the Mob, there are certain guidelines you must go by and people you have to answer to. He answers to nobody. You will also be expected to earn money for the family. The funny thing is, the mobsters are always asking your grandfather if he has anything in the works that *they* can get involved in. If your grandfather needs anything, all he has to do is pick up the phone and call whoever he wants from any of the families. He can do business with them without reporting to a crew boss. You grandfather taught me at a young age that you make more money and life is much easier if you don't become a member of the Mafia. So I do exactly what he taught me, and it works out great.

"But," he continued, "the only reason it's so easy to do this is because South Florida is an open territory. No single family has any claims to Florida like they do in certain parts of New York and Philly. This is what the Five Families and other families agreed to. For example, in New York, if you're running your own bookmaking operation on any one of the family's turf, if you're lucky they'll only break your legs and make you pay. And if you get caught doing it again, they'll kill you. Down here it's not that way. It's who you know, and we know a lot of people. I'll explain more of this to you when you are older."

"This is way better than school!" I thought. Who makes this much money selling chocolate?

Every time I went out with my dad, he taught me something I knew I'd be able to use in real life but that I would never learn in school. What a score! I made $2,500 selling chocolate and I was only eleven years old. I couldn't even imagine what I'd be making when I was fifteen.

4 | Organized Crime: The Mob, the Catholic Church, and the U.S. Government

When I was about fifteen years old, my dad sat me down and told me what to expect in life. He'd had a few drinks in him and figured it was time. He knew I hated school and probably wouldn't last much longer. I just wanted to make money and wasn't afraid of hard work. I didn't care how I did it, as long as it didn't involve hurting innocent people (and "innocent" had a very broad definition.)

By the time I was fifteen, I was a very good painter. During the summer, my dad would send me out with his men on painting jobs so I could learn the business. Grandpa was a very successful painting contractor and owner of Newport Painting. He painted most of the high-rises still around today, including the famous Fontainebleau in North Miami, the Diplomat in Hallandale, and the Newport Hotel in Sunny Isles Beach, to name a few. My dad also had a very successful painting business, and it was likely I would end up with my own painting company (along with other things). The Mafia was very involved in making sure that people they knew would get the contracts so they could get a kickback. Other contractors were often threatened not to bid on the jobs my father was bidding. This guaranteed my father the job at a high price. That's just the way it was back then. It was a great way to make legitimate money and a perfect cover for illegal earnings.

On this particular day, he gave me a quick history lesson on the Mafia in New York, Chicago, Philadelphia, etc. He told me about

Lucky Luciano, Al Capone, Meyer Lansky ("The Jew"), Bugsy Siegel (another Jew), Jimmy Hoffa, and the Five Families (Bonanno, Colombo, Gambino, Genovese, and Luchese).

In a Mafia family, there was first an affiliate. This is someone who wasn't directly in the Mob but affiliated in some way. It could be anyone: a crooked cop, a drug dealer, or a member of another organized crime family like the Chinese Tongs or Triads. Affiliates weren't bound by the rules that Mafia families were bound by. Affiliates could do whatever they wanted as long as they didn't violate their agreement with the Mob. When an affiliate made a deal, they stuck to it or they could get whacked.

The next level up was the associate. Those were the people who were trying to climb the Mafia hierarchy. Usually they were the ones who did all the grunt work, including running errands, collecting money, slapping people around, and most importantly, trying to earn the crew some money. When an associate was given an order, saying no wasn't an option.

Then there were the soldiers. Once the books were open (meaning the Mafia was officially taking new members), you had to be sponsored by your capo in order to get made. To get made, your name was put on a piece of paper and sent to the other families for approval. If anyone had an objection, there would be a sit-down and a final ruling. Traditionally, you usually had to earn your button, or make your bones, before you could get made. This usually meant you had to carry out a hit that was ordered from the top. Your target could be anyone, even your best friend. The hit would be ordered, and the associate had to carry it out. After a successful hit, the associate would have "made his bones."

After all this—the books being opened, getting a sponsor, and completing a hit—new members were required to take the oath of Omerta, or the Mafia code of silence. Once the soldier had taken the code, a ceremony took place where they pricked your finger and put your blood on a card with a picture of a saint, then lit the card on fire. You then had to say a few things and answer some questions, including making a promise to put the Mafia before God and your blood family…and bada bing, bada boom, you were a made man!

The most important thing to the Mob was money. Always has been and always will be. The bosses and capo wanted soldiers and associates who could earn money and come up with new ideas on how to make money. An associate who earned a lot of money for the family could possibly become a made man without making his bones (whacking someone). However, becoming a made man by executing a sanctioned hit showed the family your loyalty and demonstrated that you had balls. Becoming a made man because you earned a lot of money for the family didn't really prove you had any balls—it just meant you were useful as a good earner. Money earned by a crew of associates and soldiers was divided and kicked up to the capo, under boss, and boss. The crew was responsible for making the money at the street level and sending it to the top. Some guys were real earners, while others were just muscle or part of the group.

Crews were typically run by a capo. It was the capos job to make sure the crews were earning money and to hand down the orders from the boss or under boss. There was a chain of command in the crews, however, and not every crew member could talk directly to his capo. This way, if one of them got arrested and decided to cooperate with the feds, they couldn't testify that they had direct orders or information on a capo.

Next up was the consigliere, and his role was a little different. He was an adviser to the boss. Since there were rules in the Mafia, there had to be someone who could decide if a particular rule had been broken or if there was a grey area. Sometimes there were feuds inside the family, and the consigliere would act as the mediator as an unbiased third party. Consiglieres also recommended punishments. The final decision, however, was always the boss's.

One step up from consiglieres were the under bosses. There was usually one or two under bosses. He was second-in-command and stood ready to take the place of the boss in case of sudden death or terminal illness. If the Boss was sent to prison for a long time, the under boss became the acting boss.

Obviously, the boss sat at the very top. The boss was in charge and made *all* final decisions. Bosses didn't get directly involved in any of the street-level activity. Bosses had to be very discrete (as should everyone). Guys usually had to work for decades to become boss, so it was smart for bosses to fly under the radar until they retired. However, not every boss was so discrete. Some of them flaunted who they were, making displays of their power and lifestyle. That kind of behavior was guaranteed to piss the government off.

Once a boss or anyone went down, the life they lived was gone. In prison, every single day you're told when to eat, sleep, exercise, clean your room, and more. The prison has complete control of you, and if you don't like it, they just throw you in the hole (solitary confinement) and let you rot until you realize how good you really have it. Because mobsters are charged with particular crimes, they usually ended up in a federal prison, and the feds made sure not to put too many Italians in the same place or eventually they'd end up running the joint regardless of their smaller numbers.

Contrary to what the public may believe, a boss in prison doesn't have the same influence in prison as they do on the street. There are more niggers and spicks in prison than Italians, and it was a hard transition. Before prison, bosses were usually rich, living a lavish lifestyle and surrounded by beautiful women and crew members who would carry out any order. Facing life in prison with nobody to protect them or take orders, the real man came out. This is why so many mobsters—all the way up to bosses—have turned into government witnesses. Not many bosses die at home surrounded by their family and friends—they usually end up in prison and die there, unless they cooperate. That said, there have been many true Mafia bosses and high-ranking members who showed they were men until their dying day. John Gotti and a dear friend of mine, Jerry Chilli, were just a few of those men.

After my dad told me all this, I had to wonder. Why in the world would someone want to be a slave to an organization that was based on taking orders from someone else and making money for your boss? I thought the whole idea of being a gangster was that you didn't have to work for someone else. Why would someone become a member of an organization that could take everyone down just because *one* person didn't have the balls to go to prison? Your whole life was in other people's hands. Everyone knows that when someone is facing a life sentence or a very long time in prison, most people will do what's best for them and put their blood family first, before they protect a criminal organization. Then the so-called sacred oath of Omerta would fly right out the window.

My dad continued, "Son If you ever end up on the FBI's radar and the government decides they want you, there is absolutely nothing you can do about it. If they want you to cooperate, they will go to the lowest, most disgusting lengths to get what they want, even if they have to fabricate it themselves. For example, they could concoct a lie and tell your wife you're cheating on her, hoping she will fall for it in order to extract information from her. Or they could tell people in your neighborhood that you're wanted for child sex crimes, plant false evidence on you, or even have other people already doing long sentences make up lies about you so they can get their sentence reduced. They will do or say anything, and they will not stop until they destroy your life or get what they want. That is our government, and nobody is off limits, not even the president of the United States.

"Sadly, lots of good men cave and become government informants because of those tactics. So to minimize your chances of getting pinched, I think it's much smarter to keep your associates to a minimum and involve the least amount of people in any crime you're going to commit. It only takes one person to take down and entire empire."

He then explained some of the basic rules people in the Mafia are expected to go by: never use or sell drugs, and never look at a man's wife with ill intentions. If you get caught doing anything disrespectful with her, you're a dead man. Even if they're divorced, she is off-limits, or you die. And the list went on. The funny thing is, those rules were broken all the time. But at the age of fifteen, I made a point to remember the rules in order to be a stand-up man, both "personally" and "in business." By this time I had seen how they operated firsthand.

It was great having all those connections at the age of fifteen. If I ever needed anything the average person could not get, I could usually get it with just a couple of phone calls. Tickets to a football game, anything that fell off a truck, throw someone a beating…anything! Somebody always knew somebody.

After listening to everything my dad had to say about the Mob, I asked, "Dad, what do you think God would think about all this crime and killing?"

He looked at me and said, "Son, that is the whole reason Jesus came to this world. We live in a fucked-up world full of evil, and God knows it. That is why he sent his Son to die for the sins of the world. A sin is a sin is a sin. Look what Cain did to Able. Cain clipped Able just because he was jealous. And what did God do to Cain? Nothing! He gave him a pass and sent him on his way. Then he said that if anyone killed Cain, they would be punished seven-fold. God protected Cain even though he had killed his own brother. The same rules still apply. And remember, just because you might break the law or are a so-called criminal, it doesn't mean you have to be a scumbag. Some of the nicest people I have met are criminals."

"So it's okay to kill people?"

"Absolutely…just don't get caught!" he laughed. "But all bullshitting aside, if you're gonna whack someone, make sure you have a damn good reason. If you read the Bible, it says an eye for eye and a tooth for a tooth. The Bible says you shall not commit murder, that is killing someone without a just cause. However, there are multiple times God commands that people be killed when certain laws are violated. The Mafia has its own laws, and if you violate certain ones, you'll get whacked. But if you're in the Mob, this is no surprise to you. You take an oath and accept the consequences. Look at joining the Mob like sky diving. You jump out of a plane, hoping that the parachute will open while your adrenaline is pumping, knowing it's possible it won't, and if it doesn't…SPLAT…you hit the ground. You know the risks and the consequences, but you do it anyway. Same rules apply when you join the Mob. As soon as you're in, hope for the best but always be prepared for the worst. All you can do is follow the rules and be a stand-up man, then you will be respected. But remember, no matter how much you play by the rules and do the right thing, a hit can be put out on you and you'll never see it coming."

He handed me his empty glass and said, "Freshen this up for me, I'm too drunk to do it myself." Then he continued, "Before you ever do anything stupid, think about the chain of events that can follow. If you slip up, you could end up in prison for the rest of your life, paralyzed in a wheelchair drinking out of a straw, or any number of things. So think before you act."

"Okay, Pop."

His face grew serious. "You want to know who the real criminals are?"

"Who?"

"The fucking government…Listen carefully and pay close fucking attention. What's a crime?" He was slurring by now.

I thought it was a ridiculous question, but I answered anyway. "It's when you break the law."

He looked at me like I was a moron and let out a sigh of disappointment. "And who makes the laws?"

"The government."

"Who else?"

"The states?"

"And how many states do we have, genius?"

"Fifty," I answered, not sure where he was going with this.

"Bingo! Fifty fucking states and each state has their own laws. One state you go to prison for thirty years for a couple of ounces of cocaine and another state you get three years. And if the feds pick up the case, which they won't because it's too small, you might do six months. Now you tell me, how the fuck is that possible if we're called the UNITED STATES OF AMERICA?"

"Uhhh, I don't know, Pop."

"Uhh I don't know, Pop," he mimicked me. "What are you, a half a fucking retard? The state and the federal government decide what a crime is by making the laws the way they do. Whoever came up with the words to the Pledge of Allegiance obviously had no idea how the United States of America would turn out. We should be one nation under God, but instead we are one nation under the biggest organized crime syndicate in the word. The American government." I could see he was angry, so I didn't interrupt while he went on. "When the fucking government says something is okay then it's okay. But if they decide they don't like something because it's not in their best interest, they just make it illegal. If the government wanted to make smoking illegal, they could. They could easily pass a law that says possession of cigarettes is a felony. The government does whatever it wants and nobody can stop them. Let me give you a prime example on how crooked our government is. Between 1920 and 1933, the government made alcohol illegal. You could not make, buy, sell, or drink any kind of alcohol. If you did, you went to prison. That was the eighteenth amendment to our Constitution. I'm sure glad I wasn't around back then!" He laughed and took a sip of his scotch.

"Are you serious? *Alcohol* was illegal? Get the fuck outta here!"

"It sure was."

"So what would have happened if Jesus was there and turned water into wine?"

"Those cock-sucking feds would have tried to lock him up!" he said with disgust. "Now you tell me who the fucking criminals are? The only reason they made alcohol legal again was because organized crime syndicates were making a killing and half of the crooked government officials were buying booze from the Mob. Your grandfather made a lot of money at a very young age running booze for the Mob. Then in 1933, it became legal again and the government put a tax on it. Not everything that is illegal is wrong, Son. Look at prostitution. It's the oldest profession in the world. If you're a hooker in Las Vegas, you're safe. But hookers in Florida go to jail. By law, it's okay to take a broad out and spend $500 on her, then take her home and bang her. However, if you don't want to go through the hassle of taking a girl out and just want a piece of trim, paying for it is a fucking crime. I'm not saying you should go pay for a hooker, but I sometimes wonder if a hooker would be easier to deal with than a ball-breaking woman." He stopped to laugh at his own joke. "But seriously, it's her body and she should be able to do whatever she wants with it. It would be much safer for her in a brothel than being on the streets under some pimp. This whole fucking system is a scam. I'll give you one more thing to think about. Marijuana has been around since God created the Earth. It's a plant that is 100 percent natural, and there are good people doing life sentences for selling it. Families are torn apart and kids lose their fathers. And with no father around, kids usually turn out fucked up, especially girls. But in twenty years from now, mark my words, they will make it legal just like alcohol, so the government can get their piece of the action by taxing it. And the poor bastards who are doing time now will be long gone and forgotten, after rotting in prison their whole lives. And for what? A plant? Have you ever heard of someone beating the shit out of their wife after smoking a joint? I know I haven't! But people who can't hold their liquor beat the shit out of women and kids every day. It's all about money… our slimy government wanted a piece of the action so they just put a tax on alcohol and badda bing, it's suddenly legal again. As the government makes new laws, what was once considered a crime often becomes legal. It's a god-damn circus. Do you know what the RICO law is?"

"I've heard of it, but I'm not exactly sure what it is."

"It was made specifically for the Mafia and directed at sanctioned hits. But now they use it on anything, especially if you're Italian. Let's say a boss orders a hit. He puts a name on a piece of paper and gives it to the underboss. The underboss has a sit-down with a capo to discuss who should carry out the hit. Then three men are used to carry out the hit, but only one man pulls the trigger. Then the trigger man gets caught. Using the RICO statute, the feds can indict everyone involved, including the boss. And nine times out of ten, the trigger man gets a very light sentence for his cooperation. Now the entire ship sinks because as soon as one person starts to rat, the others follow. What started out as a single murder ends in a fifty-count indictment with over one hundred men being charged with all sorts of crimes."

"Get the fuck outta here," I replied in disbelief.

"The government can do whatever the fuck they want!" he said. "So my advice to you is, keep the friends you have and do your own thing like your grandfather did and I do. You're a clever kid, and there's a good chance someone may try to recruit you one day. Don't get too close to our friends, but don't distance yourself either. And one more thing, and this is important. You listening, knucklehead?"

"I'm all ears," I said.

"If you ever have to make a problem go away, make sure you do it alone. Anyone you involve can be a potential witness against you. Before you know it, you'll be digging holes all over Hollywood trying to get rid of people who can cooperate against you. You understand what I'm talking about?"

"I understand perfectly."

"And please, if you ever have any questions, you come to me, nobody else!"

"Damn right I will!"

"The way things are going with this RICO law, in the next twenty to thirty years there will be no Mafia. The government will keep passing new laws and handing out life sentences like fucking Girl Scout cookies. Bosses will flip like fucking pancakes and the whole goddamned thing will collapse. Eventually the Mob will have to go legit or they will be extinct. If you work alone, only you're responsible for you."

"I get where you're coming from, Pop," I said, thinking he was right about everything. I would rather stand alone than be part of a crew. If I did my own thing, my chances of going to prison were much less. There were just too many people involved when you joined the Mob. That shit was not for me.

"I got a question for you, Pop, did you go to prison? You told me and Marc that you had to go to some special military camp."

"Yeah…those motherfuckers sent me away, but that's what you tell your kids when they're too young to understand. I knew it wouldn't take long for you and your brother to figure it out, besides it's kinda like a military camp except the food is fuhgeddaboudit." He made a disgusted face and stuck his tongue out. Then he looked me in the eyes and said, "Prison is prison. The days are long, and it seems like they all roll into one. The food is garbage, and you're surrounded by a bunch of loud-mouthed animals who argue like a bunch of schoolgirls over the fucking television or who's next in line. I swear if it wasn't for the prison uniforms and the cells, I'd think I was in a fucking daycare. You got guys in there doing twenty years for armed robbery but then turn around and work for the prison at twelve cents an hour. If you ever get pinched, keep your fucking mouth shut and do your time. This way, once you've completed your sentence you can come home with your head held high. If you rat, nobody will even look at you, not even me. You'd be known as Tony the Rat, and you might as well be dead."

5 | Pulls A Gun and Puts It To Your Mother's Head

Sometime after our conversation, I was at my dad's house one night for dinner. He had a few scotches in him, and as the alcohol started to kick in, his eyes became bloodshot. He was looking through old photo albums and thinking about old times.

"You still want to know why I got pinched and sent to prison?" he asked after a few minutes of thinking about the old days with his photo albums.

"You finally gonna tell me?" I said.

"Why not? Remember the golden rule? Never rat?"

"Yeah, of course I do."

"Okay, then explain it to me."

"It's simple, no matter what happens, you never rat on your friends and never cooperate with the police."

"Close, but that sound like something you saw in a fucking movie."

"A movie? What do you mean?"

"Okay, let's have a little pop quiz."

I thought, "Oh boy, here we go."

Pop continued, "Let's just say one night you go visit your mother and you end up spending the night. While you are sleeping some motherfucker breaks in, thinking she's all alone. You're woken up by the sound of your mother screaming so you run into the room and he is beating the shit out of her."

"Jesus, Pop, couldn't you come up with a different scenario?"

"Shut up and listen...When you come in, you see his face clearly. But he pulls a gun and puts it to your mother's head, and there is nothing you can do. He drags your mother by the hair to the front door so he can escape while your mother is kicking and screaming. Once he has a clear path to escape, he shoots her in the head and kills her. Now, I'm using your mother here because it's the second worst thing you could possibly witness."

"The second worst thing I could witness?" I said. "What the fuck would be the worst?"

"If it happened to ME instead of your mother!" He laughed until he choked on his drink, then got serious and went on. "So what do you do next? The police show up because it's a shooting and they want to talk to you. Do you cooperate?"

"Uh," I stammered. "I dunno. This is a trick question."

"Exactly. Use your brains. What do you do?"

"Okay, then my answer is no. You never cooperate with the police."

My pop scoffed at me. "What da fuck's the matter with you?" he said. "Are you sure you not half fucking Pollack? Maybe the hospital gave your mother the wrong kid."

"This is why I quit school…I hate quizzes."

He laughed a little, but answered me anyway. "Under these circumstances, you would not be cooperating with the police to give them what *they* want, you putz. You're helping them so you can get what *you* want."

Now I was totally confused. "How is that getting what I want?"

"Follow along. You give them every detail you know about the guy and they do their investigation and hopefully find him. When they do, you'll be called in to identify him. But when you see him in the line up, you say, 'That is not the man who shot my mom!' They'll have to let him go, but then two things will happen. First, he'll think he got away with it so he won't leave town *and* you'll know exactly who did it. Then you clip that piece of shit yourself, like you should!"

"Ohhhh," I said. "That's pretty dam clever." Just like Pop had said years ago: nothing is ever what it seems!

"So remember," he said, "if you ever have to talk to the police, make sure nobody gets pinched, questioned, or becomes a suspect because of what you said. But there are times that cooperating with them will actually benefit you or a friend. A friend of ours may get arrested for something and one of us may have to go down to the station and give our friend an alibi to get him out of a jam. There are some legitimate reasons for speaking to the cops."

"Yeah, I never thought about that one."

"I got another one for you," he said, his words slurring a little.

"Enough with the fucking quizzes!" I said. "You have a couple drinks and suddenly you're a college professor?"

"Shut up and just listen, ya greaseball, you may actually learn something here. You are at a grocery store and some chigger robs the store with a gun."

"A what?"

"A chigger! A goddamm chigger!"

"What the fuck is a chigger?" I was starting to get aggravated by his quizzes.

"Oh God help me! I think my son is retarded. I'm taking you to Mayo Clinic tomorrow to get your head checked out."

"C'mon, Pop, you gonna tell me what the fuck a chigger is before your drown yourself tonight?"

"It's a goddamned Chinese nigger son! Now can I please continue with my quiz?"

I busted out laughing for the next ten minutes, until I could finally catch my breath again.

"A couple shots go off while this chigger does his bit. A stray bullet kills a little girl. You happen to know who the shooter is, and he is a real piece of shit and you want that motherfucker to pay for what he did one way or another. When the cops question you, what do you say?"

"I didn't see nothing. That's what I say."

My pop looked up at the ceiling. "Thank you, Jesus, you healed my son...Now do you know why you don't cooperate in this scenario, like most dumb fucks would?"

"Because we don't rat!"

"Goddammit. Again with your comic book answers. True, we don't rat but there are other reasons you don't get involved in other people's problems, no matter how bad things seem. In this situation, if you were to cooperate with the cops and they arrest this person, you will be called in to testify against him in court. Now you're now a key witness. No witness, no case! That's why witnesses disappear all the time. If he has a relative who wants to keep you quiet, or if he's a member of another crew, you just put a bullseye on your head or maybe even someone you love. So now you become a target and could get whacked just because you saw something and didn't keep your mouth shut. The cop's promise witnesses all the time that they will protect their identity and they will be safe. Tell me, how the fuck can you protect someone's identity when the first thing they make you do in court is raise your right hand and state your full name for the record before you testify? They use people to get convictions all the time, then just give them a thank-you when the trial is over. And if that person who testifies sends someone's, father, husband, or brother to prison, what do you think happens?"

"They get a hit put on them!"

"Bingo!" He stopped to take a sip. "But getting back to my story… the reason I went to prison is because I kept my mouth shut. The charges had absolutely nothing to do with me. The feds subpoenaed me to testify in front of a grand jury…their plan was to try and put the squeeze on me. They gave me two options: either I give them information that would get our friend Tony Plate indicted, then make me cooperate against him at trial, or lie to the grand jury, perjuring myself so they could indict me. So I took the hit and lied to the grand jury."

"Hold on, Pop. You went to prison only because you wouldn't cooperate with the police?"

"You got it."

"Don't they know that your corporation would have gotten you killed?"

"Of course they do, but me getting killed would have put a smile on their faces…Like I have always told you, the system is one big fucking circus and rigged from top to bottom. Had I cooperated, Tony Plate would have gone to jail and I would have gotten whacked. The feds would have taken out two birds with one stone and then opened a new case looking for the guy who clipped me. Round and round, like a fucking Ferris wheel. The dirty, cocksucking Feds are nothing but a bunch of motherless cunts…" He let that trail off, then asked, "Anthony, do you remember Tony Plate?"

"Do I remember Tony Plate?" I said. "How can I forget him? He was my favorite out of all the guys. I could always tell when I should stay away from him because his face would change and he looked a little mean. But besides that, the few times I hung out with him at the bar, we had a blast.

He told some great stories and really made me laugh. The strange thing was, when I was with him, if anyone ever said hello to me he would usually tell them to fuck off and leave the kid alone. I never did understand that.

"He was very protective of you and liked you a lot, so I felt comfortable leaving you with him," he said.

"So, what ever happened to Plate?" I said. "He used to come by the house for dinner and Christmas…then he just stopped coming."

"He broke a lot of rules and brought the heat down on some very important people. Plate was a tough and crazy son of a bitch, but there is always someone tougher that will do the work to prove their loyalty to the family. Plate used to always complain about how uncomfortable his shoes were, so one day he was given a brand-new pair of cement boots by a close friend of his and asked if he could swim in them…" He chuckled.

Then he handed me an old picture from one of the albums he was leafing through. It was a picture of my Mom and Dad when they were young. They were dressed up real sharp, and in the picture with them was Tony Plate and some other woman.

"I refused to testify against Plate," my dad said. "I told the government that I don't know nothin' 'bout nothin'. The problem was the feds had me on audio saying something' a little different." He pulled out a copy of a court transcript and handed it to me. "Before you read it," he said, "first let me explain a few things so it makes sense, because it's one big circle jerk. He started reading out loud from a few of the documents in his hand.

"Wednesday, June 11, 1975. John E. Scalzitti and Louis J. Maricondi were found guilty in the sixteen-count indictment for racketeering, conspiracy, and mail fraud. Scalzitti was known to be a part of the Pittsburgh La Cosa Nostra, and Maricondi was an associate with deep Mob ties in Pittsburgh and South Florida."

"Hold on a second…Maracondi, as in Uncle Lou? That Maracondi?"

"Yeah, that Dago cocksucker."

"Get the fuck outta here? He's in the middle of this shit too?"

My pop took two big sips of his scotch and chuckled before continuing. "Now this is where things start to get interesting…Sometime between 1977 and 1979, Maricondi became an undercover government agent. Can you believe this shit, one of my closest friends and I didn't even know it? But whaddya gonna do?"

"You gotta be fuckin kidding me! Uncle Lou was a rat?"

"Fuhgeddaboudit! He told the feds that he could put together another case against Tony Plate and possibly help make a case against Aniello Dellacroce, who was the underboss of the Gambino family and had some legal problems of his own. Now Plate was already on the FBI's radar for the murder of Dick." My dad shook his head. "The whole goddamn town knew Plate whacked Dick because he liked to brag about it when he got a few drinks in him. On top of that, Plate loaned Dick $50,000 about a year before he got killed and wasn't keeping up with the payments. Then to top it off, Dick orchestrated the robbery at Anthony Gaggi's house. Unfortunate as it was, Dick got what he deserved.

"Now that you got the story," he pointed at a section of the court documents and said, "start reading read aloud from here."

I focused on the paper and began reading, "Before becoming an undercover government agent, Louis Maricondi borrowed $15,000 from Tony 'T.P.' Plate, a reputed Florida loan shark, at a usurious rate of interest. Maricondi stated that he paid $400 interest per week on the $15,000 loan. Over a two-year period he paid about $40,000, including payments on the principal, and yet still owed Plate $10,000. Maricondi had asked Caucci's father, Pasquali Caucci, to borrow the money from Plate, so Pasquali Caucci obtained the money from Plate for Maricondi, ostensibly to open a new business. Maricondi went to Florida as an undercover agent on a government investigation of Plate and others. Maricondi asked the government to advance him the unpaid amount of the loan because, as he told the government, it would be very difficult to start a business in Florida while he was indebted to Plate. The government asked Maricondi to find someone who could verify the existence of that loan and also renegotiate its repayment terms with Plate. In a recorded telephone conversation, Maricondi asked Anthony Caucci to talk to Plate about the debt; Maricondi and Caucci disagreed on whether the debt was $10,000 or $15,000. During the conversation, Caucci stated that he, Caucci, owed Plate $1,000 and referred to a prior debt he had owed to Plate and which he had paid. In a second recorded conversation, Caucci told Maricondi that Plate had agreed to new terms concerning Maricondi's debt that were more favorable to Maricondi.

"A grand jury investigating Plate and others subpoenaed Caucci to testify concerning Plate's loan-sharking activities. Caucci testified under oath that he had never borrowed any money from Plate and that he had never told anyone he had borrowed money from Plate. In addition, he testified as follows:

> **JUROR:** You said you never borrowed any money personally from Anthony Plate. Have you ever had any associates of yours that ever borrowed any money?
> **THE WITNESS (CAUCCI):** Not that I know of. If anybody did, they didn't tell me about it. People don't really tell those type of things if they borrow money like that.
> **Q. (By Mr. Schwartz):** Nobody ever told you that he owed Plate money, a loan-sharking loan?
> **CAUCCI:** Not that I know of, and if they did, I wouldn't want to pay any attention, wouldn't want to know.

"The first count of the three-count indictment charged that Caucci had made a false declaration before the grand jury when he said that he had never borrowed money from Plate. The second count charged that he had lied when he testified that he had not told anyone he had borrowed money from Plate. The third count charged that he had lied when he stated that none of his associates had ever borrowed money from Plate. The district court did not explain its reasons for entering its judgment of acquittal on counts one and two, but evidently the court concluded that the government had failed to establish beyond a reasonable doubt that Caucci had borrowed money from Plate."

"Further, Caucci told Maricondi that Plate was 'not gonna bother nobody' because, 'He's got enough heat on him' and added that, 'If you wait, they're liable to put him away.' From the evidence that Caucci knew of the terms of Plate's loan to Maricondi and that Plate was a loan shark, the jury was concluded that Caucci knew that Maricondi's loan was a 'loan-sharking loan.'" When I was done, I dropped the documents on the table and my jaw dropped.

"YOU GOTTA BE FUCKIN' KIDDIN ME!" I said, staring at my pop. "You did a good thing, Pop. Damn, you couldn't catch a break on this one."

"Son, that's only the beginning of the story…it gets better from here."

I thought for a second, then said, "Pop, you said Maricondi was an undercover agent and they recorded you on the phone with him talking about the loan to Plate. Why did they call you into to testify to the grand jury? All they had to do was get Mariondi to testify to the grand jury and Plate would have been indicted. He's the one working for the government."

"Badda bing!" he said. "Because they had me by the balls and they knew it. They knew I was going to lie and that gave them a reason to put me in jail. Once I didn't talk, Mariondi went to the grand jury to testify against Plate anyway."

"What a bunch of scumbags these prosecutors are."

"Well, Son, that's what happens when you have a little dick and can't fuck a broad. You fuck the world instead."

Looking back, even though I was young when my dad told me this story, I can still vividly remember the look of disappointment on his face when he looked at pictures of Tony Plate and his "best friend" Maracondi. But he was right: there was much more to the story, which I learned later through transcripts and other records.

The truth is, by the time my dad told Mariondi to wait it out because Plate already had heat on him, he already knew that Plate was going to get whacked because he was running his mouth about what he did to Dick, which would eventually bring the heat on him and everyone around him. Plate was also earning money on the side and running side deals and not reporting it to his capo. He had gotten a little too cocky and was not conducting himself like a made man. Plate may have been a friend, but my dad was wise enough not to trust him. Maracondi, on the other hand, was like a brother to him, so when my dad was recorded saying Plate was close to being put away, he didn't mention the likelihood of Plate getting whacked. He simply wanted to reassure Maracondi that Plate had some trouble coming and not to worry. My dad knew better than to get involved in other people's business and would never repeat what he knew about the coming hit on Plate. If my dad was not the tight-lipped man he was and had mentioned the hit on Plate to Maracondi on that tape, it would have opened up a brand new can of worms.

After my father testified in front of a Grand Jury and lied on Plate's behalf, Plate had no idea what my dad said behind closed doors because grand jury proceedings are sealed. Plate didn't trust anyone—if he even suspected he had a problem, he'd just get rid of it. The feds had intentionally put a bullseye on my dad by making him appear in front of a grand jury to testify against a made man from the Gambino family, a guy who had over a dozen hits under his belt. My dad always said the feds were a bunch of motherless cunts—and he was right.

While all this was going on, Plate and Dellacroce had already been indicted and were waiting to go to trial on charges of racketeering and murder. Dellacroce had ordered Plate to murder Charles Calise (a loan shark) at a meeting in a Manhattan restaurant. Calise was suspected of being an informant for the FBI. However, the last thing Dellacroce wanted was to be sitting next to Plate during a murder trial. Dellacroce looked like a sophisticated businessman, but Plate looked like a cold-blooded psychopath. Dellacroce felt he had a much better chance of being found not guilty if he went to trial without Plate. He was sure a jury would take one look at Plate and think "Guilty."

On top of that, Dellacroce wasn't sure if Plate would flip on him to get his sentence reduced. So to make his life easier, Dellacroce had put the hit out on Plate.

Sometime after my dad testified at the grand jury proceedings and before he was charged with perjury, he was at Manero's, sitting at the bar as usual, when the bartender handed him the phone and said he had a call. On the other end, he heard Joe Sonken, the owner of the Gold Coast in Hollywood.

"Hey Caucci, what ya doin?" Sonken started.

"Whaddya think I'm doing? I'm having a drink, then I'm going home. It's late."

"No, don't do that…Come by the restaurant. I need to talk to you."

My dad knew it must be serious for Sonken to ask something like that, so he went to the restaurant and met with Joe in his office. Sonken's office was down a narrow hallway close to the kitchen, and he usually left the door wide open. The office was very small, crammed with what looked like junk, and very disorganized. There were cases of booze stacked almost to the ceiling. He had notes and newspaper clippings pinned all over the walls and sat behind and old wooden desk. If you were to judge him by the look of his office, you would think he was a slob. He looked like one too. Joe never wore anything fancy and it almost seemed like he wore the same clothes every day, usually a white short-sleeved button-down shirt with black slacks.

When he wasn't in his office, Joe sat at the same table every day with a cigar in his mouth right next to his bulldog. When you looked at Joe and his dog, you couldn't help but to think they were related. Joe always looked grumpy, and most of the time he was. Just like his dog, the skin under his eyes sagged so bad you could see red veins. His face also drooped, and when he spoke it sounded more like a grumble.

After they said hello, my dad and Joe took a small, antique secret elevator with a gate that could only fit two people to a hidden office on the second floor. It was a safe place to conduct serious business.

"What's going on, Joe?" my dad asked once they were alone.

"Your name is on a piece of paper, Tony."

"Get da fuck outta here. It's past my martini time!" My dad thought Joe was joking—there was no reason for there to be a hit on him, so he was busting Joe's balls a little bit.

"Caucci, listen to me, Plate is going to kill you. I'm being serious right now."

"Joe, you're a real ball-breaker, you know that? What's really inside that cigar?"

Joe put his hands on my father's shoulders. "Listen, you stubborn Wop, Plate thinks you're gonna flip."

"Flip my balls…My case is bullshit. I'm gonna be charged with perjury. If I'm convicted, I'll get twenty-four months max. I can do that standing on my ear."

"Yeah, but Plate is concerned. He thinks you know too much about him, especially that thing with Dick Byron. You know Plate doesn't like loose ends."

"The whole goddamn town knows about that thing with Dick Byron! Even the kids at the school for the deaf, dumb, and blind talk about it. Once he gets a few drinks in him, he tells anyone who will listen. This doesn't make any fucking sense, Joe! Why would I mention Dick to get out of a twenty-four-month sentence? This is bullshit. I've known Plate for ten years now. He went to both of my kids' baptisms and is the godfather to little Anthony. Where did you get your information?"

"Listen, Caucci, I know it's bullshit and so does everyone else. Why the fuck do you think you're standing here? If anyone thought it was true, you'd be worm food by now. Between you and your father you got a lot of friends and make a lot of money for people around here, so they'd rather keep you around. Just do everyone a favor and lay low for a while. Plate's gonna be getting some swimming lessons very soon. And lucky for you Plate has such a big fucking mouth, because if he didn't you would have never seen it coming."

Now my dad believed it. "Thanks for the heads-up, Joe."

"I didn't tell you this because I like you, Caucci," Joe said, busting my dad's balls a little bit. "You still owe me 10k and I'll never get my money if you're dead." They laughed over that.

After hearing his old friend wanted to kill him, my dad was not very upset that Plate was about to get whacked. Besides, there were other things going on. After my parents got divorced, Plate showed up at my mother's house one day. Her father had just passed away, so she was grieving—and had just inherited a lot of money. Plate was trying to schmooze her to see if he could get some money out of her, so he invited her out to dinner. My mom was a sharp lady and knew exactly what was going on, but decided to go to dinner anyway. She knew it would get back to my father, and she wanted a little payback for all the times he had cheated on her. So Plate and my mom went to the Upstairs Downstairs lounge in North Miami. Plate acted like a real gentleman that night and was very respectful, but he hinted several times about possible business opportunities. She knew Plate's angle and said she would think about it, but she never did any business with him and never intended to. My dad never told Plate he knew about that night, but he never forgot either.

My dad ended up getting sentenced to twenty-four months in prison, and just like he said, Plate was long gone by the time he got out. One day, Plate was seen in a car leaving a realtor's office with some friends and that was that—he wasn't a very good swimmer after all. It was later discovered from an informant for the FBI that John Gotti (soon to be acting boss), along with Angelo Ruggiero, got the order to take out Plate. They did everyone a huge fucking favor getting rid of that filthy mutt.

Now that I knew why my dad went to prison, and why Tony Plate and Lou Maracondi had stopped coming around for family dinners and special holidays, I thought about something else my dad said a lot: you can't trust nobody.

6 | My Childhood: I'll Hit You in The Head With A Goddamn Hammer

From a very young age, I was interested in martial arts. My uncle Steve (my mom's brother) used to come over and show me some kick boxing moves. Uncle Steve was very cool and fun. One day when I was about nine years old my mother took us to Winn Dixie to do some grocery shopping. I remember seeing a sign on a store in the same place: "TAEKWONDO." My eyes light up and I asked, "Mom can you please take me to check out that school? It must be new, because I haven't ever seen it before."

"Absolutely not!" my mother said, like I was crazy. "You keep fucking up in school and now you want me to take you to karate? You never do your homework and you don't pay attention in school. I have to get a daily report signed by all the teachers because you act like a goddamn moron in class. Do you know how embarrassing it is to have to always go to these teacher conferences because you act like a fucking clown and never do what you're told? If I was strong enough, I would punch you right in your goddamn head and knock some sense into you."

But I wasn't giving up. "I promise I'll do better, Mom, let me at least check it out, please..."

She pointed at me and said, "Okay, but were only looking. That's it."

We went in, and it was just as awesome as I'd hoped. Different colored belts and weapons were hung on the wall, and people were doing amazing kicks while jumping, spinning, and flying through the air. I begged my mom to let me join, but she said ,"Definitely not…school is more important, and at the rate you're going you'll graduate when you're forty. I'll have to tell all my friends that my son is half retarded. Do you know how embarrassing that will be?"

I was devastated, and the whole drive home she didn't say a word. This was unusual. She usually never denied me or my brother anything, but this time she seemed serious. A few hours later, she called me in to her bedroom. That only happened when it was serious. She was sitting on the edge of her bed and waved for me to sit next to her, but she had a smile on her face. She was up to something, but I wasn't sure what is was.

"You still want to join karate?" she asked.

"More than anything in the world!"

"Okay, starting tomorrow I want all seven teachers to give you a good grade on your daily report card. You fuck this up one time and the deal is off. You do this for two weeks and then you can join. But going forward, your schoolwork is first, or karate is out! And if you make me regret this, I'll hit you in the head with a goddamned hammer! You understand me?"

"Deal, Mom! You're the best!"

It was hard, but two weeks went by and my scores were perfect. I behaved in school and did all my homework—I finally had something to work toward. The big day finally came for me to sign up for karate—and I loved it! I went to every single class. I loved learning all the fancy high kicks to the head. Unfortunately, after about one year the school closed down, and that was that. No more karate, but at least I had earned my green belt. My schoolwork slowly went downhill after that, because I had nothing to work for. At least my mother let me put up a punching bag and a few pieces of martial arts apparatus in the garage, so I could keep training what I had learned.

A few years later, I was watching a Bruce Lee movie called *The Chinese Connection*. In the movie, Bruce walks into a Japanese karate school and kicks the shit out of all of them. And then right before he leaves, he holds up his fists and says, "CHINESE BOXING!"

His fighting looked a little different from what I had been taught, much faster, and I had never even heard of the term "Chinese Boxing." So I immediately went to the Yellow Pages and start looking for martial arts schools, but all I found was karate and taekwondo. Then, in the bottom right hand corner of the page, I saw a small advertisement and the name of a school: "CHINESE BOXING INSTITUTE INTERNATIONAL."

I couldn't believe it. There were no other schools anywhere that taught Chinese boxing, but Bruce Lee had said "Chinese Boxing" and I knew he was one of the greatest fighters ever. By now I was around twelve years ago. I asked my Mom again to take me and this time she said yes without hesitation, as she knew how much I loved it and how I had done better in school when I was learning martial arts. I wanted to learn more. When we arrived at the school for the first time, I saw a sign on the door that said "Christian Church," but next to it on the other window there was a sign that said "Chinese Boxing."

I walked in with my mom, not knowing what to expect. The first person I met was Sifu (teacher) Kenny Mills. He was the instructor of the kids' class. He explained that Chinese boxing was nothing like karate or taekwondo. It was designed for lethal combat only. He said that if the wrong person was taught this style of fighting, they could abuse it. Before I was able to join the school, I had to take four private lessons with Kenny and pass a character test. That made me laugh. I'd been hanging out with Mobsters for over seven years, and now I had to take a character test? You gotta be kidding.

However, one thing the Mob had taught me was to obey the rules and be respectful, especially to my superiors. I passed the character test easily and promised that I would only use what I was taught if it was absolutely necessary. The school was very different from my previous school. For one thing, all the instructors were very devout Christians—not Catholic but some other kind of Christian. And except for Kenny, all the instructors looked soft, not like fighters. I learned very quickly that you don't need to look mean or be big and full of muscles to be dangerous. These guys were great fighters...they were deadly. But you'd never know it. In fact, most of them were from Tennessee and carried around Bibles, so they kind of looked like Bible-thumping hillbillies. They were just "good ol' boys" who could rip you a new asshole and pull it over head before you could say, "Praise Jesus."

Sifu Kenny's technique was so different than what I'd been taught before. He told me that a real fight without rules should only last one or two minutes tops—sometimes only seconds after the first encounter. He explained how in Chinese boxing, you're supposed to go for the finish and aim for the eyes, groin, or throat. Then, once you closed in on your opponent, you were supposed to grab their head, jam your fingers into their eyes, and slam their head on the floor. This made a lot of sense.

One day, Kenny asked me to spar with him. Since I was still new to the school, he went at my pace, staying just a little above my skill level. I think he wanted to see how good I was—and maybe show me how much I had to learn. Every time I tried to kick him in the head with a fancy kick, he would quickly kick me in the nuts so I'd go down like a ton of bricks. This kept happening until I couldn't spar anymore.

The founder of the Chinese Boxing Institute International was a man named Christopher Casey who had been given the name Kai Sai, which meant "Victorious in every encounter," by his Chinese teachers. He had a photographic memory and had studied under many of the best grandmasters in the world. Mr. Casey integrated many Chinese fighting styles into his own style. He called it Kai Sai Chinese Boxing.

Mr. Casey had only one senior student, James Cravens, who was known as Professor Cravens. Professor Cravens lived in Tennessee and often came down to teach seminars or three-day bootcamps. When Professor Cravens came down to teach, I noticed something very different in how he demonstrated Chinese boxing. His objective was the same (finish your opponent), but his method was quite different. I wanted to learn more, but it was almost impossible to get a class with Professor Cravens.

Then, in 1988, Professor Cravens moved to South Florida and began teaching full time at my school. By that time, I was one of Kenny Mills top students and had been studying Chinese boxing for about five years. I loved it; I loved to fight. I loved the art of combat, and meeting all the different types of people who trained with us. They were so different from the guys I usually associated with.

Professor Cravens was a man of few words—and that's being generous. He did not look very athletic, was soft-spoken, and barely even smiled. He was a very devout Christian who had married his first love and high school sweetheart. Kenny Mills did the same. These people were real Christians. It was strange being around people like them. They were so kind and humble and did not seem to care about money or materialistic things. In some ways, I didn't understand them. Professor kept to himself outside of teaching and rarely complimented anyone. He once told me "there is more room for improvement than there is for compliments. Once you think you have mastered something is the day you stop learning." Even getting him to say, "Not bad" was a huge compliment.

Shortly after Professor Cravens moved to Florida, Kenny asked Professor if he would mind watching us spar. I wasn't too keen on the idea as I knew Kenny was going to go very hard to impress Professor Cravens, while I did not want to go full speed against my teacher as I felt it would be disrespectful. But Professor Cravens said he would, so the fight was on. We both fought very hard, kicking and punching until exhausted. Once we caught our breath, Kenny looked at Professor and said, "What do you think?"

Professor sat there for a few seconds with a blank stare on his face, then said, "That was intense and fast, but definitely not Chinese boxing." Then he got up and walked into the back room without another word. We looked at each other in surprise, then Kenny said, "We'll ask him what he meant on our next private lesson."

The next night during the group class, Professor Cravens asked, "What is Chinese boxing?"

"Lethal combat!" I said, excited.

"There are plenty of styles that have lethal techniques," he said, like he was disappointed with my answer. "But what is Chinese boxing as we teach it?"

The class was silent.

Then Cravens said, "Well, I will tell you what it's not. Chinese boxing is not just punching and kicking as hard and fast as you can, exchanging blows with your opponent."

Kenny and I just looked at each other, knowing this was directed at us due to our poor sparring match.

Cravens continued, "Chinese boxing is about finishing your opponent as efficiently as possible, using any means necessary." He went into great detail about the Chinese boxing approach and philosophy. I got that message loud and clear.

As time went on, Kenny and I continued to get private classes from Professor Cravens as often as we could. Eventually Kenny did what great teachers do: he gave me a senior student certificate and spoke to Professor Cravens about taking me on as his student so my Chinese boxing skills would improve. From then on, I became a student of Professor Craven's and took my Chinese boxing skills to another level.

Besides Chinese boxing, my teen years were when I discovered my other great passion: reptiles. Snakes in particular. After school my Mom often dropped me off near the woods or I would catch a ride with my friend George to the Everglades so we could catch snakes. I became quite good at it and often sold them to the local reptile shop for extra cash. I always had at least two or three really big boas or pythons at home, usually eight feet or longer. They only needed to eat once a week, their water bowl got filled and cleaned every ten days or so, and best of all, they didn't make any noise. Very efficient pets, just like Chinese boxing.

One evening when I was around age twelve, I went on a snake hunt with George. George had a driver's license, so we would drive a couple hours deep into the Everglades. During the winters, the snakes would come out at night and lay on the roads, which were still warm from the sun beating on them all day. As we drove down empty streets one night, we spotted a few snakes. George and I both got out of the car as fast as we could and ran for the catch. The problem was, George had the flashlight and I had left mine in the car. I didn't care—I grabbed the first snake I reached, and it immediately bit me. This wasn't a big deal; I got bit all the time. But this time it stung.

George ran over with the flashlight and aimed it at the snake on the ground. It was a fucking diamond back rattle snake! We looked at my hand and saw two fang holes in my finger. "Great," I thought, "I'm gonna die!"

There was no way I would make it to a hospital in time. My hand was swelling up fast. We drove for two hours at full speed to Pembroke Pines Hospital. When we got there, they didn't know what to do and didn't have any anti-venom. It turned out I was their first rattlesnake bite, so they had to call another hospital to deliver the anti-venom. By the time the anti-venom arrived, my arm was twice its normal size and they had to move quick. They did a skin test to see if I was allergic to the anti-venom, but the results weren't clear and they had no time, so they shot me up with it.

Well, let me tell you, that shit almost killed me. It turned out I was *very* allergic to the anti-venom. My whole body broke out into hives and my head swelled up like a pumpkin. I could barely breath and I started sweating profusely, then my temperature dropped to freezing cold. I was going into anaphylactic shock. My mother was there by now, crying as she watched the nurses and doctors run around. I was turning blue from lack of oxygen when I heard my mom say, "Is my son going to die?"

Next thing I know, they injected me with something else—I don't even know what—and in two seconds, I went from almost suffocating to death to being able to breathe. That was great, and at least I knew I wasn't going to die right then, but the experience wasn't over yet. I ended up staying in the hospital for six weeks, waiting to see if gangrene was going to set in and they'd have to cut my hand off. Thank God I made out okay.

That was a horrible experience and gave my poor mom a few more grey hairs, but it didn't stop me from catching snakes or being interested in animals and reptiles. Right around that same time, I got a job at our local vet, where I was allowed to assist Dr. Ferber during surgeries, handing him instruments. Dr. Ferber could see I had a love for animals and was a mentor to me. At one point, I even wanted to be a vet—but things don't always go the way you plan.

By this time—around age fifteen or sixteen—my life was pretty good. I was getting better at Chinese boxing, plus I was catching and selling snakes, going to bars and making cash with my dad, working with a few painting companies, and hanging out with my then-girlfriend. Little did I know things were about to drastically change.

7 | "You Trying to Get Me Killed?"

By age sixteen, I had saved enough money for a car, which meant I didn't have to depend on anyone. I had dropped out of school completely at this point, and all I wanted to do was make money. Around this same time, my Uncle Steve from my mother's side had just gotten out of prison.

Like my mother, Uncle Steve had inherited a good chunk of change when my grandfather died. My grandfather had invented and patented a new type of drivetrain for boat engines and made a killing. He was also a developer who had built about half of Hialeah, including Miracle Mile. My grandfather died when I was around four years old and had left my grandmother before I was born, so I never really got to see how my mom grew up, in a twenty-thousand-square-foot house in Miami Shores with maids, nannies, and all kinds of shit. The maid quarters in my mom's house were bigger than our whole house.

My mother tried to do everything the right way. She was raising two boys all alone. So, she took her money and bought us a decent house in a good neighborhood, then she opened up a sporting goods store. She was very successful until a super store opened up right next to her and put her out of business in a matter of months. I knew my mother was stressed and very upset, but there wasn't much I could do at the time. She had no other option but to file bankruptcy. This was a big blow to her, but she handled it as best she could. Eventually she had to get a job waitressing just to pay the bills. I remember the day I came home to an eviction notice taped to the front door. That's when I decided something really drastic needed to change.

My uncle, on the other hand, took his money and bought speed boats and decided to smuggle marijuana and cocaine into the country. He became heavily involved with the Cocaine Cowboys, but that story is for another day. He did this all in the early '80s until about '86. He finally got busted with a very small amount of cocaine and went to prison. By the time he got out, all his connections were either in prison or dead, so he lost everything and had to move into our house. Then, to top it all off, my maternal grandmother had her house taken from her because my mom and uncle could not afford to keep paying for it. So Grandma moved in as well. Now the entire family was living with us—we were like a criminal version of the fucking Brady Bunch.

It actually wasn't so bad…I was very close to my Grandma, and Uncle Steve was always fun to be around. He got me interested in martial arts and I looked up to him. However, I knew he was miserable. Just a couple of years before he had millions of dollars, and now he was sleeping upstairs in our loft on a sofa.

At the time, there was a kid who lived down the street from me who everyone called Fat Man, even though his name was Alex. He was about eighteen and owned his house—I'd heard he paid cash for it. He also had a brand-new, very expensive car every month, like a Porsche or a Ferrari. I wasn't sure what he did for a living, but he for sure had a lot of money. One day my uncle asked me, "How well do you know Fat Man?"

Curiously I replied, "Pretty good, why?"

"Do me a favor and see if you can get an ounce of coke from him."

"What makes you think he sells coke?"

"If he's not selling coke he knows someone who does," he said.

"Okay, I'll give it a shot."

So I walked down the street, knocked on his door, and he invited me in. Fat Man already knew about my uncle's involvement with the Cocaine Cowboys and seemed interested. After some small talk, I said, "Alex, can you get me an ounce of powder?"

Alex's demeanor went from cool to very serious as he asked, "Who is it for?"

"My uncle."

"Sure no problem. But I'm giving it to you, not your uncle, so you're responsible for it. You understand?"

"Absolutely. How much do you want for it?"

"It'll be $425."

"Okay, can you give me a week to pay you?"

"Sure, not a problem. But remember, you're responsible...got it?"

"It's on me, I got it."

Alex went to his bedroom and came back with a sandwich bag that had a white shiny rock in it. He gave it to me and said, "I'll see you in a week."

I walked back to my house and gave it to my uncle. He opened the bag to check the quality.

"It looks great, but let's see how good it really is," he said. He walked into the bathroom, put a line on the counter, and snorted it. "Wow, this is good some really good shit!"

Although he did not offer it to me, and I had absolutely no desire to try it, I remembered my dad telling me to never use drugs or nobody will do business with you. "Hey, how much can we sell it for?" I asked.

"Well, if we bag it up into grams and sell it for $50 per gram, there are twenty-eight grams in an ounce, so that's $1,400. We'll make $975 on this ounce."

"How long will it take to sell?

"Since we are just starting and it is only an ounce, no more than a week."

"Sounds good to me!"

Since my uncle sold all his cars and did not have any transportation, I had to drive him everywhere in my low-key 1979 Toyota Corolla hatchback. As I drove him around, I also met all his friends/clients. These were not drug dealers...just normal people with good jobs and a lot of money.

After a week went by, Fat Man pulled into my driveway in his Corvette as I was cleaning my car. He had very serious look on his face as he asked, "Where's my money?"

"Hold on, let me go get it." I walked inside and yelled to my uncle, "Steve...Fat Man is here! It's time to pay up." I got no answer so went go upstairs to wake him up. "STEVE! STEVE! Wake the fuck up. Fat Man is outside, and he wants his money."

Uncle Steve started to scramble in a half-drunken stupor and pulled out a wad of cash and handed it to me.

I count the wad and realized it was short by $150.

"What the fuck is this? It's $150.00 short!" I yelled.

"Uh…some people owe us money," Steve mumbled with his face buried in the pillow.

"We agreed that we would not front to anyone, cash on delivery. My name is on this deal, not yours." I was so fucking mad I wanted to kick his ass and I probably could have. At that age, I had five years of Chinese boxing under my belt. But I didn't kick his ass. Instead, I had to go outside and face Fat Man. I was not afraid of him, but I was ashamed that I had broken my word. When I approached his car, I looked him in the eyes and said, "It's short by $150."

By the look on his face I could tell he was pissed. But he was right. Before he started the threats, I changed the direction of the conversation and said, "Let's go to your house and talk." I knew this would make him feel like he had the home advantage.

"Jump in."

We drove one block to his house and sat in his living room. "Alex," I said, "before you say anything, here I am, in your house…all alone. I'm not running or trying to make excuses. I'm a man of my word, and my name was on that deal. The only reason I don't have your money is because I didn't know the people to sell it to, but now I do. My uncle took me everywhere and introduced me to everyone. These people are all good, working-class people with a lot of money, not junkies."

"Then why don't you have my fucking money?"

"To be honest, I think my fucking uncle spent some of it and snorted the rest. Give me one more ounce and put $50 on top of the money I owe you. I'll go back to my house and take his beeper and I'll sell this shit myself. Deal?"

Alex sat there for a minute or two, contemplating my offer, then said, "Okay, deal. But this time, it's all on you. We agree that your uncle is not involved going forward."

"You have my word."

I went back to my house and found my uncle still sleeping on the sofa. I yelled at him at the top of my lungs and scared the shit out of him. "You trying to get me killed?" I said. "This fucking Cuban is not playing any games. Give me your fucking beeper. I'm gonna do all the dealing and handle all the money from now on, and if you don't like it you can get the fuck out of this house. If my mom finds out what you did, she'd stick a fucking gun up your ass and blow your brains out."

Of course my mom had no clue what I was doing, especially my uncle's part in it.

"Okay…I'm sorry, I fucked up," he grumbled.

Within three days, I had the ounce sold and collected all the money. I went back to Fat Man with the cash and told him to give me two more ounces. By now, I knew this was what I wanted to do. I was my own boss. I didn't need to join the Mob and risk my life and freedom just to be a part of some organization. I wouldn't have to kick up the money I made to higher ranking members. I could do this on my own. I didn't have to prove my loyalty to a family, take orders, follow their rules, or worry about getting whacked. I remembered all the things my dad had taught me: how to make money, how the street works, and all the unwritten rules that separate "low-life scumbag criminals" from the rest of us.

I didn't need to be a member of the Mafia to know that you never steal from friends, always keep your word, never rat on anyone, and never fuck with another man's girl. You can break the law and still keep your honor. After seeing how drugs had affected my uncle and ruined his life, I also understood why the Mob did not do business with anyone who used drugs. I knew I would never use drugs because I did not like things to control me. I was never even tempted, not once. Even though I was dealing drugs and going my own way, I still had the luxury of all the Mob connections I'd known since childhood and was always treated like a son by them. They looked the other way as far as the drugs went; I had a free pass.

I had just made $1,750 in three days without breaking a sweat. It was easy money. This kind of work could either get you killed or locked up for a very long time. But what were my choices? I either took things into my own hands and made as much money as quickly as I could, or my entire family would be homeless.

In most businesses, it's a matter of supply and demand. Same with drugs. There were more junkies than there was coke, so it was a no brainer. If I stuck with the upper-class working people, the chances of me getting pinched were much lower. If you dealt with junkies, you had to be pre-pared for all the shit that came with it.

Within two months, I was making $500 a day and was able to get our house out of foreclosure.

As my business grew, I knew the word would eventually get out, and some of the Mob guys I didn't know well would try to muscle in on my action. So the day came when Steve Maruca wanted to see me. Steve was a respected made man in the Bonanno family and a very close friend of me and my dad's. All my childhood memories of him at his diner in Hollywood were great. I remember him telling my dad, "Caucci, all that soda he's drinking is poison. He's better off having a cup of coffee with a little cream and sugar, at least it's natural." So at about seven years old, I had my first cup of coffee.

Steve was not one of these guys who made their way up the hierarchy by being a big earner. He was made the old-fashioned way, the way it was intended, by "making his bones." Steve was not one of those guys you wanted to fuck with. He was known for muscling in on other crews from other families and demanding a cut of their rackets. He had dozens of sit-downs because of this, and the majority ended in his favor. The other families knew that if Steve did not get a cut, he would make it very difficult for their crews to do business. They had two choices, either whack Steve (which would have caused a war) or give him a cut.

I had a feeling Steve was going to put the bite on me and try to take a cut of my business. I knew all I really needed to do was reach out to any number of my friends, who would call him off and put the word out that "the kid is off-limits," but that's not how I wanted to play this. I didn't want to be making a phone call every time I ran into a problem. I was on my own, so I needed to stand up for myself or this type of shit would never end.

So Steve called me in for a sit-down, but it was more like a shakedown. There I was, just sixteen years old, all alone, and sitting down with a very dangerous made man.

I walked into the familiar diner and remembered sitting at the counter and getting free milkshakes as a kid. Steve was sitting in the back booth, waiting for me. He was wearing his black leather jacket and a pair of gold-framed, tinted reading glasses. He looked like a true Mobster. I should have been nervous, but I was surprisingly calm. I knew the routine, I'd seen it a million times, but this was the first time I'd been on the other end of it. I greeted him with a big hug and a kiss on the cheek. Then, after some bullshit small talk, he says, "I heard you're doing real good, kid."

"I'm doing okay, just paying the bills like everyone else."

"The word on the street is you're making a lot of money. There's a lot of guys, not friends, talking about making a move on you."

"Get da fuck outta here. People wanna make a move on me?"

"They sure do…but I can easily put a stop to it."

"Yeah…and then what? We become partners and I have to kick up to you every week?"

"Nothin's for free, kid."

I sat silent for a minute or two, then I leaned forward, looked him straight in the eyes, and said, "Steve, I've known you since I was a knee-high little turd. I know you're concerned and trying to look out for me. You're like an uncle to me, and I love you. But please do me a favor…you tell every one of those half-breed greaseball guinea fucks that if they want a piece of my action, they're gonna to have to earn it the old-fashioned way, and it won't be easy."

"Listen, kid, you know they'll come after you."

I discreetly pulled a 9 mm handgun out of my waistline and put it on the table. Steve raised his eyebrows in surprise as he looked down at the gun on the table. Then I said very calmly, "How 'bout this…you put the word out to anyone who has the balls to come and get it. And make sure they know that I don't have to go by the rules. Steve, nobody's gonna muscle in on me, it will never happen. I will never kick out a dime. If anyone comes after me or if I even think that someone's gonna make a move on me, I will turn them into a fucking pencil full of lead."

Steve leaned back in his seat and folded his arms. He stared at me for a minute without saying a word, but he had a huge smile on his face. "Look at you," he finally said, "all grown up now." He leaned forward, pinched me on the cheek, and said, "Attaboy…don't ever let anyone get in your way and always stand your ground. I'll put the word out on the street. I'm proud of you."

"Steve, I have the utmost respect for you. If you ever need me for anything, I will always stand with you because I know you will do the same. And when the day comes when you're too old and you need some work done on someone, you call me. Just point the finger, and I'll take care of the rest."

After that, Steve spread the word that I was to be left alone and that if anyone approached me they would have to answer to him. And from that day on, nobody tried to put the squeeze on me again.

A few weeks later, I walked into Joe Sonken's restaurant to meet my dad. When I got there, I saw Steve sitting at a table with a couple of the guys. He'd already had a few drinks and they were telling stories as usual. He told me to pull up a chair and ordered me a Coke. Steve told them about the sit-down we'd had a few weeks earlier. Then he said proudly, "Do you believe I tried to put the bite on this little prick and he pulled out a piece and put it on the table and basically tells me to go fuck myself!"

Everyone laughed, then Steve put his arm around me, pulled me real close, pinched me on the cheek, and kissed me on the head. "You got balls, kid."

"What the fuck's wrong with you, Maruca?" one of the other guys said, busting Steve's balls a little. "Trying to put the bite on little Anthony? Next you'll be shaking down old ladies at the bingo hall!"

"Ah, quit breaking my balls, I was three sheets to the wind and had a bad day at the track. So I thought I'd give it a shot. Plus, I wanted to see what the kid's made of."

My dad had heard the story himself earlier in the week and wanted to see me. Luckily, he'd had a few drinks already when he finally walked into the bar. "Hey you," he said, "come have a seat, I wanna talk to you. I heard what you are doing, and for the record I think it's a bad idea. I don't like the idea of you dealing that junk. Just promise me you'll never start using that shit."

"Pop, I don't even drink alcohol," I reassured him, holding up my soda. "I'd never put that shit up my nose."

He ruffled my hair. "Okay, Son, just be careful, and whatever you do, learn the laws on that shit in case you get pinched."

"Okay, Pop, I'll make sure of it."

Pretty soon, I was selling a lot of cocaine, at least for a sixteen-year-old. I averaged about a kilo a month. Not only was I selling to the upper-class users, but I also supplied some dealers. I didn't like selling ounces to the dealers because the profit on an ounce was about $350. If I broke it up into smaller quantities, grams and eight balls, the profit on an ounce was about $1,000.

Selling the coke was not a problem—the big problem was being able to supply my clients. My coke came straight from Columbia, and once it arrived in Miami, I got it from Fat Man who got it from Carlos, who actually brought it into the country. Since I was so close to the people bringing it in, the quality of my cocaine was the best on the street. It was usually around 95 percent pure. This not only made my clients and other dealers happy, but it also made it difficult to stock. It went out as fast as it came in.

8 | Operation Cherokee: Broward County Organized Crime Task Force

In June 1985, the Broward County Sheriff's Office put together a task force that would end up having a major effect on my life. It was called the BSO Organized Crime Task Force. You see, the FBI wasn't going to waste its time on low-profile crimes, but the BSO (along with Hollywood police) drooled when they got a crack at arresting anyone affiliated with organized crime.

Dave Green was an undercover detective on the task force. He used the name Danny Ledford. The guy was like a splinter in your asshole. He made a big name for himself taking a lot of people down, so I had to agree when my dad said, "I hope that cocksucker dies from asshole cancer."

Detective Green made his name during Operation Cherokee, and now he was determined to infiltrate the South Florida Mafia. Det. Green became very close with Anthony "Guv" Guarnier, a capo in Pennsylvania's Bufalino crime family. Once Green was seen a few times with Guv, the other local Mobsters thought he was okay.

When it came to organized crime, South Florida did not have territories like New York and other states. Any of the families could do business anywhere and with anyone, as long as they were good people. This made infiltrating the Mob in Florida much easier since there were so many crews around and new people always showing up to get a piece of the pie. Danny (Detective

Green) often visited the same restaurants and bars my father and other Mobsters went to. After a few months of hanging around, buying drinks for people, one day Green approached my dad at Joe Sonken's restaurant in Hollywood.

"Hey, Caucci, you know anyone interested in a truckload of Dom Perignon?" Green asked, no doubt knowing the answer before asking the question.

"Let me ask around," my dad said. "How much are you asking?"

"Twenty bucks a bottle."

"I'll see what I can do."

"Sounds good."

They had a few more drinks and my Dad told Green to meet him back at Sonken's the next day. On his own, my dad went around to his usual places, talked to all the guys and owners of the restaurants, and by the end of the day confirmed that all the champagne could be sold. The next day, my dad met up with Green and said he'd take the entire load. They organized a time for the following day to do the exchange at Sonken's.

The exchange went smooth. My dad met with Green at the bar, gave him the money, and Green gave him the keys to a truck that was parked outside. My dad went outside and did a quick case count, plus taking a couple cases for himself. As he was unloading the champagne from the truck into his car, the task force was across the street in a hotel taking pictures. I have to say, whoever took those pictures was one damn good photographer. They took some of the best picture I have ever seen of my dad.

After he was done, my dad took the truck and went around to the local hangouts to get rid of the champagne. It was a nice, easy $20,000 score for him.

Detective Green was just sitting back and adding names to the list of guys he was going to take down. When it came time to pull the plug on Operation Cherokee, Detective Green had been working on it for some time. Mobsters ended up getting arrested for a variety of crimes: bookmaking, loansharking, extortion, credit card fraud, and more. In the process, my father was arrested for buying stolen alcohol. When my father went to court, his attorney filed a motion to dismiss on the grounds that Detective Green had never told my dad that the merchandise was actually stolen.

When the detective took the stand, and the judge asked him whether or not he had informed my dad that in fact the champagne was stolen, he replied, "Since I was selling $100 bottles of champagne for $20, he had to know it was stolen."

"But you never actually told him it was stolen?" the judge said.

"Correct, Your Honor."

My dad caught a break and the case was thrown out.

My father and I have the same names, so the fact he was on the task force's radar didn't help me much. But I thought I was clever and had a master plan. I was only sixteen, and I had no criminal history. As long as I didn't get caught committing a vicious act of violence, I figured I was safe. If I got pinched selling coke as a juvenile, as long as it was under 28 grams I would get a slap on the wrist.

As I mentioned, I had a few dealers I sold to. One was a friend named Tony Lopez, who often wanted an ounce, or 28 grams. Because of my plan, I only sold quantities of 27.5 grams, so it was never a full ounce. Tony was a few years older than me and seemed like a standup guy. One day he called and asked for two ounces of coke. I told him I only had one left until next week, thinking he would take his usual ounce. He said, "Never mind, I really need two ounces. I'm going to bring it up north and triple my money. I can wait until next week."

A couple of weeks went by and we continued talking over the phone. Every time I talked to him, I gave a different excuse why I could only give him one ounce. I didn't want to offend him, but I was sticking to my 27.5-gram golden rule. Finally, he said, "FUCK IT. I'll get one and now buy the other one when you can get it." Sounded good to me...

We arranged to meet in a parking lot outside K-Mart in Hollywood on Highway 441. My girlfriend Michele, who was eighteen at the time, was with me in the car. I had met Michele at Hot Tracks, a nightclub in Hallandale. I told her I was eighteen, and by the time she found out I was only sixteen it was too late. She was studying to be a paramedic and had her head on straight. She did not drink, smoke, or do any drugs, which was one of the things I liked about her...

Michelle knew she could never come with me when I conducted business, for her own good. But on this particular day, she was already dressed up for dinner and insisted. I talked myself into letting her come. She had nothing to do with the deal, if anything was to go wrong, I would take full responsibility and say she knew nothing about it.

When I arrived at K-Mart, I saw Lopez standing out front. I pulled up, and he got in the car.

"Hey, Lopez, what's going on brother?"

"Same old shit. How about you, Caucci?"

"Eh, you know."

We drove around the parking lot to find a secluded place, and I pulled into a parking space with no cars on either side. We made some bullshit small talk, then he pulled out the $800 for the ounce and gave it to me. I did a quick count, then reached into my pants where I kept the coke and handed it to him. He opened the bag and said in an unusually loud voice, "This is some good shit."

"Fuhgeddaboudit…"

Then out of nowhere, a big black van with blacked-out windows skidded to a stop right in front of my car. The van's side doors slammed open, and six heavily armed men dressed in black wearing SWAT gear rushed toward my car with their guns drawn and pointing at us. Their faces were covered with what looked like ski masks.

9 | I'll Blow Your Fucking Head Off

Four of the masked men aimed their guns at my head and yelled, "Don't move, or I will blow your fucking head off!"

The other two masked men ran toward the passenger side of my car and opened the door while aiming their guns at Michelle's head. They grabbed her by the hair, threw her to the ground, and drove their knees into her back. Then they did the same to me. I was on my stomach looking at her from under the car. I still didn't know what the fuck was happening. One guy drove his knee into her back again and kept a gun pressed against the back of her head. God no, please don't let him pull that trigger. I could see the pain and fear in her face and mouthed, "I love you." She stared at me and, without taking her eyes off me, said, "I love you."

What had I done? I just got us both killed. I knew these guys meant business because of the intensity and violence they were using. As I squirmed around, trying to get a look at their faces, I think I called them every swear word in the book. Then one of them stomped on the back of my head and slammed my face into the concrete. He put the gun to my temple, pulled my head back by my hair, and said very calmly, "I said don't move or I'll bow your fucking head off! Hollywood police, you're under arrest."

I felt a short-lived rush of relief knowing it wasn't a rip-off and we weren't going to be killed in the robbery-style execution that had been common lately amongst drug dealers. For the first fifteen seconds or so, I had been paralyzed with fear because I didn't think they were cops and thought we were dead.

As the cops squeezed the handcuffs on me as hard as they possibly could, one screamed at me, "What's your fucking name?"

But I remembered what my dad said: "If you ever get pinched, keep your fucking mouth shut until your lawyer is there."

So I didn't say a word. I just looked at Michelle, who had tears in her eyes as she was pinned to the ground in pain. Then another heavy knee in my back knocked the wind out of me.

"I said what's your fucking name?"

I thought, "If you think I'm gonna say or do anything to assist you fucks in my own arrest, you're some pretty goddamn stupid police."

While I was getting roughed up, the other cops looked through my car for drugs or guns. I heard one on the radio say, "We got him! We got Caucci!"

"Son of a bitch!" another one said, slamming his fist on the hood of his car. "He's only sixteen."

"No fucking way," one replied in disbelief.

"Here's his fucking driver's license. He's a juvenile."

What a relief those words were! I knew this day could come, but I didn't think it would come so soon. You can grow up with some of the toughest sons of bitches on earth and learn a lot, but nobody can teach you how to act or feel when you have a gun to your head.

They yanked me to my feet by the handcuffs, nearly dislocating my shoulder, and slammed me against my car. My mind started racing, and I could feel the heavy pounding of my heart in my chest as my adrenaline pumped through me. I thought back to everything my dad and friends have ever taught me. Then I remembered the law: anything under twenty-eight grams on a first offense did not carry a minimum mandatory sentence, and I was a juvenile.

And Michelle had nothing to do with this, so I figured they couldn't do anything to her either. Looked like all this was for nothing...what a bunch of fucking clowns.

Then one of cops said, "You're not going to do any time because you're still a juvenile, but your girlfriend is eighteen. She'll be taken down to the county Jail, booked, fingerprinted, and charged with trafficking cocaine and conspiracy to traffic cocaine. Her bail will be set at $50,000."

What the fuck was going on? She had absolutely nothing to do with it. She just sat there in the car and didn't say a word. How could they charge her? And just like that, it went from THEM being clowns to ME being a fucking idiot. I knew what their angle was going to be and how they would try and squeeze me into cooperating on her behalf. But little did they know, it was only 27.5 grams. Worst-case scenario, Michelle would get probation, but this would be on her record for the rest of her life.

Michelle had no idea what to say or do. She didn't know the laws and had not been schooled from an early age like I had been. I knew they would try to scare the shit out of her by telling her she would go to prison for at least three years if she didn't talk. I also knew she didn't know anyone else she could cooperate against...except me. But since I was only sixteen and likely to get off with a slap on the wrist, cooperating against me would not help her at all.

While they had me bent over the hood of my car, I overheard the cops telling her, "Your scumbag boyfriend is going to be sleeping in his own bed by tomorrow night while you rot in the county jail waiting for someone to pay your $50,000 bail. You think your boyfriend is gonna pay that kind of money to get you out? He doesn't give a fuck about you, he'll let you sit in there and he'll be sleeping with a new girl by tomorrow night. We see this shit every day."

My heart broke hearing the words that were coming out of that pig's mouth. I wanted to strangle the life out of him with my bare hands. I was so angry and ashamed of the position I had put her in. I couldn't imagine what was going through her mind.

Then I heard her say, "Okay, okay, I'll talk."

Oh shit...what was she going to say?

Very nonchalantly, she said, "First let me say that I have no idea why you are arresting me. One minute I'm sitting in the passenger seat of my boyfriend's car and the next you have both of us on the ground with guns to our heads. It takes six armed men to arrest an unarmed sixteen-year-old? You guys should be ashamed of yourselves. And as far as me rotting in jail over a measly $50,000, uhhhh I don't think so. When I get my one phone call, his father will bail me out quicker than you can blow your load watching gay porn." Then she finished sarcastically, "You do know who his father is, don't you? Or did you accidentally arrest the wrong Caucci?"

I couldn't believe my ears.

They put a black bag over her head, threw her into the back of a police car and took her away. What the fuck had I done? I had ruined her life and embarrassed my family, taking down my girlfriend with me. It would probably be better if I just stayed in jail. I was never gonna hear the end of this one.

"You stupid fuck, you know better than this." I could hear my dad's voice echoing in my head.

I knew I'd never forget the look on her face when she was handcuffed, staring at me from under the car. I would always regret letting her come with me that day...

The cops duct taped my mouth, put a black bag over my head, and threw me into the van on my stomach. It was an unforgettable ride but a short one since the Hollywood police station was just around the corner. As they were taking me to the station, I could hear the detectives calling into the station: "We have a white male, Anthony Caucci, DOB 11/14/71 5'8" en route, ETA seven minutes."

During that ride, I realized what had happened. It was so fucking obvious...I should have seen it coming. Lopez had insisted so many times on buying two ounces of coke instead of his normal one. The cops were trying to make sure I had over an ounce when they busted me, so that I would be facing a three-year minimum mandatory sentence.

I later found out from mutual acquaintances and my attorney that Tony Lopez (confidential informant CI 1315) had gotten busted with a couple of ounces over a month before. I had been dealing with him for quite some time, and he seemed like a solid guy up until he got busted. Lopez was nineteen or twenty at the time of his arrest. It was his first offense. However, he was not a juvenile, so he wasn't getting off so easy. As soon as the handcuffs went on, he apparently cried like a little girl. The thought of going to jail turned him into a little bitch and he sang like a canary.

He gave up so many names that the cops didn't even like him. One cop joked, "We almost had to slap him so he would stop talking!" Little did he know that once he mentioned my name, things would get really bad for him. Now the police had Anthony Caucci's son on their radar. Lopez told them about my connections and that I got my coke from a guy down the street from me who went by the name Fat Man and could get hundreds of kilos of cocaine. He told the police that Fat Man and his father were some of the biggest Cuban drug dealers in South Florida. The Hollywood police were psyched. They thought they were finally going to get a Caucci to flip and get Fat Man too. That would be a huge score for them.

When we arrived at the station, they pulled me out of the van, the black bag still over my head and my mouth taped. I was disorientated, but I had just enough time to pull myself together before they pulled the bag off my head. They wouldn't see any fear in my eyes. I would make sure of it.

They took the bag off and one of the officers said, "Caucci, hold still so I can take this tape off your mouth nice and slowly or it will really fucking hurt."

Okay. I stood still and he started to peel it off ever so gently. Then, once he got a good grip on it, he ripped it off as quick as he could, pulling what little mustache hair I had right out. I screamed, "Your mother's a whore, you fucking pig!" The bag went back on my head, but at least I could curse them out after that. The other cops just laughed as it was just another day for them. That was the first and last time I ever had my mustache waxed, and it hurt like a son of a bitch.

This was where the men were divided from the pussies. Keep your head up, show no fear, and don't talk. They escorted me through the underground parking lot, into the elevator, and into the booking area. Then they took that fucking bag off my head. One of the officers read me my charges (trafficking cocaine 28 grams or more and conspiracy to trafficking 56 grams of cocaine) and asked me if I understood my charges. At first I thought, "No, it was only 27.5 grams, scrotum breath," but out loud I said, "Nope, I don't understand nothin."

"Oh, so you gonna be a smart ass?"

"Nope, but do you think you can move a little faster? I'm gonna be late for dinner."

"I can see this is gonna be a long fucking day."

"Just get to work, you fucking shoe shine boy. I don't have all day."

They took my fingerprints and mug shot. Since it was picture time, I thought I'd have some fun since I didn't plan on being there long. I put a real cocky look on my face as they took my picture. Then they told me to take my shirt and shoes off. Suddenly I remembered…ohhh shit, I had another 14 grams under my balls that I had completely forgotten about during all the chaos. If they find the 14 grams and add it to the 27.5 grams, I'd be way over the limit. On top of that, having 14 grams in separate baggies would not look good in front of a judge. The whole story I had come up with that this was the first time I have ever done something like this would not fly. I wasn't feeling so cocky anymore. I said a quick prayer in my head: "God, I know you're there and I probably don't deserve it, but how about a hand here?"

They checked my shirt, shoes, and socks real good, but I still had my pants on. Then an officer got in my face and said, "Put your hands in the air and spread your legs." So I did. He gave me a quick pat down, up and down and between my legs. He didn't go too close to my balls, so I was in the clear. Then he put his arms around me and his hands down the back of my pants, pulling outward on my underwear until he came to the font. When his hands got closer to the front of my body, he pulled them out and told me to get dressed.

Thank you, Jesus, I owe you one!

Now I was trying to look real cool with no more smart fucking remarks from me. I still had 14 grams between my legs. How the hell was I going to dump this shit? Then he told me to go sit over on a bench. As I was walking to the long wooden bench, I looked through the glass into a holding cell. There were four concrete block walls and a long bench along the wall and a stainless-steel toilet bowl in the corner. I had to get to that toilet.

"Officer...Officer, I need to take a shit," I said, bending over and grabbing my stomach.

"Hold on," he said dismissively.

"There ain't no holding this one! If I don't get this one-eyed ass monkey out of my ass, I'm gonna have a code three blowout!"

"Okay, stand up and pull your pants down."

Fuck. Busted.

I pulled my pants down to my ankles without hesitation, hoping he wouldn't say underwear too. Then he says, "Pull 'em up." He opened the door to the holding cell and slammed it behind me. The only person in there was a very shy, skinny white boy about fourteen or fifteen years old who seemed like he didn't have much confidence in himself. I asked him, "Why are you here?"

"I was trying to steal a Coke from a machine," he replied with a slight redneck accent.

"Get da fuck outta here! You got locked up for stealing a Coke?"

"Sure did. Dem dam cops don't give a fuck 'bout nobody."

"Don't worry, you'll be out of here soon, it's just a soda."

"No I won't, this is my third arrest. They're gonna send me back to juvenile detention for at least twenty-one days and them damn niggas gonna take my food and whoop my ass every single day. Us white boys don't stand a chance in juvi! Dem niggas run the place."

"What were your other two arrests?"

"Trespassin'."

I knew from the look on his face that he was scared of where he was going, and it wasn't going to be a good thing for him.

"So what's your name?"

"Freddy," he replied softly.

I put a big smile on my face said, "Nice to meet you, Freddy, I wish the circumstances were a little different. Listen, Freddy, I'm in a jam here. I need you to do me a favor, okay?"

"What is it?"

"I need you to look out that window and tell me if the pigs are coming. I have to use the toilet."

"Dem pigs don't care if you use the toilet."

"Freddy, just do me a favor and let me know if you see someone coming. When we get to juvenile hall, if anybody messes with you, I got your back. If we get outnumbered, so be it. There is nothing wrong with taking a beating. Just take it like a man, don't fold, and always fight back. If you don't fight back, they'll never stop picking on you. They thrive on weakness. Just watch the door, okay?"

Freddy's face lit up with relief as he said, "Okay, man, I'll keep a lookout."

My heart raced as I sat down on the seat because I knew they could come in any minute. I pulled the big plastic bag with the fourteen smaller bags of cocaine from under my balls. I had to open each one and rinse it in toilet water before I flushed. I contemplated flushing the whole thing in one shot, but figured I was definitely not the first person trying to flush dope down the toilet in the police station. I would bet there was some sort of filter that would catch the plastic baggies and I'd be screwed. Better to be safe and open each one so I could dissolve the coke in the water. Then, as I'm starting to open individual bags, I heard the sound of keys jingling and heavy footsteps getting closer to the cell.

Freddy whispered, "Whatever you're doing, hurry up, the cops are coming!"

I was moving as fast as I could, but it's not easy opening one-inch bags when you're sitting on the toilet and your adrenaline is racing. "Stall them!" I said.

"How'm I sposed to do that?"

"Use your fucking head, Freddy! Figure something out."

Freddy fell to the floor and curled into the fetal position with his hands over his heart, looking like he was in a lot of pain. He started screaming, "Help! Help!" The cops came rushing in to see what was going on.

"What's wrong, Freddy?" one of the officers asked while the other called for paramedics on his radio.

Gasping to get the words out, Freddy said, "I don't know...I have...a pain in my chest." Now this fucking kid was one good actor—he had me convinced for a second that something was really wrong. As they were concentrating on helping him, I was on the other side of a three-foot privacy wall, sitting on the toilet so all they could see was my head. With all the commotion of the paramedics arriving and checking Freddy's heart, I was able to open the bags and get rid of everything. After about ten minutes, I gave the toilet a final flush. I was in the clear. The 14 grams were down the toilet and I was back in the safe zone, just under an ounce.

Once Freddy heard the toilet flush and saw me stand up, he let out a very loud burp and jumped to his feet. "I'm ok," he said. "It was just a little gas. It happens sometimes, especially when I drink too much stolen Coke."

10 | I'll Kill You with My Bare Fuckin' Hands

While all this was going on, Detective Dave Green got word that Caucci's son had been arrested—and he couldn't wait to call my father.

"Mr. Caucci," he said, "this is Detective Green with Broward Sheriff's office."

"Heeey!" my dad said, happy for another chance to bust Green's balls. "Mr. Green, where the hell you been? It's been quiet around here. Everyone is really starting to miss you."

"Actually I've been very busy now that I got your punk kid in custody here at Hollywood police station."

"Hey, watch your fuckin' mouth, you mutt! Who you calling a punk? My kids got more balls than you'll ever have, you motherless rodent."

"I guess we are gonna see how tough your kid really is, aren't we? I bet you a G-note I get him to cooperate."

"Fuuuuuck you! What are you charging him with?"

"Trafficking cocaine. It carries a three-year minimum mandatory. See, Caucci, your son might not do any time because he's a juvenile, but if he doesn't cooperate, his girlfriend Michelle will. She got arrested with him. I thought you would have taught your son better than that...getting his girlfriend involved in illegal activity. Your friends are really gonna like that one, hey Caucci?"

"You know something, Green, you fucking cops are pathetic. You blew your shot at arresting me so you go after my son! You deserve a fucking plaque! As a matter of fact, I'm gonna have one made for you that reads, 'Lifetime achievement award, Detective

Green has dedicated his life making our community safe and has finally captured the notorious sixteen-year-old Anthony Caucci.'"

"Go fuck yourself, Caucci."

"Yeah yeah yeah, that's a real classic. Why are you calling me?"

"I need you to come down to the station so we can question him. We can't talk to him without you being here."

"Yeah, I know the drill. Give me a couple of hours to get down there."

"A couple of hours? The station is two minutes from your house!"

"I know where the fucking station is, I can smell you from here. You woke me up out of a dead sleep. I was dreaming that I was sitting at the bar with your wife, having a martini. I was just about to take her back to my place when you called."

"Fuck you, Caucci."

"Before I come down, I'm gonna pour myself a martini or two. And listen, Green, you keep your fucking mouth shut. Not a word to him until I get there, you understand?"

"Okay, Caucci, look forward to seeing you again."

"Yeah, me too, you fucking schoolgirl."

My dad walked over to his freezer, dressed in his white terry cloth Ralph Lauren bathrobe, and grabbed the ice-cold bottle of vodka out of the freezer. He walked back to the living room, took a seat at his well-stocked bar, lit a cigarette, and poured himself a nice double martini with three olives. He then played his favorite song, "I did it my way" by Frank Sinatra, raised his glass and toasted, "Okay, kiddo, let's see what you're made of."

Then he took three big gulps and went right back to sleep.

Back at the police station, the arresting officers showed back up in the tank with big fucking grins on their faces. "Your father's on his way here so we can talk to you, so you better get your story straight," one of them said to me.

"My dad said what? He's coming *here*, so *you* could question *me*?"

"That's exactly right…he knows we got you by the balls."

"How long until he gets here? Did he say?"

"Yeah, a couple of hours, he wants to have a martin before he comes. I think we made him nervous." They laughed.

"Oh, thank God…that's a huge relief. I thought he would just leave me here to rot."

I couldn't believe these stupid pricks thought he was coming down here to talk to them. They took me back to the holding cell to wait. It was getting late, so I grabbed a roll of toilet paper and took off a few sheets to use as a pillow. It was gonna be a long night.

After the two hours passed, Detective Green called my dad again.

"Hello?" my dad answered, his voice hoarse from sleeping.

"Hey, Caucci, it's Detective Green. Where the fuck are you? We've been waiting here for two hours."

"Hey, Green, how you doin'? Two calls in one night? I was just dreaming about you, would you believe that?"

"Oh really? Dreamin' about what this time?"

"It was a strange…it was like you and a couple of dumb fucks were sitting down at the police station waiting for me to come talk to you about something. Strange thing was, youse were all wearing pink tutus. I don't wanna be rude, but you're gonna have to let me go back to bed because I can't wait to see how this ends."

"CAUCCI, YOU MOTHERFU—"

Click.

My dad hung up and rolled over with a huge smile on his face and slept like a baby.

A few more hours passed until I heard my name called. "Caucci! wake your fucking ass up and let's go!"

"Let me guess, you guys been waiting here all this time, thinking my dad was actually gonna sit down with you so you can question me? What fucking cop school did you go to? The Mickey Mouse Police academy?"

"You're a real fucking smart ass, aren't you, Caucci? That's okay, we got a little something extra for you. We'll see who gets the last laugh."

They slapped the handcuffs back on me extra tight and we headed for the juvenile detention center. On the way out the door, I said to Freddy, "Keep your head up, kid. I will see you soon."

He smiled and said, "Okay, okay, yeah, I will see you soon."

In the back of the squad car, I had so many thoughts going through my head. My poor mother was going to be heartbroken. What was my dad going to do when he heard I got busted for drugs? Is this going to embarrass him and our family to our friends? What are people going to say about my father when they hear his son got busted selling cocaine? Will anyone still come around? How would I face him? Did I really want to face him or was I better off in jail? I had really fucked this up. My heart was also breaking for Michelle—I could not imagine what she was going through in the county jail with all those scumbags. All in all, I'd rather get slapped in the face with camel balls on national TV.

When I arrived at the juvenile detention center, they put me in a room and made me strip completely naked this time. They told me to spread my legs, raise my hands, turn around, and open my mouth. They stuck their fingers in my mouth (while wearing rubber gloves), then they ran their fingers through my hair. They told me to lift up my balls, then drop my balls and lift my dick. Next, they ordered me to turn around, bend over, and "spread dem ass cheeks, boy, let's see what you ate for dinner. Now cough!"

Boy, was I glad they didn't do that at the station!

When they were done, they handed me a pillow, a blanket, toothbrush, toothpaste, shampoo, bar of soap, comb, and a jump suit. Then a black guard who was about 6'4" and twenty-five years old, made of solid muscle, said, "Hurry up and get dressed, you cracker."

Oh boy, this was going to be interesting. I figured it was payback for two hundred years of slavery, but whaddya gonna do?

They escorted me down a hall to a pair of double doors, where we were buzzed into a room the size of a basketball court with about fifteen kids between the ages of fifteen and seventeen just running around, making noise, and having fun. It seemed like they enjoyed being there, but to me, they looked like a pack of wild dogs with zero discipline. As I started to walk toward my cell, the place got really quiet and I got nothing but dirty looks. Then I heard one of the black kids say, "Fucking pussy ass cracker." And another, "Fuck boy, soft-ass pussy bitch white piece of shit."

I stopped dead in my tracks and slowly set all my shit on the floor. Then I calmly walked up to one of them who was running his mouth. As I approached his chair, he stood up with his fists up and said, "You want some of this, you white piece of shit?"

I raised both my hands as if I was surrendering and said in a low voice so nobody could hear but him, "I don't want to have a problem with you. Just calm down and stop making so much noise…you're gonna attract the guards."

"I don't give a fuck 'bout no pussy ass guards," he says, holding his sagging pants up and making hand gestures.

"Listen to me very carefully and look me in the eyes. You got the wrong fucking cracker, you bitch-ass nigger. If you wanna try your luck with this cracker, let's take it to the room nice and quietly so nobody knows what's about to go down." Then I leaned forward and whispered, "Come to the room with me and I will kill you with my bare fucking hands."

I could tell he was nervous and didn't know how to react. So I said, "You wanna squash this or we taking a walk to the room?"

He put his fists down and sat back down.

"By the way, the last time I looked at a piece of shit, it wasn't white, so get your fucking facts straight, you stupid coon."

I turned around, picked up my shit, and thought, "Where the fuck are all the white people?"

I found out when I got to my room. There were two white boys lying in their beds. From the fear in their eyes, it was obvious they were afraid to come out. Then I remembered the words of my father: "Son, it's okay to be scared. It's how you act when you're scared that separates the men from the boys."

My dad would have been ashamed of me if I sat in this room, hiding from the niggers. So I put my shit on my bed and went back into the main area, walking around as if I fit right in. Again, it got quiet and the dirty looks kept coming. I grabbed a chair and put it in the corner so nobody could sneak up behind me. I studied each person one at a time. There is always one person running the joint who everyone is afraid of. I had to find out who it was. Usually it's the loudest and most disrespectful person in the group. But nine times out of ten, that is just a sign of fear. The ones you really have to watch out for are the quiet ones who don't bother anyone.

Within minutes, I picked my guy out. They call him Beast. He was controlling the television, which was tuned to what he wanted to watch and fuck everyone else.

I knew from my dad that the best thing for me to do was just keep to myself and wait to get bailed out, but I thanked God that I had stuck with my Kai Sai Wing Chun training for as long as I had.

Early the next morning, at about 6 a.m., one of the guards yelled, "Chow time! Line up!"

We lined up as usual, nothing but a bunch of fucking noise and people acting uncivilized. The food was shit too, just like I expected. I looked around for a place to sit and, lo and behold, there was Freddy sitting directly across from Beast.

I remembered the promise I had made to him at the police station, so I walked over and sat down next to him, giving him a pat on the back.

"Hey Freddy, how you doing, my friend?" By the look on his face I could tell he was not doing good at all.

"Hey, uh, what's your name again?"

"Caucci."

"I'm doing okay, I guess."

Across the table, I saw the Beast staring us down, while Freddy did his best to ignore him. Freddy hadn't even touched his food yet—he was scared shitless. My adrenaline kicked in. I had a bad feeling something was about to go down.

"You gonna eat that, fuck boy cracker?" the Beast said as he stuck his finger right into Freddy's cake.

"I'm really not that hungry, you can have it," Freddy said, too afraid to look up.

I could not believe the blatant disrespect this nigger was showing. What kind of human being would do something so low? I was angry, but I remained calm because I didn't want to give Beast any warning about what was coming his way. I had to position myself in a way that he would be at a disadvantage, but since he was on the other side of the table, he would have had plenty of time to react if I made a move on him right then. Plus, he was about 6'2" with an athletic build and long arms. I was only about 5'8" and 170 lbs.

He wasn't expecting Freddy to make a move, so I planned to do a "mind hit" (a temporary distraction of one's mind) and catch him off guard. I pretended I was scared and said in a timid voice, "Excuse me, but you can have mine too if you'd like. I'm not hungry."

Without looking at me, he quickly reached over and took the cake off my plate and said, "I'm taking your fucking milk too, soft-ass cracker"

"Of course you can have it, just don't hurt me. I don't want any trouble."

He sneered and thought, "Perfect, he thinks I'm soft and weak." I took a quick look around the cafeteria to see if anyone was watching. There were two black guards watching the whole thing, but they just laughed when I looked at them. I leaned forward and whispered to the Beast,

"Listen, man, when it's time to buy commissary, if there's anything you need just let me know. Whatever it is, I'll get it for you."

He looked at me with a mean grin on his face, showing off his gold teeth, and said, "Bet cracker." That was street slang for done or deal.

Now he thought he had me, that I wasn't a threat. The mind hit had worked perfectly so far. I politely excused myself from the table and told Freddy to come along. I grabbed my tray and walked away, toward Beast's blind spot. When I was alongside him, I turned my tray sideways and swung it as hard as I could, hitting him right across the nose with the edge of the tray. He howled and covered his bloody nose with both hands.

While he was still hunched over and bleeding, I circled around and punched him in the base of the skull, knocking him out of his seat and onto the floor. He curled into the fetal position, so I jumped on top of him and started punching him as hard and as fast as I could. I knew I only had seconds until the guards took me down. I wasn't able to land a solid blow to the face because he was covering up pretty good, so I stupidly began punching him in the skull, thinking I could crack his head open. Unfortunately, his head was much harder than my knuckles, so I broke a few.

Within seconds, the guards blew their whistles and all the other inmates quickly hit the floor, lying face down with their hand behind their heads. The guards rushed me, tackled me, and handcuffed me. They picked me up, one on each arm and leg, and escorted me straight to the hole, using my head to open the double doors.

Once I was alone and had calmed down, I had time to think about what had just happened. At the time I thought I had to do something to protect Freddy. But now he was all alone. What if I had made it worse for him? What if the other niggers had already beat the shit out of him because of me?

Then I remembered what my dad had said: "Son, if you ever go to jail, mind your own business, lay low, keep your eyes and ears open, and never get involved in anyone else's business, no matter what. Don't try to be a hero."

I was such a fucking fool. First I got my girlfriend busted and now I was involved in other people's problems in jail. I was a disgrace to the Italian race. My dad was going to be so disappointed with me.

After a week in the hole, they pulled me out and sent me back to my unit. I figured this wasn't going to go well for me. I was probably outnumbered fifty to one.

I went through the double doors, and everyone stopped what they were doing and stared at me. I just stood there, waiting to see what was coming next. It was so quiet, you could hear two mosquitoes fucking. The tension was thick, but at least nobody was talking shit under their breath about me being a soft-ass cracker. Even the guards were staring me down, and it was obvious they wouldn't have minded if something went down so they could fuck me up. So I just waited…but nobody said or did anything. Just like day one, I calmly walked around as if I belonged there and acted as if nothing at all had happened. Luckily, nobody made a move, so I casually strolled back to my room. When I opened the door, the same two white boys were sitting there, still afraid to come out of the room. I put my shit away and asked, "Have you come out of this room since I went to the hole?"

"No fucking way, man. We've been stuck here for a week now."

"So you mean to tell me that you eat, shower, and go hide in this room?"

"Damn straight," one of them said. "We ain't going out there…dem niggers said they're gonna fuck us up if we come out."

"Is this your first time here?"

They both answered yes.

"How many times you think I've been here?" I asked.

"Uh, a couple at least. You walk around like you're used to this shit."

"Well, you're wrong about that, this is my first time too and to be honest with you, I'm scared too…I'd be a goddamn moron if I wasn't. But I'm not gonna let the niggers know that. We are outnumbered about fifteen to one. Look, guys, you have two choices. Either you can sit in this room and hide like a bitch, or you can be a man and grow some damn balls. Staying in this room will only guarantee that even the weakest nigger in here will fuck with you when they have the chance. So why don't you tighten the fuck up and accept where you are and be men? The worst thing that can happen to you is you get your ass kicked. And if that is the case, just make sure you fight back as hard as you possibly can, make them think you're crazy. When you fight, the others will be watching, and if you fight back hard and don't back down, the others will think twice before picking on you. If you don't fight back and just take the beating, they will take turns picking you apart until you break. This entire place is run by the blacks, and most of the guards know the inmates from the streets. It's obvious they hate us, and rightfully so. Two hundred years of slavery and you'd be a little pissed off too. All we can do is stick together and send a message."

"Oh yeah, what message might that be?"

"Just because you're white doesn't make you soft! So put your fucking shoes on and let's go out there and do something."

They agreed reluctantly. We got some stares out on the unit, but everyone quickly went back to doing whatever they had been doing. One group of black kids was slap boxing. They weren't trying to hurt each other but were just having some fun. Since I loved fighting, I studied how they were positioning their hands, if they telegraphed their strikes, if they were covered or wide open, if their footwork was any good, and most importantly if anyone was good at controlling their fighting distance. One kid really had the advantage. He was very tall, at least 6'4", but he was real skinny and fast with long arms, so his reach was ridiculous. He was not very good technically but since he was so tall and fast, the other kids had no chance against him.

Me and the other two white boys had our backs against the wall, watching them all take turns at him and lose. Then he looked over at me and said, "Come on, cracker, show me what you got."

It didn't seem like he was challenging me in a bad way so I said, "Looks like fun, I'm in." He had a few advantages, especially his height and reach, but I felt that if my timing was perfect, I could give him a light slap on the cheek before he could react. I hoped he'd keep it fun and wouldn't try to knock me out with a real punch.

Now the whole place was watching, even the guards. It was no longer a fun slap boxing match; it was black against white. As we squared off, I kept my head way back while I used my footwork to position my lower body closer to him. Once I was in range, I needed to create an opening because his long arms were covering his head. It would be very difficult to get past them without getting hit. I threw low, fast kick to the inside of his thigh, just hard enough to get his attention. It landed about five inches from his groin. He immediately dropped his hands, so I lunged in and gave him a light tap on the face, then jumped back before he could react.

The look of surprise on his face was a moment I will never forget. The niggers went nuts and the whole place burst out in laughter. "Damn, that cracker got you!" they yelled. Even the cops were buckled over laughing.

From that moment on, the racism and tension stopped. I was no longer the fuck boy cracker and they were no longer niggers. We were just a bunch of kids, black and white, doing our time the best way we could. It's remarkable how sometimes not showing fear can change the way people perceive you.

Interacting with the black kids could be entertaining. They often wanted to slap box with me and asked questions about my martial arts, making really funny comments about me doing some of that "crazy Bruce Lee shit." Once I was able to understand their street slang, I laughed harder than I ever had. They were some funny sons of bitches. They treated me with respect and were helpful, as most of them had been there more than once. I introduced them to my two "cracker" cellmates and everyone seemed to get along.

A couple of days before my court date, my dad came to visit. After some small talk, he said, "Don't worry, it's your first offense. You'll probably be out in a few days." Then he leaned over the table, covered his mouth, and whispered, "Do you remember Tom Lynch?"

"Of course I do. You were partners with him when you opened Ticon Construction."

"Well, his son is a judge. He's going to reach out to the prosecutor and put in a good word for you." I knew he was saying this just to make me feel better, but what else could he do?

The day finally came when it was time for me to go to court. I was certain that I was going home that day, especially after all the other stories I heard from other inmates. One black kid with two prior arrests got caught with two kilos of crack and was released after ten days. Another black kid stole a car from a dealership and got busted with a kilo of coke and a gun and only got thirty days. After I told some of the other inmates my story, they were all certain I was going home.

Pretty soon, I was at the courthouse in a holding cell with eleven other kids who were going before the same judge as me. A guard opened the cell door and handcuffed us all together by the wrists and escorted us into the court room. We were seated in the jury box. As I sat down, I noticed a plaque sitting on the judge's bench with his name on it "The Honorable Tom Lynch." I couldn't fucking believe it. How did my dad pull this off? My stomach started doing cartwheels, but I had to remain calm. I couldn't wait for this thing to fall into place and the judge to say, "Time served" and release me. This would go down in history.

Then the judge walked in and took a seat.

11 | You're Italian...They Want to Make An Example Out of You

I was so excited. I couldn't wait to get the fuck out of there. Then the judge said, "I have to bring it to the court's attention that my father, Tom Lynch Senior, is a very close friend of the defendant Anthony Caucci's father. I have also met the defendant Anthony Caucci many years ago. Therefore, I must recuse myself from this case."

Recuse??? What da fuck does that mean? I had never even heard of such a word. Then the black kid sitting next to me said, "You and your daddy know the judge and he didn't let you go? That's some straight bullshit. You can bet yo mutherfuckin' ass if I knew the mutherfuckin' judge and da mutherfuckin' judge was a nigga, my black ass be'd going home today."

I couldn't believe my ears—me landing in front of Lynch was just a fucking coincidence! Now what? I had to wait a few more days to be seen by a different judge? This WAS some straight bullshit. My dad would have never thought in a million years this could have happened. Most of the kids went home that day, and a few with more serious charges were sentenced to a couple of months of juvenile detention. So, I thought...worst case scenario would be I get a couple of months.

After hearing the charges the other kids had, I was a saint. A few days went by, and I heard my name called: "Caucci." That usually meant you're going home. For a second, I got really excited, then the guard said, "You got a visitor." Visitor? Couldn't be my dad…it wasn't visitation day. The guards brought me into a very small room and sat me down in one of two chairs facing each other. Then a very well-dressed black woman in a white suit walked in carrying a bunch of folders. She sat down across from me and introduced herself. "Hello, Mr. Ka hu chi. I'm Mrs. Washington. I'm with the state and I am your case worker. So, let me start by saying…I have some good news and some bad news."

Shiiiiit, I did not like the sound of that—bad news coming from the state was definitely going to outweigh the good news. "Okay…what is it?"

"Would you like the good news or the bad news first?"

"I'm pretty sure the order you tell me is not going to make me feel any better so…why don't you start with the bad news and then hit me with the good news so you can cheer me up and make my day?"

"Okay, Mr. Caucci, the bad news is the state has decided to direct file you."

"Direct what?"

"Direct file. This means you are going to be charged and tried as an adult. If you are convicted, you will be sentenced as an adult and sent to an adult prison."

I could not believe my ears. I remember the police being pissed off when they arrested me because I was only sixteen and saying I "would be out in a few days." But that one scumbag cop did say they "would get the last laugh." And now I was getting charged as an adult? My dad was right, the government could do anything they wanted and there was nothing you could do about it. Who would believe they would stoop this low to see if they can get me to cooperate? Then I said to Mrs. Washington, "If I ask you a question, will you be completely honest with me? Please be straight with me, no bullshit."

"I will do my very best to answer you, Mr. Caucci." She looked a little perplexed and said, "Let me look in your file to see if anything out of the ordinary stands out." She started to flip through my papers and read the police report, then said, "Okay, let me see here, this is your first offense, it's a nonviolent crime, you didn't have a weapon, and you only had one ounce of powder cocaine. Actually 27.5 grams, but that doesn't seem to matter. I don't see anything out of the ordinary except that you're a white boy with an Indian last name."

"INDIAN? Do I look like a horse-riding featherhead to you, Mrs. Washington? Where in the world did you get that from?"

She covered her mouth and looked down at the floor as she laughed uncontrollably. It was obvious she was embarrassed that she was laughing, but she just couldn't hold it in.

It had been a while since I had a good laugh, so I kept it going. "Mrs. Washington, can you imagine me riding on the back of a goddamn horse wearing war paint with feathers in my hair chasing a white man for his scalp?"

She got up and excused herself and went out into the hallway until she regained her composure.

"Okay, where were we?" she said when she came back in.

"You had just called me an Indian."

"Well, Ka-hu-chi sure sounds Indian to me."

"No, ma'am, I'm Italian."

"Well then, Mr. Caucci, there's your answer."

"What's my answer?"

"That's why they're charging you as an adult…you're Italian. Very few Italians come through the juvenile system here in Florida. They want to make an example out of you!"

"Get da fuck outta here…"

"Welcome to the world of discrimination, Mr. Caucci. There are plenty of blacks, whites, and Hispanics who come through the system, but when they get an I-TALIAN the prosecutors act like a kid in a candy store. You can thank all them people who make those Italian Mafia movies. Usually a juvenile is direct filed when it's a crime of violence, a weapon is involved, sex crimes, murder, or the person has a prior felony arrest. But for one ounce of powder cocaine on a first offense, this is the first time I've ever seen this happen. I'm guessing you have something they want."

"Since you're my case worker, is there anything you can do?"

"I'm sorry, Mr. Caucci, if there was anything I could do to help you I would, but all the power lies in the hands of the state attorney's office. Unfortunately, the judge doesn't even have the power to send it back to the juvenile court. Your charge carries a three-year minimum mandatory sentence unless you cut a deal, and that usually means cooperating with the police."

"So I just went from three weeks as a juvenile to a three-year minimum.? What's the maximum, the electric chair?

"If you don't cooperate and take it to trial and lose, you could get fifteen to thirty years. But if you plead guilty, they will probably offer you the three-year minimum."

This was not looking good. "Please, Mrs. Washington, knock me off my feet with the good news now?"

"The good news is they will be sending you downtown to the county jail to process you and take your fingerprints. Once that's done, your bail will be set at $50,000."

At this point I was in the same boat as Michelle and knew she could cooperate against me if I went to trial. But I had nobody to blame except myself. I broke a golden rule and had to face the consequences, whatever they may be. When it got down to the last hour and it was either me or her, I would insist that she cooperate against me if it prevented her from going to jail! Or maybe she would refuse and keep her mouth closed.

I also knew for a fact that I had sold 27.5 grams on the dot, which changed our charges to possession of cocaine, which did not carry a three-year minimum mandatory. I figured once I got a lawyer, the charges would be reduced to possession and I would be in a much better position.

The next day, they called my name: "Caucci! Pack it up!" Then they sent me downtown to the county jail. When I arrived, it was the same shit as the Hollywood police station, except the deputies were surprised to see a sixteen-year-old getting charged as an adult.

The next morning I was brought into the judge's chambers, along with my attorney. With my attorney's permission, the judge asked me a few questions off the record before the prosecutor arrived. He seemed very sympathetic. "Son, is this your first offense?"

"Yes, Your Honor, it is."

"Did you have any weapons?"

"No, Your Honor."

"Did anyone get hurt during this…let's say incident?"

"Besides me getting my face slammed into the ground and my shoulder nearly dislocated, no, Your Honor."

"Young man, did you resist arrest?"

"Absolutely not, Your Honor. Who would resist arrest with a gun pressed up against their head? I thought I was going to be killed."

It was obvious that the judge did not like what he was hearing. He quickly flipped through my paperwork like he was looking for something important. After the prosecutor arrived and the hearing began, the judge asked, "Am I missing something here?"

"Uh, what are you referring to, Your Honor?"

"Are there any underlying circumstances that I'm not aware of that would persuade the state to charge this young man as an adult?"

"He does not conduct himself like the average sixteen-year-old, Your Honor."

"Really? Please explain."

"From the information provided by the arresting officers, the way he conducts himself during his criminal activities is a lot more sophisticated than the average sixteen-year-old and is extremely mature for his age."

"Well, I have seen plenty of sixteen-year-olds who have shot people, committed home invasions, car-jackings, and all other sorts of violent crimes who did not get direct filed on a first offense. This would be the first case I have ever had in front of me where the accused is a nonviolent, first-time offender and is being direct filed because he was sophisticated. Before we proceed, I'm going to take a few minutes to review the statute." Then he read out loud:

A MANDATORY DIRECT FILE

(a)   With respect to any child who was 16 or 17 years of age at the time the alleged offense was committed, the state attorney shall file an information if the child has been previously adjudicated delinquent for an act classified as a felony, which adjudication was for the commission of, attempt to commit, or conspiracy to commit murder, sexual battery, armed or strong-armed robbery, carjacking, home-invasion robbery, aggravated battery, or aggravated assault, and the child is currently charged with a second or subsequent violent crime against a person.

(b)   With respect to any child 16 or 17 years of age at the time an offense classified as a forcible felony, as defined in s. 776.08, was committed, the state attorney shall file an information if the child has previously been adjudicated delinquent or had adjudication withheld for three acts classified as felonies each of which occurred at least 45 days apart from each other. This paragraph does not apply when the state attorney has good cause to believe that exceptional circumstances exist which preclude the just prosecution of the juvenile in adult court.

(c)   The state attorney must file an information if a child, regardless of the child's age at the time the alleged offense was committed, is alleged to have committed an act that would be a violation of law if the child were an adult, that involves stealing a motor vehicle, including, but not limited to, a violation of s. 812.133, relating to carjacking, or s. 812.014(2)(c)6., relating to grand theft of a motor vehicle, and while the child was in possession of the stolen motor vehicle the child caused serious bodily injury to or the death of a person who was not involved in the underlying offense. For purposes of this section, the driver and all willing passengers in the stolen motor vehicle at the time such serious bodily injury or death is inflicted shall also be subject to mandatory transfer to adult court. "Stolen motor vehicle," for the purposes of this section, means a motor vehicle that has been the subject of any criminal wrongful taking. For purposes of this section, "willing passengers" means all willing passengers who have participated in the underlying offense.

(d)1.   With respect to any child who was 16 or 17 years of age at the time the alleged offense was committed, the state attorney shall file an information if the child has been charged with committing or attempting to commit an offense listed in s. 775.087(2)(a)1.a.-p., and, during the commission of or attempt to commit the offense.

When he was done, the judge stared hard at the prosecutor. "From what I've just read, this young man does not fall under a mandatory direct file, would you agree?"

"Yes, Your Honor."

"Okay, then, what statute is the state using to transfer him to the adult system."

"Your Honor, it's the state's discretion."

DISCRETIONARY DIRECT FILE

With respect to any child who was 16 or 17 years of age at the time the alleged offense was committed, the state attorney MAY file an information when in the state attorney's judgment and discretion the public interest requires that adult sanctions be considered or imposed.

Again, the judge went on, "So the state is charging him as an adult not because he meets the requirements of a mandatory direct file but rather because the state thinks and it's at their discretion that this sixteen-year-old, first-time, nonviolent offender should be punished as an adult?"

"I understand, Your Honor, I'm just doing my job as directed by my superiors."

"Well, at this point I still have control over this case. The state has not filled out the paperwork in its entirety. If they fail to do so, I will be releasing him in the next thirty minutes!"

That was good news, but short-lived. Fifteen minutes later, all the paperwork was filled out and I was officially charged as an adult.

I was taken back to the county jail where I was able to make one phone call to my dad. He told me he was working on getting me out, but I found later on he wasn't really working on it at all. All it really took was one phone call to a friend who owned a bail bonds company and I would have been released immediately. He let me sit there for two weeks, just long enough for it to soak in. He was trying to teach me a lesson; he was letting me see what life would be like if I chose the life that got me in this jam in the first place. I was only sixteen and it wasn't too late for me to make a change. I think he felt a little responsible for what had happened and the direction my life was going, but he was also proud that I took the pinch like a man and didn't snitch.

Two weeks went by in county with nothing exciting to talk about except fights. Then, on Friday at about 10 p.m. I heard my door unlocking electronically and my name came over the intercom. "Caucci, pack it up..."

Now this was a day to remember. It took just as long to get released as it did to get booked...about six hours. Then they escorted me downstairs still wearing my beige jail pants that were five sizes too big, a white T-shirt, and some cheap shower slides. My dad was sitting in the lobby with a group of long-time Mob friends: Jerry Chilli, Al Salerno, Steve Maruca, Tommy the Beard, and Natty Passaro. My welcome-home committee was an impressive bunch. When I walked out of the elevator, they all stood up clapping their hands and shouted like a big celebration was happening. "Hey...! There he is..! Come here, kid...! Get over here, you... your vacation's over!" All of them gave me a hug and a kiss on the cheek. A get-out-of-jail party...man, it was great.

"Let's go have a drink!" my dad shouted, even though they were already half-tanked. Me, I couldn't wait to have a Coke and a burger.

12 | The Hanging Judge

The next two years of my life were boring as far as illegal activity went, but I still wanted to be as prepared as I could be for prison, just in case things didn't work out the way I was hoping. One day my dad sat me down and said, "Listen, until we get this bullshit case thrown out, you have to keep your nose clean. These fucks will lock you up for jay walking. Your lawyer is going to argue that you are only sixteen, it's your first offense, and you were set up by an adult. So don't do anything stupid to give the state prosecutor a reason to fuck you any more than they already have."

"Okay, Pop. So what's the next step?"

"First your attorney has to file a motion for discovery. This is where he will request copies of all the evidence they have against you. Everything they plan on using against you at trial, they have to give to your attorney. This way he can dispute any of their claims and possibly get some, or maybe all, of the evidence thrown out. A lot of times, the prick cops break the law in order to make an arrest stick and hope the attorney doesn't find out."

"So what happens if the cops did something dirty?"

"Then the whole case is thrown out and they're onto the next one."

"Then what happens to the cops?"

"FORGET ABOUT IT...they can do whatever the fuck they want to guys like us and nobody gives a shit."

"What about that fuckin' rat Lopez?"

"We'll find out everything there is to know about the snitch, his full name, his address, the reason he cooperated. We're gonna find out how many times a day he takes a shit and which direction he wipes his ass."

"Really?"

"We'll know more about that spick than his own parents."

"Whaddya say about his address?"

"Don't get any smart ideas, genius. If you go anywhere near that fuckin' stool pigeon, they'll revoke your bond and you'll sit in the county jail awaiting trial and that can take years. We're going to work this thing from two angles. One from the court, and the other from the street. If, for some reason, he mysteriously doesn't show up to court, the charges will be dismissed. You follow?"

I nodded. Things didn't seem too bad, but I still wanted to be prepared for the worst-case scenario. In the meantime, all I had to do was stay out of trouble. Maybe it was time to start thinking hard about the direction my life was headed. After paying for mine and Michelle's attorney and $100,000 in bond money, I didn't want to spend what I had saved. So I started painting for my Dad again.

I also started training extremely hard in Chinese boxing. I had the key to the school and would usually train in the middle of the night for hours and hours. Professor Cravens was often at the school past midnight, working on his book. As I practiced, he sometime left his office and watched me train for a few minutes. Then, without saying a word, he would go back to working on his book. Once in a while he corrected me, but he never gave me any compliments. Still, the fact that he stopped what he was doing to come watch me meant a lot.

One night I came into practice and asked him if he would mind if I worked on the wooden dummy. Hitting the dummy is very loud and might distract the average person trying to write a book.

"Sure, go ahead," he replied. So I spent the next thirty minutes hitting the wooden dummy as hard as I could, trying to impress him—and to be honest, I could hit the dummy very hard.

He walked in and stood next to me and said, "You're hitting it wrong."

"Really? Can you please explain?"

"You're too tense and you're relying too much on the strength of your arms. You're not projecting your energy into the dummy, so your hits are dead."

I looked at him, a little confused.

"You need to throw your energy into the dummy using a unitary shock force. Use your whole body. Push from the ground with your legs and hit the dummy square with follow-through and a small circular recoil while your arms and body remain relaxed." Then he demonstrated how I was doing it and then how it should be done. "Can you hear the difference? One sounds like a whip and the other sounds like a CLUNK."

I hit it for a few minutes and he looked at me with a blank face and then said, "Yes, that is how it is done. If you can keep that whipping sound up, I'll finally be able to concentrate on my writing." Then he turned around and walked away. Now I knew I had to hit the dummy perfectly or he wouldn't be able to concentrate…the pressure was really on.

Twenty years later he asked, "Do you remember the night I corrected you on the wooden dummy while I was writing my book?"

"Of course I do! I'll never forget it!"

"That night was a turning point in your hitting power."

I thought, "Well, it only took you twenty years to tell me, but I'll take that as a compliment."

I continued to train almost every night, preparing my mind and my skills, just in case I got sent to prison. A few weeks went by, and it was time for my first court appearance. I ended up in front of Judge Thomas Coker. My attorney said, "This does not look good at all. From the looks of this, they want you bad. You have literally ended up in front of the toughest judge in the entire United States of America. He is known as the Hanging Judge. Between 1981 and 1982, he sentenced seven people to the electric chair."

"Oh great! You just made my day…that's just what I wanted to hear. I feel so much better now, Thank you for sharing that wonderful news with me."

We entered the court room and the clerk called my name. The judge asked me how I was going to plead and I replied, "Not guilty." The judge next asked the state why I was sent to the adult court system. They said it was due to the nature and sophistication of the crime.

"One ounce of powder cocaine with no prior arrest?"

"Yes, Your Honor."

"Well, I hate seeing a young man's life ruined over something like this when no violence was involved, but my hands are tied."

I was ordered to return in three months for my next court appearance. After a month or so my attorney called me and said he had received the discovery and would like to talk to me. When my father and I arrived at his office, he was sitting behind his desk with two big boxes full of papers and some tape recordings. He said, "Here's the discovery…and it sure is a lot of stuff for such a small case, but the bottom line is the charges. You are being charged with trafficking cocaine of more than twenty-eight grams but less than two hundred grams."

"Wait a second, stop right there. More than twenty-eight grams?"

"Yes, thirty-one grams to be exact."

"That is total bullshit! I always sold my ounces light…27.5 on the dot. Where did the 3.5 extra grams come from?"

He looked at me and raised one eyebrow and said, "Where do you think?"

My dad's face turned beet red. "Those cocksuckers. He is only sixteen, and they won't even be honest about the charges."

"I was hoping it was more like 28.5 grams," my attorney said, "then we could have it sent to a lab to have all the water weight taken out of it and that possibly could have brought it down to under the twenty-eight gram mark. Since they added 3.5 grams of cut to it, it will never get below an ounce.

"Can't they take the cut out?"

"I wish that was the case, but the law states 'a substance containing cocaine.' You could have sold a kilo of flour that only had a gram of cocaine in it and you'd be charged with the entire kilo. Prosecutors make deals all the time. First we will try to get the case thrown out, and if that doesn't work hopefully they will let you plead guilty to a lesser charge that doesn't carry the minimum mandatory. Then your last options are to cooperate with the police or go to trial."

"No, I would never agree to cooperate with the police. I could not image the embarrassment to my family and the disappointment of our friends. Or looking at myself in the mirror every day."

"That's not an option and don't ask that question again," my dad said.

"Okay, but I have to let you know the penalties if he gets convicted. He would be sentenced as an adult to a minimum of three years, and he could get more. He'll be doing time with people doing life. And just so you are aware, people doing a life sentence have nothing to lose, so things could get complicated inside for you"

"It is what it is. We have friends inside too, ya know," my dad replied with confidence. "Our reach is very far! If anyone makes problems for him, they'll wish they had the death sentence."

My attorney nodded and started looking through his paperwork. My dad looked at me and gave me a wink, which meant he had a plan and wanted to reassure me.

After getting the discovery, we learned everything we needed to know about the RAT. The word was on the street and all of our friends were looking for this guy, but he was nowhere to be found. The few months passed quickly, and it was time for me to return to court. My attorney filed a motion for dismissal and argued that the amount of cocaine was not 31 grams but only 27.5 grams and that the police added the 3.5 grams to make sure it would be a trafficking charge. The state argued that our accusations were totally false and there was no evidence to support our argument. We lost the motion to dismiss, but the judge did say something peculiar: "This the first case I have had where the defendant has given away extra cocaine free of charge."

After the hearing, the case was postponed for a couple of months and then several more postponements came after. In fact, the case was postponed for two years.

During that time, I kept painting for my dad. I enjoyed the hard work and the feeling of fulfillment on a Friday. It wasn't long until I started thinking about how I could make as much money as possible painting. I was just what I said I would never do; I was busting my ass to make someone else money, but at least it was my dad. I started watching the way my dad ran his business and learned all the ins and outs. Some things were beneficial, other things I thought I'd do differently. I also remembered how my grandfather ran his much larger and successful painting business.

But it was the day I saw my dad writing invoices that really got my attention. One in particular was Barnett Bank…he charged them $2,500 for something that took me four hours. My dad had made a $2,400 profit while sitting at the bar. That was the day I realized this painting thing may not be a bad idea. I could make good money and do it legally. Besides, it was the Caucci family's "other business," and we used all the connections we had to get work. It was a no-brainer.

After work, I spent most of my time studying all the textbooks I needed to get my own painting contractor's license, and within a few months I was the youngest person in Broward County to have a painting contractor's license. My dad didn't even have one—he couldn't be bothered with all the bullshit associated with having a license. Before long he was using mine, and everything seemed to be falling into place...except I had the damn court case hanging over my head.

By the time I went to trial, I was eighteen years old. I could not help thinking that the reason it was postponed for so long was so I would actually look like an adult at trial.

On the day before the trial, the judge asked the state prosecutor, "Can you and Mr. Caucci's attorney please go out in the hallway and see if you can come up with some sort of plea agreement, so we can avoid a trial and wrap this up today? It's been two years now, and trial is set for tomorrow."

This was music to my ears. It helped when the judge saw everything I had accomplished in the two years I'd been waiting for trial. I wasn't sitting on my ass like some bum. I'd actually been working hard, and it showed. Until then, the only deal the state had ever offered me was to cooperate with the police. But now the judge was telling the state to cut me a deal. All they had to do was let me plead guilty to a lesser offense like possession of cocaine with intent to distribute and still charge me as an adult. I could be going home on probation that day.

After a five-minute discussion in the hallway, my attorney came back with the news. "Plead guilty as a youthful offender and you will be sentenced to four years with no minimum mandatory and a recommendation of bootcamp, which would reduce your sentence to only ninety days once you start bootcamp."

"Ninety days! That's a walk in the park."

"Yes, only ninety days once you get to bootcamp. But it's only a recommendation, there is no guarantee you will get in."

"Who makes the final decision on whether or not I get in?"

"If you take the deal, you will be sentenced to four years. Then, once you get to prison, the Department of Corrections will make the final decision."

"GET DA FUCK OUTTA HERE! There ain't no fucking way they're gonna let me out in ninety days. One phone call from this pencil neck prosecutor to the Department of Corrections and bootcamp will be out the window. The state has been fucking me like a prostitute and refusing to pay for the past two years, but now their gonna pay me and give me a kiss? I'd have to be a complete moron to fall for that. What are my odds if we go to trial?"

"Fifty-fifty."

Those aren't good odds when your freedom is involved. "So, what's in my favor?"

"I am gonna try to get the jury pissed off with the state by proving they used an adult to set up a minor so the adult could gain his freedom. We need a few mothers on the jury panel who will have sympathy and understand that the state is going to ruin a young man's life over a one-time crime with no victims. We want the jury to believe that you are the victim and the state is the one committing an injustice here."

"That sounds pretty damn convincing to me. What jury in the world would convict me?"

"Like I said, it's a 50/50 chance, but the state made it clear they want you locked up. So we can expect them to be very aggressive at trial."

"Really…they said that?"

"Yes, they really want to put you away. And the cops are pissed off that you refused to cooperate. So for them this is personal…they put a lot of time into this investigation and got nothing."

The reality suddenly sunk in. This was some serious shit. There was a good chance I could go to prison. My dad put his arm around me and said, "Son, I won't tell you what to do here. This is your decision."

"Well, if I plead guilty I'm going to prison for sure. If I go to trial, I have a 50/50 chance. Fuck 'em…let's take 'em to trial."

He pinched me on the cheek and said, "I'm proud of you son." His eyes got a little watery as he held back tears. That was the first time in my life I saw tears in my father's eyes, and I couldn't believe it. Suddenly I got choked up too. The fucker almost made me cry. I told him I loved him and let him know I was going to be okay no matter the outcome. Since we were in a court room and had friends there, I had to keep it together. Besides, I didn't want the prosecutor to think he broke me. My dad said to the attorney, "Fuck those cocksuckers, we're going to trial."

"Are you sure you want to go to trial?" he asked.

"Positive…what jury in the world is going to convict me knowing I'd be going to prison for at least three years?"

With a disappointed look on his face he said, "You are correct, a jury would probably never convict you if they knew how much time you were facing. However, the jury will never know. They have no idea you'll be going to prison if convicted. As a matter of fact, they'll probably think you'll get a slap on the wrist if they come back with a guilty verdict. They'll only be instructed to come back with a verdict or guilty or not guilty and not to consider what the penalty may or may not be."

"This is some fucking justice system we have here. Arrest juveniles, charge them as adults, take them to trial, and the jury has no clue what's going to happen to the kid if convicted. What a load of shit."

It was time to start. Judge Coker asked the prosecutor, "Have we come to an agreement concerning Mr. Caucci?"

"No, Your Honor. They have refused our offer."

"And what was your recommendation?"

"Plead guilty to four years as a youthful offender, with a recommendation of bootcamp."

"You couldn't come up with something a little better than that? This case has wasted a lot of the court's valuable time."

"Only if he provides substantial assistance."

"I see."

Then the judge asked me, "Is this what you want, Mr. Caucci? Are you declining to cooperate in order to get your sentence reduced, and you have declined to plead guilty as a youthful offender with the state recommending a four-year prison sentence?"

"Yes, Your Honor, that is correct."

"Okay, the trial is set for tomorrow at 9 a.m. Mr. Caucci, do you have any questions?"

"Yes, Your Honor, I do. May I approach the bench?"

With a perplexed look on his face he asked the state if they had any objections. They did not. "Okay, Mr. Caucci, you may approach the bench."

I walked over to the bench with my attorney and my dad by my side and the state hovering over us. Nobody had a clue what I was about to say, and actually neither did I. I just wanted to talk to the judge face to face. I wanted him to see me as a person, not just another case.

"Do you have a question?" the judge asked.

"Yes, Your Honor, I do."

"Go ahead, young man."

"Let's say that I agreed to cooperate with the state..." That caught everyone off guard, especially my dad, but the prosecutor smiled. "And let's say I did exactly what someone did to me. Now that I'm eighteen and I'm legally considered an adult. What if I agreed to cooperate with the police and found some kid who was poor and really needed the money to help his mother with the bills and that kid was only sixteen years old. Then the state does the same thing to him that they did to me."

There was a moment of silence and the judge said, "What is your question?"

"Sorry, Your Honor. My question is what type of man would that make me?"

"I'm sorry, Mr. Caucci, I cannot answer that question for you."

"Oh, I'm sorry, Your Honor. I was just looking for your opinion as you see this type of stuff every day."

"Is there anything else, Mr. Caucci?"

"No, Your Honor, that is all."

"Okay, trial is set for tomorrow at 9 am."

As I was walking away from the bench, I felt that the judge actually saw me as a person. He may have been called the hanging judge and handed out the harshest sentences to criminals who had victims, but I was the victim here. At least that's what I wanted him to think. It was worth a shot.

After court, we headed for a local bar. My dad was doing everything he could to play it cool, but it was clear he was very worried. That made me nervous too. He sucked down a couple of scotch on the rocks and said, "You did real good in there…I want you to know how proud I am of you. You have a lot of people out here rooting for you, and most of our friends will be there in the court room during the trial. You may not know it, but this is a real big thing, son. Not many guys take it to trial."

"What do you mean, Pop?"

"You know…all the guys you have known since you were a little boy have called and checked in on you. Everyone you know has asked me how you're doing and said to keep your chin up. Those are real friends."

"Okay, Pop."

"Son, you need to know something, and this is very important. Everyone we know is waiting and watching to see how this turns out. They are waiting to see how you carry yourself and what decisions you will make in the face of the worst possible outcome. Because when it's all over, how you carry yourself will stick with you for the rest of your life. Keep up what you're doing and be a stand-up man, you will be respected even more and new opportunities will open up for you. But if your balls shrivel up, people will pretend they don't even know you. It doesn't matter what direction your life goes in after this is over, whether you go legit or still hustle, your name will be shit and nobody will come near you."

"Okay, Pop. I understand."

"Son, when this is all over, one day one of our friends will try to recruit you. They will want you to be a part of their crew."

I took a sip of my Coke, looked my father in the eyes, and said, "Pop, I would rather be on my own. I'd prefer to do my own thing. I have great respect for all our friends and the connections are great, but there is no way in the world I'm gonna put my ass on the line to earn money for some crew boss. I don't have to prove myself to anyone, I'm my own man! Like you said, most of the guys we know have never gone to trial and just a handful went to prison. Look, I'm only eighteen and I took the pinch like a man and I'm going all the way with it. Once this is all over, I'm on my own. If anyone ever wants a piece of my action, they're gonna have to earn it."

"It's not that easy, kiddo. If they see you making money, someone is gonna want in on your action. When you were younger it was different. But you're not a kid anymore, so the rules change. On top of that, you're Italian and the whole town knows you. But if you decide to go legit, then nobody will expect a dime from you. Working the streets is what they do."

"Thanks for the tip, but I've been thinking about this for quite a while and I already know how I'm gonna handle things."

13 | They Want to Crucify Me

The day that could change my life forever came quickly. I had been on the streets for two years and had finally gotten my life in order. I had studied hard to get my painting contractor's license. I was working full time and making decent, legit money for the first time in my life.

I'd also had the same girlfriend for about two years; her name was Denise. Michelle and I had broken up mainly because of the case and her not knowing what was going to happen to me. I think she wanted to overcome her feelings for me just in case she was forced to cooperate with the state. I was in a very difficult situation between Denise and Michelle. Sometimes, Michelle would just show up at my house out of the blue while Denise was there. Obviously, this made Denise very upset, but the last thing I wanted to do was piss Michelle off and give her another reason to cooperate against me. I told Denise, "You have to just let this pass, Michelle has the power to guarantee I get convicted. So put your pride aside until the trial is over." So she did—she was a good girl from a nice Italian family. They knew my circumstance when I started dating their daughter, and they didn't hold it against me at all. As a matter of fact, this was one solid family. I will never forget all the Cardellas did for me.

When the trial day came, I was as nervous as a turkey on Thanksgiving but I was trying to act normal. Not tough, not soft…just normal. I walked into the courtroom wearing a nerdy outfit so the jury would look at me like I was some regular kid. The prosecutor came in and whispered to my attorney, "The arresting officers are here and they said they want to crucify him."

That was not good to hear and really a fucked-up thing to say. They were acting as if they had arrested John Gotti. My case was fucking peanuts in the grand scheme of things.

The judge asked my attorney one last time, "Are you sure we can't resolve this today?"

"We would love to, Your Honor, but the state won't budge."

The first day of trial was not exactly exciting. There was jury selection, some opening statements, and the officers were called to the stand. The prosecutor brought up the fact that I was only sixteen at the time of my arrest and asked the officers to compare me to other sixteen-year-olds they had arrested before.

"He is not your average sixteen-year-old drug dealer," said arresting Officer Brundy. "From the language he used while speaking on the phone and the way he conducts his business, it is clear to us that he has been in this business for a very long time."

Obviously, my lawyer objected, but it got us nowhere and I had a bad feeling. After that first day of trial, they had *me* convinced I was guilty.

"The jury has only heard their side of the story," my attorney said to me at the end of the day. "Tomorrow we're up to bat, and when I put you on the stand they'll see a scared young man who made a mistake. Do you understand what I'm saying?"

"Oh, you bet your ass I do."

Day two of the trial came, and when they called me to the stand I was instructed to answer only yes or no. As the prosecutor was firing off his questions, it was obvious he was trying to get on a roll. The questions were coming very quickly. As soon as I answered one, he would ask another without taking time to breathe. So I decided to slow him down—I wanted to control the pace and break his rhythm.

"Mr. Caucci, isn't it true that you delivered a bag of cocaine containing twenty-eight grams or more to Tony Lopez in the parking lot at K-mart in Hollywood?" he asked.

"Uh…that's not exactly true…"

The judge ordered, "Answer the question either yes or no."

"Your Honor, I have to tell the whole truth and can't leave out anything, correct?"

"Correct."

"Then I'm gonna have to say the answer is no."

"Did you say no?" the prosecutor said angrily.

"Yes, sir…my answer is no."

The prosecutor quickly walked over to the table where the evidence was laid out, grabbed the bag of cocaine, and held it in the air above his head and said, "Did you or did you not deliver this bag of cocaine to Tony Lopez?"

I calmly replied, "With all due respect, if you want 100 percent honesty from me, I would have to say I cannot give you a definitive yes."

"Do you think this is funny, Mr. Caucci? Is this some sort of game to you?"

It was clear I had pissed him off, but I wanted to throw him off his game. I turned to the jury with a scared and confused look on my face and said, "I do not think this is funny at all, or a joke. I am facing a minimum mandatory sentence of three years in prison with a maximum of thirty."

"OOOBBBJECTION!" the prosecutor yelled, slamming papers on his table.

I looked around the court, pretending to be confused and scared. I glanced at my dad, who was sitting in the back of the court with a few friends. Everyone had turned beet red and was doing everything they could to stop from laughing. The judge then asked my attorney and the prosecutor to come to the bench.

"Would you like to motion for a mistrial?" the judge asked the prosecutor.

He thought about it and said, "No, we'll continue as long as Mr. Caucci doesn't pull anymore stunts like that."

Then the judge turned to me and said, "Mr. Caucci, you are not permitted to talk to the jury about any penalty you may be facing."

I sat for a second pretending to be confused, then I said, "I don't understand, Your Honor, are you saying I can't say that I'm facing a three-year minimum mandatory sentence if I'm found guilty?"

"OBJECTION! Your Honor?" The prosecutor's face was red. My dad and a few others headed for the door before they burst out in laughter.

The judge looked at me and said, "Mr. Caucci! This is your last warning."

I bowed my head as if I was defeated, but I knew that I needed to get one more in. What were they going to do, charge me with contempt of court? No minimum mandatory for that…

"I'm sorry, I'm sorry, Your Honor. I'm just so nervous up here. The state wants to put me in prison for a very long time."

"OBJECTION!"

"Your Honor, I just said prison for a long time. That is not in the sentencing guidelines, is it? A long time?"

"Overruled!" The judge sighed. "Mr. Caucci, I will not tell you again. I do not want to hear one more word pertaining to any duration of time that you think you may or may not be sentenced to, understand?"

"Yes, Your Honor, now I understand." But the jury heard it and there was no mistrial. I just hoped it sank in…

"May I please continue with questioning the witness, Your Honor?"

"Please proceed."

The prosecutor again held the bag of cocaine up in the air. "Mr. Caucci, did you or did you not deliver this bag containing twenty-eight grams or more to Tony Lopez?"

"I have two answers for you, sir. The first one is I'm not 100 percent sure, and the second answer is no."

At this point, the prosecutor was completely exhausted and looked like he was barely hanging on. "Your Honor, please?"

Then judge said, "Will the counsel for the defense speak with his client and instruct him to answer the question with a yes or no answer or I will hold him in contempt?"

My lawyer walked up to me on the witness stand, covered the microphone, and whispered, "Just answer the fucking question. You're pissing off the judge."

I explained what I was thinking to my attorney. He shook his head and sighed. "Okay."

My attorney turned to the judge and said, "Mr. Caucci is being very honest with his answers. I think if you let him explain, then maybe the state will reword the question."

The judge leaned back in his chair and turned toward me with a curious look on his face. "Mr. Caucci, this better be good…please explain to the court your answer."

"Your Honor, the first question the prosecution asked me was if the bag he was holding in his hand was the same bag I delivered to Tony Lopez. The answer to that question is I honestly do not know if that is the same bag. It has been in the state's possession for the last two years. How can I testify that that is the exact same bag? Secondly, the state asked if I delivered twenty-eight grams or more to Tony Lopez. The absolute truth to that question is NO! I delivered 27.5 grams on the dot. Then someone added the other 3.5 grams to make sure it was over twenty-eight grams."

"OBJECTION! Calls for speculation...Your Honor, please!" the prosecutor roared.

"Wait just a minute...you asked for the truth but don't want to hear the truth?" I said. "Well THAT is the truth! And if someone added 3.5 grams, then they probably switched the bag too."

"Okay, Mr. Caucci, hold on right there," the prosecutor said. "Let me get this correct."

He walked around the courtroom with his hand on his chin in deep thought.

"So, Mr. Caucci, did you or did you not deliver a bag of cocaine to the informant Tony Lopez?"

"Yes, sir."

"And how much did Mr. Lopez ask you for?"

"One ounce."

"And do you know how many grams are in an ounce?"

"Yes, sir. Twenty-eight grams."

"Okay, Mr. Caucci, if there are twenty-eight grams in an ounce, then why would you only give him 27.5 grams?"

Oh shit...he had an angle, but I wasn't sure what it was. "Your Honor, may I consult with my attorney please?" I asked.

"You may."

My attorney walked to the witness stand and leaned in so nobody could hear. "What's going on?"

"I have a bad feeling on this question. I'm just killing some time here, trying to think. If I tell him that I knew the law and that I intentionally sold it light just to get under the minimum mandatory sentence, he's gonna say I'm not the average sixteen-year-old, just like they said."

"You're absolutely right about that."

Then I saw my mother sitting in the back of the courtroom. She gave me a wink and put her hand over her heart, letting me know she loved me. But she didn't know she also had just given me an out. "I got it!"

"What is it?" my lawyer asked. "Please, no more surprises."

"Trust me on this, ask the judge to have my mother go out into the hallway for a moment. There is something I don't want her to hear."

The judge allowed it and my mother left the room. The prosecutor looked very frustrated.

Then the judge said, "Mr. Caucci, you may answer the question now."

"I'm really sorry for this delay, I know everyone's time here is valuable," I said. "It's just my mother already feels terrible about what's happening to me, she feels like she's the one to blame. The reason I shorted the ounce by a half of gram is…I was going to take that half gram and sell it for $30 to help pay the electric bill. Not all of it, but enough to keep the lights on. Money was very tight, my mom was working two jobs at the time, so I was doing everything I could to help her out. If she heard this, it would break her heart."

My attorney gave me an approval nod of the head. Then I looked at the judge, and it was clear he felt sorry for me.

But the prosecutor was another story. "Mr. Caucci, do you really expect the jury to believe that you weighed out 27.5 grams so you could sell the other one gram for $30 just so you could help out with bills?"

"Have you ever had your water or electric turned off?" I asked.

"Objection, Your Honor."

"Sustained. Please answer the question yes or no, Mr. Caucci."

"I expect the ladies and gentleman of the jury to believe the truth, so my answer is yes."

After my testimony, both sides rested, and the jury went back to deliberate. The judge instructed us to stay close by and wait for the verdict. My dad asked my attorney if there were any good bars close by so he could get a drink and something to eat. I had absolutely no appetite—my nerves were completely shot. In a couple of hours I would either be a free man or I'd be in prison for who knows how long.

I was praying for a not guilty verdict, but whatever came down, I had to keep my head up.

About four hours later, we got the call and headed back to the courtroom. The judge said a few words and asked the jury to read the verdict.

"We the jury find the defendant guilty of trafficking cocaine in the amount of more than twenty-eight grams but less than two hundred grams."

Then the strangest thing happened. Suddenly I felt the weight of the world lift off my shoulders and a voice in my head said, "Today is the first day toward your freedom. Everything is now put behind you."

The judge asked the bailiff to take me into custody, but as they started putting the cuffs on me, my girlfriend's sister Lisa screamed at the top of her lungs to the prosecutor, "I'm going to fucking kill you, you scum bag!" She jumped out of her seat and went after the prosecutor as my girlfriend Denise broke down in tears. Her father Vinny and the courtroom deputies had to restrain her and escort her out. The judge then asked the deputies to escort the prosecutor out since his life had been threatened. But before he left he had to get his two cents in. As he walked by me, he stopped, looked me in the face, and said, "You should have taken the deal."

"Maybe so, but what would that make me? A little pussy just like you, so go back home to mommy and suck on her tits, you little sissy. "

I looked over at my mom. She was sobbing, with her face hidden on my brother's shoulder. I could also see the tears in my father's eyes.

"It's all downhill from here, Pop," I said. "I'm finally on my way home! I will see you soon."

As for Michelle Carvin, my girlfriend who got arrested with me, she stood solid and refused to cooperate with the police in any way and was sentenced to probation.

14 | Before We Kill Him

After the guilty verdict, I was sent to the North Broward Detention Center for six weeks while they were putting together my pre-sentencing investigation report. When I arrived at my cell block, I stuck out like a sand nigger in a synagogue. The emotions of the prisoners were written all over their faces. Some who had been in the system several times looked as hard as stone, while others looked very comfortable and relaxed. Others looked scared, not knowing what to expect, while some were sad knowing they would lose their families during their long sentences.

The cell blocks were old and had a musty smell; the walls were painted mustard yellow with three dark brown metal picnic tables in the center for the prisoners to watch TV, play cards, and eat. There was a small TV in the right corner. It was encased in plexiglass so it couldn't be taken down and slammed over someone's head. In the other corner was a security camera so the guards could monitor us from their station down the hall. The guards did rounds once an hour and looked through the bars to make sure everything was calm. There were two blue phones on one wall that we could use to call our families or attorneys. Each cellblock had four cells, and each cell housed six people. Inside each cell there was three solid steel bunk beds that were painted battleship grey with the names of past prisoners and tally marks counting down the days carved into the paint. In the corner was one stainless steel toilet bowl connected to a sink for brushing your teeth, with a polished piece of steel bolted onto the wall above it that served as a mirror. When we had to use the toilet, we used it in front of all the prisoners in the cell with absolutely no privacy. But instead of being embarrassed about it, we often joked about the smell to lighten up the mood. "Damn son, that smells like some good old-fashioned county jail food…how 'bout a mercy flush?"

Once I got settled in, something very strange and unexpected happened: I was treated very well by the other prisoners. The majority of them were grown men and fathers. It wasn't anything like I thought it would be. But then again, it wasn't prison. One day while I was on the phone with my dad, this fucking Jamaican disconnected my call and said, "I'm using the phone now, cracker." I wanted to kill him, but my attorney told me not to get in any trouble prior to sentencing so I just bit my lip and went back to my cell. A few minutes later, Thomas, a black prisoner about thirty-five years old who had become a good friend of mine, asked me what had happened. As I was telling him the story, he started to get real fidgety and kept looking at the Jamaican. Then he said, "Let me handle this."

Thomas calmly waited for the Jamaican to finish his call. Once the Jamaican was back in his cell, Thomas walked in behind him nice and calmly. Thomas had two other inmates stand at the doorway to keep a lookout for the guards and other prisoners. The security camera in the main area could not see into our cells, so if things were done the right way the guards would never know what was happening. I sat on my bed so I could see everything that was going on in the cell across from mine. Thomas walked up to the Jamaican and said, "Hey, homeboy, let me holla at you fo a minute." Before the Jamaican could get a word out, Thomas hit him with an uppercut and that shattered his teeth. He was completely unconscious before he landed face-first on the concrete floor. Then Thomas and about ten other inmates went into the main area and started screaming through the bars, "Officer! Officer, get this motherfucker out of here before we kill him!"

The guards came running in with batons in their hands. "What the fuck is going on, here?" one of the officers yelled.

"You get that motherfucker out of here before he gets killed!" Thomas shouted. Some of the other inmates joined in, screaming at the guards to get him out. The guards ran into the Jamaican's room, handcuffed him, and dragged his badly beaten and bloody ass out.

When Thomas came back into the cell, he laid down on his bed and with a smile on his face said, "That's how you get rid of tough guys."

When I was able to get back on the phone, I told my dad to keep an eye out for a letter from me and that I needed a favor. In the letter I asked my dad to send Thomas $200 for commissary because he did a good thing for me. A few days later, when it was mail call, they called out, "Inmate Thomas! Thomas!"

He wasn't paying any attention to mail call because he never got any. So I said, "Thomas, you got mail."

"Mail? I ain't got no motherfuckin' mail...nobody knows I'm here!"

"Yes, you do, they called you twice."

As he walked over to get the envelope, I pretended I was looking at a magazine. Then he came back to the cell, sat on his bed and opened the card when he saw the yellow commissary receipt inside. "Money? Some motherfucker sent me some mutherfuckin' money!" Then he took a closer look. "Two hundred dollars! Somebody sent me two hundred mutherfuckin' dollars!" He sat with a huge smile on his face, repeating the words "two hundred dollars" and trying to figure out who had sent him the money. Then he said, "There ain't no mutherfuckin' name on the card, it just says thank you." He held the card in front of his face and stared at it, like he was talking to it. "No...thank you, motherfucker, whoever you are!" Then he got up and did a little happy dance, and the whole cell started laughing.

A few minutes went by and he said, "Hey, Caucci...?"

I looked up at him from my bottom bunk as he pointed to the receipt and gave him a wink and a nod to let him know it was from me. He gave me the thumbs up and put his finger over his lips, signaling to keep this thing quiet because sending money to another inmate would get you separated and thrown into the hole.

A few very long, boring weeks went by until one day...a day I will never ever forget. There had been a white-boy fag in our cell for some time now. He didn't try to hide the fact that he was gay but instead flaunted it. He walked around in his underwear after showering, constantly made jokes about gay encounters he'd had on the streets, and just acted like a girl. One day as he was walking around in his underwear, Thomas said to him, "Hey boy, why don't you come over here and suck my dick?"

Everyone in the cell laughed at the joke, but the fag replied, "You got no chance, Thomas. Come talk to me when you get some real money. I don't go out with broke boys!"

Thomas jumped up out of his bed and quickly advanced on the fag. He wrapped his arms around him, putting him in a bearhug, and tried to kiss him. It all seemed like a joke and everyone was laughing. But as the fag tried to push him away, Thomas got more and more aggressive. The fag started to get really upset and kept saying, "Please, Thomas, stop!" It was all funny and entertaining but in one second, everything changed. It went from funny to very serious.

Thomas slammed him on the floor as hard as he could, knocking the wind out of him. As the fag tried to catch his breath, Thomas gave him a couple shots to the face then ripped his underwear off and positioned himself between the fag's legs. I could not believe what I was seeing—and neither could anyone else. Thomas looked at me and said, "Watch the door."

"Okay, I got it."

As the fag started to scream, Thomas punched him several times in the face and said, "You punk bitch, you gonna walk around here with yo underwear on and tease a nigga? Shut your motherfucking mouth and take this dick."

In a matter of seconds, Thomas had his pants down and his fully erected dick out with his hand around the fag's throat. The fag was pleading, "Please don't!" but he could barely talk because of the grip Thomas had around his throat.

Then Thomas jumped off him and said, "Come near me one more time walking around in your underwear shaking your little white ass and I will split you wide open."

The fag jumped up, put his clothes on, and went into the main area of our cell block and called out to the guards to tell them what had happened. They immediately took the fag out and put us on lock down. Minutes later the guards showed up in their riot gear and went from cell to cell questioning all the prisoners. When they got to our cell, they asked me what had happened. I stuck to the same story as everyone else. I said, "Nobody touched that punk, he owed Thomas his dinner for two nights because Thomas gave him a couple of Snickers bars. But when it was time to pay up, the punk told Thomas to fuck off. This motherfucker thinks he can get away with that shit by making up some bullshit story. That punk has been causing problems with everyone since he got here. He still thinks he's on the streets and he's going to get hurt if you don't get him out of here."

The prison guards knew there were prison rules, including unspoken rules between inmates. After questioning everyone, they put the queer in the hole and things went back to normal. After it was all clear, I started thinking. I really didn't know Thomas or anyone in there. One minute Thomas was as cool as a cucumber and the next he was close to raping someone, and then he acted like it had never happened. Then I thought, "If that fag had just acted normal and not told all those disgusting stories and just blended in like everyone else, life would be much easier for him. What Thomas did was fucked up, but in prison everything is fucked up. If you're going to tell stories about sucking dick to a group of angry prisoners, some of whom are probably homosexuals who will be spending decades behind bars...be prepared for the worst. The whole scenario was completely fucked up, but whaddya gonna do?"

15 | The Maximum Sentence

After a long six weeks went by, the day to be sentenced finally came and I was so damn nervous. I had been offered four years if I pleaded guilty with a recommendation of a ninety-day boot camp program that would have had me out in about six months—but I didn't take it. The maximum sentence was thirty years. What was the judge going to do to me? If I got five or less, I would be okay. Any more than five and forget about it!

When the deputies brought me into the courtroom, I saw my dad sitting between Jerry Chilli and Steve Maruca. The courtroom was filled with friends. I looked over at them and got a few winks and a couple thumbs up. They were there to let me know they were in my corner. The deputies escorted me over to the jury booth and handcuffed me to the chair. My attorney walked over to me and said, "The prosecutor said the arresting officers are going to request that you get the maximum sentence."

"What the fuck? Why?"

"Not sure, but they have a real hard-on for you."

That was not good news and made me feel even worse, but I had to keep calm and not look nervous. I started to think, what if the police got what they wanted? I would be almost fifty years old when I got out! That would almost be my whole life. I shook that thought out of my head and remained calm. When the judge walked in, he asked if everyone was present. The prosecutor said, "We are waiting on the arresting officers to arrive, Your Honor."

"I am not waiting on them," he said, "let's proceed with sentencing. State, you may proceed."

The state began to tell the judge why I should be locked up for at least ten years and how they had offered me four years, but I had refused the deal. "You Honor, Mr. Caucci had the opportunity to help himself before trial. If he had cooperated with the state, he would not be facing any jail time. Instead, he refused and took his chance at trial." They went on for about ten minutes and came up with a hundred reasons why I should get at least ten years.

Then it was our turn. My attorney said, "Had my client's last name not been Italian, we would not even be sitting here today, Your Honor. At the time of the offense, my client was only sixteen years old and should have never been charged as an adult. Your Honor, this is Mr. Caucci's first offense and it's a nonviolent offence. The only reason my client did not cooperate with the police was because he didn't want to do to another young kid what was done to him. My client was set up by an adult who wanted to save their own skin by setting up my client, who was a juvenile at the time. We ask the court to take into consideration all these facts before sentencing."

Then it was the judge's turn to speak. My knees were shaking and I was nauseated. "It does not sit well with me, having a case like this in front of me," the judge said. "We have an obligation to carry out justice, but I do not see any justice in sending a young man to prison for a crime like this when he was only sixteen at the time of the offense. This really troubles me, knowing a young man's life is going to be ruined, but my hands are tied. Due to the nature of the crime, I am bound by law to stay within the sentencing guidelines. The offense carries a minimum mandatory of three years with a maximum sentence of thirty years—"

Oh shit! This did not sound good at all...he was going to hang me.

"Mr. Caucci, you are hereby sentenced to four years in a Florida state prison as a youthful offender, followed by two years of house arrest. I also am recommending that you be sentenced to ninety days in boot camp."

The prosecutor jumped out of his chair. "Objection! Objection, Your Honor! The state offered him four years before trial and he refused the plea. The state strongly objects—"

"My judgement is final."

"But Your Honor—"

"I said my judgment is final, one more word out of you and you will be held in contempt!" The judge banged his gavel and left the bench, leaving the prosecutor frustrated. Then everyone stood and applauded the decision.

I didn't know what the hell was going on. The judge was going to hold the state in contempt? What had just happened?

My attorney said, "You made out pretty good, kid. You've been sentenced as a youthful offender, with ninety days of boot camp. Now I have to warn you, boot camp is a very intense ninety-day program, like the army but a lot more intense. If you complete the ninety days, your sentence will be commuted, and you will be released."

"Are you joking? All I have to do is ninety days of intense military training and I'm out? Fuhgeddaboudit! That's a walk in the park compared to the Chinese boxing training I've been through."

"It's not that easy, Anthony, a lot of people don't make it and are sent back to prison to finish their entire sentence."

I understood what he was trying to say, but I couldn't help feeling relieved. I had finally caught a break. I looked at the crowed and gave them a thumbs up. As the prosecutor was packing his briefcase, I noticed Jerry Chilli walking down the aisle toward the front row of seats. He stood right behind the prosecutor and looked around to see if anyone was paying attention, then whispered "Pssst!" When the prosecutor turned around, Chilli said, "Good job, you mutt, now go home and fuck your mother!" Then he walked away laughing.

Now *that* was a great ending to my day.

16 | You'll Have to Kill Me First

After sentencing, they sent me back to the North Broward Detention Center for a couple of days while I waited to be transferred to the main jail and then to South Florida Reception Center for processing. At 3 a.m. one night, I heard a guard yell, "Caucci, pack it up!"

I said my good-byes to Thomas and the others, and off I went. At the main jail, they put all the inmates who were getting transferred to prison into a separate cellblock. When we arrived, we were seated in the main area of the cell block while we waited to be assigned our beds and cells. As usual, I minded my own business. I didn't get into any conversations; I just watched and listened to what the other inmates were saying. There was one nigger who really stood out. He was way too comfortable for someone going to prison. He was full of energy, very talkative and extremely friendly, especially to the young white boys. He tried to strike up a conversation with me, but then decided to try someone else who would fall for his bullshit. He picked a young blonde kid with blue eyes who looked like a surfer with hair down to his shoulders. He looked weak, fragile, scared, and out of place. This poor bastard had no idea what he had coming. The nigger approached him and asked, "Hey, my friend, what's your name?"

"Peter," he replied softly.

"Is this your first time going to prison?"

"Yes."

"My name's Jackson. It's nice to meet you...Listen, Peter, I been to prison a bunch a times and I got a lot of homeboys in there. In prison, the more friends you have, the easier your time gonna be. You feel me?"

"Uh, yeah, that makes sense."

"Peter you make sure you surround yourself with good people so nobody will fuck with you."

I looked out of the corner of my eye to see Peter's reaction. He had a smile on his face and looked like he wasn't so scared anymore. I thought, "Come the fuck on, Peter, don't fall for this nigger's bullshit."

Jackson went on, "Listen, stick with me and I'll make sure nobody fucks with you. I'll get you extra food trays, a good job, and we can work out together so you are in good shape when you go home. You train with me and you'll have muscles on top of muscles. The girls will go crazy for you when you get out. You down with that?"

"Hell yeah, that sounds great!"

Peter excused himself and went to the restroom. As soon as he left, this sick lowlife nigger grabbed his dick and turned to one of his homeboys and said, "Man, I can't wait to fuck that tight little pink ass tonight."

I couldn't believe my ears. For a second, I contemplated going to the bathroom to tell this kid he was gonna get raped if he kept fucking with this nigger. But then the voice inside me said, "Mind your own fucking business and do your time."

When Peter returned from the bathroom, they kept shooting the shit and it seemed like they really got along. Finally the guards came and assigned us our rooms. Peter and Jackson were assigned separate rooms, but Jackson told Peter to ask the guard if he could change his room so they could be cellmates. So Peter did, but the guard said, "No, you get what you get. Does this look like a fucking Hilton Hotel to you, boy?" Then Jackson slithered over to one of his homeboys who knew the guard and asked if he could hook it up for him. After a few minutes of shucking and jiving, the guard said okay. Jackson walked over to Peter and gave him a high five and said, "You're in my room now, brother."

"Wow! How'd you do that?"

"I told you I have a lot of friends in here."

"That's so cool...I owe you one for that."

"In prison, it's all about taking care of each other because the guards don't give a shit if we live or die."

Evening came, and we were sent to our cells for the night.

They locked us in at nine and lights were out at ten. I was in the cell directly next to Peter's so I could hear every word they were saying through the AC vents. Inmates would sometimes communicate between cells by standing on their toilets and screaming through the AC vents. The problem with that was that everyone had to listen to their moronic bullshit.

At ten o'clock, the lights went out and I heard Peter and Jackson shooting the shit and laughing in the next cell over. Then Jackson said, "Hey, Peter, get down off your bed and come holla at me."

"Come on, Peter, wake the fuck up!" I thought. "How don't you see this? This poor kid is about to get his ass split." I heard a thud as Peter jumped down from his bed. Then Peter said, "What's up?"

"Come here and sit down, I have to talk to you about something." The talking turned into whispering for a few minutes.

I couldn't make it out, so I got off my bed and stood on the toilet to get closer to the air vent. I heard Peter say nervously, "You're joking, right?" There was dead silence for about fifteen seconds. Then I heard Peter say, "No way, man, I'm not gonna do that!"

"What the fuck you say, bitch?" Jackson said.

Then there was silence for a few seconds.

"Please, Jackson," I heard Peter pleading next. "I thought you were my friend."

"I am your friend, but in prison we have to look out for each other. So you're gonna look out for me by sucking my dick just like I looked out for you and got you in this room. When we get up the road, I promise I'll take care of you and I'll make sure nobody fucks with you."

"No way, man, I'm not going to do that. You'll have to kill me first."

I heard Jackson slam Peter up against the wall. "Say no one more time, bitch, and see what happens."

Peter began to cry and plead some more. "Please don't make me do this."

Then Jackson said, "Aw, c'mon man, I'm just fucking with you. I wouldn't do that to you."

Relief flooded through me. Thank God Jackson was just fucking with him. Motherfucker had me fooled too. Now that was a strange sense of humor.

I could hear Peter hyperventilating and trying to catch his breath. "Oh my God...Oh my God. I thought you were serious. You scared the shit out of me."

"Yeah, my boy Peter, I don't want you to suck my dick."

"Thank God, because I couldn't live with myself if I ever did that."

"Nah, it's cool, Petey…it's all good. I'd rather fuck you so you understand how things work in here."

My heart sank. If I'd had a gun, I would have put a bullet in that nigger's head without thinking twice.

Then I heard the sound of Peter getting hit with an open-hand slap. Whack! Jackson hit him so fucking hard that I felt it. I heard Peter fall to the ground with a thud.

"Stand up, bitch"

"God, please help me!" Peter cried out.

"Did you say God? In here, I am God!"

Then I heard another sound like a kick. Peter let out a moan and another plea, "Please, I'm begging you…I will do anything you want, just don't do this to me, please. I will send you money so your commissary is always full, anything—"

Then the all-out assault took place. It lasted about three minutes but seemed like an eternity. I heard Peter's clothes being ripped off while he begged for Jackson to stop.

"Please…please…don't do this to me! Stop! Stop! Please, God help me…"

In between Peter's begging and the sound of blows falling on him, I heard the nigger saying, "You think there's a God, bitch? If there were, you wouldn't be here."

Peter screamed as loud as he could, "Heeeeeelp!" hoping the guards would come running to his rescue, but it was impossible for the guards to hear through the solid steel cell doors. Anyway, they were stationed about seventy feet away in a bulletproof control pod. His pleas for help were useless.

"Take your motherfucking pants off, bitch, or I'll kill you right here," Jackson growled.

Then there was complete silence for about a minute. I hoped the nigger had given up.

But no, he hadn't. I heard Peter sobbing as he knew the inevitable was just a few seconds away. "Okay, okay…please don't hurt me anymore."

I was shocked. Why didn't Peter even try to fight back? Why didn't he fight for his life? At least he would have had some chance, maybe Jackson would have backed off. But not fighting at all? I just didn't understand.

"Move your ass, bitch, and get those clothes off."

I heard a couple more slaps and that was it—Peter gave up. "Okay, okay," he said. "I'll take my clothes off. Just don't hit me anymore."

While Peter was removing his clothes, I could hear him crying and praying. He made one last attempt to stop Jackson. "Please, I'm begging you…don't do this to me."

Then there was the sound of a massive blow and Peter gasping to catch his breath while the sexual assault began. On and off for the next two hours, I heard muffled crying and Peter saying, "Please not again." But Peter's first night in prison was just beginning.

This was some justice system we had. The state couldn't have put us in a separate cell block with men closer to our age and size? It was fucking disgusting. I sat on my bed for the next few hours, listening to Peter screaming and begging over and over. My eyes filled with tears, knowing I could have prevented his rape if only I had said something.

The next morning at chow time, Peter hobbled out of his cell. His face was badly bruised; the white part of one eye was red with blood. He walked over to my table and barely managed to sit down. His eyes filled with tears, but he just sat there in shame, unable to speak. When he finally did, he wouldn't look me in the eyes and I could barely hear him. I wanted to console him, but what do you say to someone who had been raped all night? He handed me a letter. "Please mail this for me."

"Okay, but why don't you do it yourself?"

"Because I won't be here."

"Whaddaya mean?"

He pulled up his shirt and revealed a shank tucked into his waist band. His ribs were badly bruised, and there were scratches all over his torso.

"Where did you get that?"

"That nigger had it under his mattress, he pulled it out on me last night. That's when I gave up. This morning when they opened the doors for breakfast, I did a quick search of the room and found it."

"Whatcha gonna do with it?"

"Whatcha think I'm going to do with it? I don't want to live anymore."

I thought about talking him out of it, but he needed to make things right on his own terms. I wasn't living in his shoes. "You do what you gotta do. I promise I'll mail this out for you, but can I give you a little advice?"

"Sure, why not."

"You can't change what happened to you, but you can make that nigger think twice before he does it to someone else."

"I'm listening."

"See that shank you got? You need to jam it right between his legs."

Peter's face lit up and he had a little smile.

"Listen, do whatever you got to do to get his pants down. Make sure you catch him off guard and at a disadvantage. You have to get his pants down to his ankles or to his knees at a minimum. Then when the time is right, drive that shank right between his legs. There's a pressure point between your balls and your asshole. If you hit that, he will drop like a ton of bricks and it will be impossible for him to defend himself. But you have to hit that spot."

"How do you know this will work?"

"Trust me, Peter, I know a thing or two about hurting people, plus I got kicked there one day by a friend wearing pointed cowboy boots. It hurt for days. Now make sure you don't kill him, because when he's down on the ground and helpless, it might cross your mind. When the guards come, you tell them what happened to you last night and how you screamed for help and nobody came. And how he tried to rape you again. Tell them you want to go to the hospital immediately so they can check you out. And call your attorney right away. After they hear your story and after the doctors examine you, you probably won't even go to prison and might have a nice lawsuit."

"But how will I know when the time is right?"

"Just be patient...the time will come. But you need to always be ready and act normal, as if nothing happened. As a matter of fact, if I were you...and I'm really glad I'm not...I would hobble my ass over to the table he's sitting at and pretend like nothing happened."

"There's no fucking way I can sit at that table with him!"

"If you can't sit at a table with him, then you definitely can't pull this off. Maybe you're just not cut out for this. Give me that letter you want me to mail."

I just dropped the subject and continued to eat my breakfast. After thinking about it for a few minutes, Peter said, "You're right...I can't let him get away with what he did to me."

"Look, whatever happens, make sure you fight until you have nothing left in you."

"Thanks for caring," he said. Then he casually strolled over to the table where Jackson was sitting. "Hey, Jackson, do you mind if I sit here with you"

Jackson stood up and gave Peter a brotherly hug and introduced him to the others sitting at the table. "You my boy, Pete, take a seat." Jackson produced a deck of cards and asked Peter if he knew how to play spades. Surprisingly he did and beat Jackson easily. I was just in earshot and could hear and see everything they were doing. To my surprise, Peter was doing a great job playing this fucker. He looked like he was having a real good time, and I started to wonder if he was actually having fun playing cards with the man who raped him. Then Jackson said, "Peter, hold my seat, I have to take a shit."

"I got you...but hurry back so I can whoop your ass some more."

After Jackson closed his cell door, Peter looked over at me and we locked eyes for a second. I gave him a slight nod, letting him know it was time to make his move. Peter casually got up and walked toward his cell, and my heart began to race. Once Peter was inside, I casually walked back to my cell, closed the door, and stood on the sink so I could hear Peter get his revenge.

"Can a nigga get some privacy? I'm trying to take a shit."

"Well, I started thinking about what you said last night, and it's starting to make a little sense to me. If I don't have protection when I go to prison, everyone is gonna get a piece of me. But since you and I are already friends, I guess it's better if I just stick with you."

"That's right...that's what I've been trying to tell you the whole time."

"So I thought since we're up here and nobody's around, I'll just go ahead and take care of you now. But we have to make it quick, I don't want anyone to see us. You look out the window and keep your pants down. If anyone comes, you can just pull them up really quick."

I couldn't believe my ears. Peter should have won an Oscar for best actor. As my heart raced, I closed my eyes and said a quick prayer for Peter.

Then I heard Jackson say, "There we go, that's what I'm talking about."

"Don't look at me, look out the window so we don't get caught."

"Okay, but hurry up! Let's get this thing going!"

"I never did this before, give me a second. Is it all clear?"

"It's all clear, nobody's around...now get moving, bitch!"

Then I heard the loudest scream I have ever heard from a grown man. It was so loud that even the guards heard it from their bulletproof pod.

"Who's the bitch now?" Peter yelled as Jackson fell screaming to the floor.

Peter continued to kick and punch Jackson for as long and hard as he could while Jackson screamed at the top of his lungs, "Help! Help! Please stop." By the time the guards got to Peter's cell, all I could hear was Jackson crying like a little baby.

I jumped off the sink and squeezed my fists together and said, "Thank you, God! Thank you!"

17 | Baptized with A Shotgun

After a week or so in the county jail, I was finally headed to the South Florida Reception Center where all the prisoners were processed. Once there, I received a psychology exam and took an IQ test. They also did my blood work and all kinds of other shit before they shipped me to my permanent prison. We rode in an old beat-up city bus with no windows so I didn't have a clue where I was going. We all wore bright orange county-jail jumpsuits and were chained together around the waist. Our handcuffs and ankle shackles were connected to the main chain, so I couldn't even scratch my nose.

A cage separated us from the bus driver, and on the other side was a filthy redneck prison guard with a shotgun who looked like he was itching to use it. He had a wad of chewing tobacco in his mouth and looked like he hadn't taken a bath for a week.

I was the youngest guy on the bus, and most of the men in there were going away for a very long time, some for life. These guys had piercing anger in their eyes and wanted revenge; they reminded me of my old friend Tony Plate.

There was a sensation of darkness on that bus I will never forget. Most of the prisoners looked like they would kill you for nothing and not lose a wink of sleep over it. Then there were some who looked like they were going to drop dead from fear any moment, people who just didn't belong there. I felt sorry for them because I knew they would have a rough time in prison. Being scared is one thing, but looking like a frightened child is another. Where we were headed, the gangs preyed on weakness, and some of these guys reeked of it.

There wasn't any talking, laughing, or bullshitting on the bus—it wasn't a game, and nobody was in the mood for jokes. Our freedom was being taken from us; we were being shipped far away from our families, and some of the men would never see their wives or children again.

When we finally arrived, we pulled into what looked like a warehouse that was surrounded by two fences with razor on top and between the lines. We pulled in and the overhead door slammed shut behind us as the bus parked in a huge cage. The bus driver yelled, "Welcome to your new home, boys!"

The filthy redneck corrections officer with the shotgun opened the back door of the bus and yelled in a thick accent, "Listen here ya'll stupid motherfuckers, ya'll do exactly as ya told and ya might just walk outta ere in one piece. Now if ya'll think I'm playing, then just one of you dumb sons of bitches try me. I'd love to fuck one of you up, it'll make my day. Now listen up, inmates! You'll be exiting your sorry asses from the rear door of the bus, startin' from da back seats first. If any of you motherfuckers makes a sound, you will be eating out of a straw for the next six weeks."

These rednecks were dead serious. They were itching to fuck one of us up, but it wasn't gonna be me. In order to exit the bus, we had to jump out of the rear door while our hands were cuffed to a chain around our waist and our feet were shackled. If you happened to be old and didn't have good balance, there was a good chance you could land on your face—but that would have just been entertainment for the prison guards.

Once we got out of the bus, they told us to stand shoulder-to-shoulder with our backs against the cage. One prison guard stood in the center of the cage with his shotgun over his shoulder and screamed as loud as he could, "Keep your fucking eyes on the ground!" Then another guard came around to take off the shackles and handcuffs. Another guard screamed, "Take all your fucking clothes off, underwear too, and throw it to the center of the floor!" There I was standing inside a cage with about eighty buck-naked men.

"Listen up, keep your hands by your sides at all times," a guard yelled. "If any of you move a muscle without my permission, you'll receive a South Florida Reception Center baptism! I don't wanna hear a fucking sound out of any one of you inmates. I don't care if ya have to take a shit or you're having a heart attack. I want complete silence so I can hear myself think. Welcome to prison, boys."

As I was staring at the ground and not moving a muscle, the prick with the shotgun was walking around screaming the rules. As he was doing this, a poor old black man lifted his hand up to scratch his nose. In the blink of an eye, the guard charged him and hit him with the butt of the shotgun right in the head, knocking him unconscious. His fell to the floor. When his skull hit the floor, it sounded like someone had dropped a bowling ball. Immediately, blood began pouring out of the huge gash in his head and from his nose. More guards joined in and kicked him a couple times. They flipped him over on his belly and handcuffed his wrists to his ankles like they were taking him to a pig roast. Then they threw him into the back of the bus like a fucking dog. One of the guards said, "Write him up for assaulting an officer and send him to the hole." They could've easily killed this man, but they didn't give a shit if he lived or died. They had to be the lowest, most white-trash pieces of shit I had ever seen in my life. Those redneck cracker prison guards were a disgrace to the human race.

"Anyone else want to get baptized?" a guard asked us.

I looked at the pool of blood where the old man had been standing, frozen in disbelief. Fuuuuck me. This was just the beginning of day one?

They next ordered us to "raise your hands above your head, put your hands straight out in front of you, and wiggle your fingers, then turn your palms up, run your fingers through your hair, open your mouth and stick out your tongue."

They walked up and down the line with a flashlight and carefully looked inside everyone's mouth and behind our ears to make sure nobody was hiding a razor blade.

"Lift up your dick, now your balls, then turn around bend over and spread your ass cheeks and cough."

When that was done, they threw our prison clothes at our feet and told us to get dressed.

After processing, I was sent to my temporary unit, where I waited to be sent to prison and then boot camp. In the temporary unit, I ran and trained with weights every day, preparing for boot camp and staying in shape for prison life. While I was there, I became friends with a young man named Juárez. He was quiet, kept to himself, and just wanted to do his time peacefully. He had a very short sentence, only eighteen months, of which he had already done three. With good time, he would be out in six.

One day as we were working out in the yard, he started pacing back and forth and I could hear him talking to himself. I could tell something was very wrong, but he disguised it pretty well. I cautiously walked up to him and said, "Hey, Juarez, what up?"

He didn't answer, but just kept pacing back and forth, fidgeting with his hands and talking to himself. For a second, I thought maybe he wasn't playing with a full deck.

Then I saw tears of rage in his eyes and realized he was fighting to keep his composure. Then he said, "That mother over there took my manhood."

What the fuck was going on with all this rape? First Thomas, then Peter, and now Juarez? And I'd only been locked up for a couple months so far! I didn't want to make the situation worse so I tried to act as normal as possible.

"Which one?" I asked.

"The Spanish dude on the bench press with all the tattoos. He just looked me right in the face and didn't even recognize me."

"'When'd this happen?"

"'Bout six months ago in the county jail, him and his homeboys jumped me and raped me."

I looked in his eyes. "Juarez, listen to me, you can't change the past, but you can make a path for your future."

"He took my manhood," Juarez said. "I can't let it go, I have to do something, or I won't be able to look myself in the mirror."

I grab him by both shoulders and looked him in the eyes, then said "He took your manhood? You look like a fuckin' man to me. The last time I checked, my manhood wasn't in my asshole, it's in my heart! HE's the motherfucker who's not a man!"

"I'm gonna kill this mother fucker."

"Juárez, you will be home in six months, with your three-year-old daughter. If you put this punk down out here on the yard, you'll have twenty people testifying against you in court to get their sentences reduced and you'll get another twenty years. Think about it…you won't be there for your daughter's birthday, you won't see the smile on her face at Christmas, and you won't be there to protect her like a father should. Besides revenge and personal satisfaction, what good is going to come out of this?"

He thought about it for a second, then said, "Caucci, you're right, I'm gonna let it go. Thanks for talking me out of doing something stupid, I owe you one."

"You did the right thing, brother. You're a better man than I am."

We worked out for about ten minutes, then he asked, "Caucci, let me ask you a question and please be straight with me." He stared me straight in the eyes and said, "What would you do if that shit happened to you and the motherfucker was working out right next to you? Be honest with me."

I hesitated, pretending to think about it as I did not want to give him my answer. As I sat there in silence for a while, I scoped out the yard and contemplated how I would take the guy out if it were me. I saw where the guards were positioned, if the cameras had any blind spots, how many people were around him, which ones were his friends, and what would be the most efficient way to execute my plan. I had it all worked out in my head in a matter of seconds, but then I thought, "Would I really do this if I had a daughter waiting for me to come home?" No, I wouldn't. I would wait until I got out and then I would track him down. He'd never see it coming.

"Not so easy to let go, Caucci, is it?"

"Juarez, you're absolutely right. But think of your baby, she needs a father. Do you want men like these dating your daughter when she grows up? You can't protect her from the inside. You want revenge, then bottle it up and thrive off it while your here. Then wait until he gets out, hunt him down, and have some fun."

But he must not have been listening, because he squatted and quickly rubbed his hands in the dirt, then grabbed a five-pound dumbbell and WHAM! He hit that scumbag RIGHT IN THE FUCKING HEAD. The weights the rapist had been using came crashing down on his throat and the alarm sirens went off. All the inmates hit the ground and not a single person went over to help that piece of shit while his arms and legs flailed around. We were immediately put on lock down while the prison guards did their investigation and questioned everyone. Nobody was allowed to leave their cells. After three days, they let us back out on the yard and I couldn't believe my eyes: Juarez was still there. With all those witnesses, nobody snitched on him. The word was that motherfucker had it coming from a few of the other inmates anyway. Juarez just happened to beat them to it. From that day forward, Juarez was and new man and was shown a lot of respect from the other prisoners. It was like the weight of the world had lifted off his shoulders and hit someone else in the head.

I later learned that some gangs believe that raping someone made you more of a man, but this phenomenon only applied in prison. Figure that one out. Their twisted logic was that the victim getting raped was a lesser man since "you are taking his manhood" and raising your status.

Once I got processed, I was finally shipped off to my permanent prison, Indian River. I had to wait there until there was an opening in boot camp. It took almost a year before I finally got to boot camp. In the meantime, I tried to get in the best shape possible because I'd heard stories from other inmates about the mental and physical torture waiting for me at boot camp. There was one inmate I remember vividly who quit boot camp and was sent back to Indian River. He said, "Fuck that boot camp shit, I'd rather do my time."

Hearing that really shocked me. "How much time you got?"

"Ten years."

"You mean you'd rather do ten years than ninety days in boot camp? Are you out of your fucking mind?"

"Damn straight. Them mutherfuckin crackers ain't playing in boot camp."

Hearing that made me nervous to say the least. This boot camp must be some serious shit if someone would rather do a ten-year sentence over ninety days. As the days went on, and as I waited to get transferred, I had no idea when they were coming to pick me up. They would come get you by surprise, and when I say surprise, I mean SURPRISE!

So there I was one night, sound asleep on the top bunk. At three o'clock in the morning, three crazy motherfucking boot camp military officers dressed like Hitler with boots up to their knees and batons in their hands kicked my door open and scared the shit out of me. They screamed as loud as they could, "Inmate Caucci! You got five seconds to get out or your fucking bed and give me two hundred jumping jacks."

"Okay."

"What the fuck did you just say, boy? Don't you okay me, you pathetic maggot! When you address me, you start with 'Sir' and end it with 'Sir.' You hear me?"

"Yes!"

"Caucci, are you one of those slow ones? Did your mother drop you on your head when you were a baby? Or are you just plain old stupid? Didn't you just hear what I just said?"

"Oh, my bad."

"Your fucking what…? You dumb son bitch. Drop down and give me some pushups until it sinks into that empty fucking skull of yours."

"Sir, yes sir!"

"Okay, now that's better, maybe you're not as stupid as you look, you poor excuse for a human being. Your mother must be ashamed to have a son like you. You're just a waste of human flesh! Now get back on your feet, you sack of cow shit. Inmate Caucci, why are you in here?"

"Trafficking cocaine."

"God have mercy on me. Inmate Caucci, you have to be the stupidest inmate I have ever come across. Get your ass back down in the push-up position! We can do this all night!"

"Sir, yes sir!"

That shit went on for about thirty minutes until I was about to puke. Then they handcuffed me, carried me by my legs and arms, and threw me into the back of a very small transport van. I was on my way to boot camp.

When I arrived at boot camp, there were thirty-four inmates in my platoon. We each got our own private room, which was nice, but for the next ninety days, they literally tried every tactic in the world to break me. Here is how an average day went. At 4 a.m. on the dot, one of the officers would blow a whistle and start counting down from five. You had to be out of your bed and standing at attention with the door closed within the five-second count. If you were late, they made you do hundreds of jumping jacks. We then had twenty minutes to clean our room, brush our teeth, and get ready for breakfast. We would then run a mile to breakfast. Once we arrived at the chow hall, there would be four inmates per table, all standing at attention. When the fourth inmate got to the table, he would yell, "Ready seat!" This started the stopwatch. We had exactly five minutes to eat everything on our plates. It had to be spotless. We had to eat all the butter, jelly, and sugar packets we had put on our plates. Absolutely no wasted food. The only way they would let you get away with not eating everything was if you vomited in your plate. Then you were excused.

Immediately after breakfast, we ran to the auditorium for morning calisthenics. That was an intense hour of military-style exercise, done on a full stomach. The rest of the day included a two-mile run around the prison immediately followed by a one-mile obstacle course. If you collapsed, they just picked you up and threw you in the back of a pick-up truck. After the obstacle course, there was one hour of military marching, three hours of picking weeds by hand in the hot sun, then a one-hour class on RET, or rational emotive therapy.

Out of the thirty-five inmates in my platoon, only eight of us made it. The others were sent back to prison, and some of them had very lengthy sentences. Not only did I make it, but I was the first to be released. See, the messed-up thing about boot camp was that some judges send prisoners there just to torture them, knowing they probably wouldn't make it, and others wouldn't release prisoners on time. The judge not only had to recommend that you be sent to boot camp, but he also had to sign your release papers. So the judge could fuck with you if he wanted. For me, that was not the case. At the end, my papers were signed and I was cleared for release.

So to Judge Thomas M. Coker, thank you for making sure the state did not hold me one more day.

18 | Your Name's on A List

I made it...I completed the ninety days and was released from prison. One day I was locked up and being treated like an animal, told when I could eat, sleep, and shit. The next day I was a free man, like it never happened. It's strange when you really think about it. You're sitting there at 8:59 a.m., a prisoner of the state, and sixty seconds later you are free.

My girlfriend Denise picked me up with her parents and took me straight to Joe Sonken's. My dad had told them he would meet us there so I could finally get a good meal. But when I walked in, I heard "Surprise!" It was shocking...it seemed as if the whole town was there, including my old friends, local wise guys, bookmakers, loan sharks, and everyone's families. There had to be at least 150 people. It was one hell of a getting-out-of-jail party. It made me feel great knowing that people recognized the fact that I didn't rat and stood up like a man.

My dad gave me a hug and a kiss on the cheek and whispered, "Make sure you shake everyone's hand and thank them for coming." As I walked around thanking everyone, every single person handed me an envelope with some cash. Some hold very large amounts, while others gave me just a twenty-dollar bill. The amount of money did not mean anything to me, just the fact that they thought about my situation and did whatever they could to help.

The biggest envelope came from Carlos Barcos. He handed me an envelope stuffed with ten thousand dollars and said, "I love you kid." He was at the top of the food chain as far as the cocaine business went, and he would have had the most to lose if I'd ratted. He had more money than everyone in the room put together and was a solid guy. Carlos also liked the finer things in life and owned more cars and houses than any one person needed, but he managed to do it with class. Just by looking at him and seeing the way he acted, you would never know how rich he was. He was not flashy like Fat Man, who had a serious case of "Look At Me Syndrome". Carlos was just a nice, down-to-earth guy who everyone in the drug business knew not to cross. The stories Carlos told me about the Colombian cartels were insane—it made the Italian Mob sound pretty damn civilized. All in all, I walked out with a little over fifteen thousand dollars. And that was the day Carlos and I became really close friends.

The thought of coming out of prison with nothing was a horrible feeling, but things were done differently back in those days. People looked out for each other and MOST people kept their mouths shut if they got pinched, especially higher-level guys. But nowadays, the vast majority of people are rats, and if you went to prison and kept your mouth shut, all you'd come out with is a couple of hundred dollars you may have made in prison performing slave labor and a bus ticket.

For the next two years I had to lay low. I had four years of probation, and if I stayed out of trouble they would possibly let me off probation in two years. So I painted for my dad, worked, and kept on training in Kai Sai Wing Chun and Chinese boxing. Denise and I stayed together for another year after I was released; she was a real solid girl. I loved her, but eventually we went our separate ways. Denise and her whole family were there for me before, during, and after prison—and for that I will never forget them.

I continued my Kai Sai Wing Chun training and was studying under Professor James Craven once again. At the age of twenty-one I received my teaching license in Kai Sai Wing Chun from Professor Cravens (he was the only senior student of the late Christopher Casey, better known as Kai Sai). Mr. Casey was given the name Kai Sai (Victorious in Every Encounter) by his martial arts instructors in Taiwan. Unfortunately, I never got to meet My Casey. He was more than just a great martial artist, he was a real thinker and had a genius IQ with a photographic memory. He actually memorized the entire dictionary. For the people who did have the honor to meet him at his home, he would often ask them to open the dictionary and pick any word. He would then tell them the definition(s) verbatim, page number, and how many listings down from the top it was. Since he loved the martial arts, and had a photographic memory, he excelled at a very unusual level. He had a black belt in every style he studied, which was highly unusual.

Mr. Casey sold international reinsurance, so his job often took him to Taiwan in the 1970s. After negotiating a very big deal that was extremely favorable for the government of Taiwan, they wanted to express their gratitude to him. So one day Mr. Casey was approached by a high-ranking government official and asked if there was anything the government of Taiwan could do for him. Mr. Casey replied, "Well, I have a passion for the martial arts. Is there anyone in Taiwan known for their fighting skill that would be a good teacher for me?"

The Chinese man chuckled and said, "Mr. Casey, right before mainland China turned to communism, all of the good Chinese Kung Fu teachers fled to Hong Kong and Taiwan. The top five in the world live here and are known as the Five Tigers of Taiwan."

"What are their names and what styles do they teach?"

"Hmmm...let me see, there is Lo Man Kam, he is the nephew of Bruce Lee's teacher Yip Man. He's the Grand Master in Wing Chun. Then there is Liao Wu Chang, he's the Grand Master of Stone Killer Monkey. Shen Mou Wei is a Grand Master in Chin-Na, Shoui Chaoi, and Shang-Tung Black Tiger and is also the chief instructor at the Taiwan Police Academy. There is a Mr. Chan who is the Grand Master in Fukien White Crane, but I do not know his full name. I will find out for you. And Wang Shujin is the Grand Master of Bagua Chang. But there is one more very good instructor here in Taiwan and his name is Tao Ping Siang. He is the Grand Master in Yang Style Tai Chi."

"That is an impressive list," Mr. Casey replied. "I would like to take lessons from all of them."

"I'm sorry, but that is not possible, Mr. Casey. You must pick one teacher, and if they accept you, you will become their student and you are not permitted to go to other instructors. This is the Chinese way."

Mr. Casey replied tactfully, "You asked me if there was anything you could do for me, and it would be a great honor to learn from these masters. Would it be possible for me to take a couple of lessons from each one so I can decide which teacher is the best match for me?"

This put the government official in a very difficult position as the Chinese do not like to lose face. He told Mr. Casey that he would talk to the masters and see what he could do. They all agreed. Cleverly, Mr. Casey had used his charm and intellect to his advantage. He showed his passion and high skill level to all his potential teachers, and all of them agreed to teach him. They gave Mr. Casey a pass because he was Caucasian and agreed that he did not have to be bound by the Chinese traditions.

To their surprise, Mr. Casey excelled in every style. He was the first person to earn a full teaching license from Lo Man Kam in Wing Chun. At that time, not even a Chinese had earned a full teaching license from Lo. Mr. Casey's skills were truly extraordinary. While Mr. Casey was in Taiwan, he went to each teacher every day to study, and in his free time he thought about each style and the techniques and principles that were useful in realistic combat. He took the most effective techniques and principles from each style and developed his own synthesis, creating a deadly fighting system he later called Kai Sai Chinese Boxing, which he passed down to one man: Professor James Cravens. Professor Cravens was not only my teacher but became a very good friend and mentor.

Because Mr. Casey had some very strong government connections inside the Taiwanese government, there was some speculation that he may have been working for the CIA, as his father-in-law was in the Agency and had tried to recruit him. But this we will never know.

After I got my teaching certificate from Professor Cravens, I decided I would like to go to Taiwan to meet some of Mr. Casey teachers, who were still alive. Since Wing Chun was my main style, Professor Cravens sent a traditional letter written in Chinese to Grandmaster Lo asking if he would accept me. He agreed. But I still had a dilemma, I had to get my probation officer and the judge to agree to let me leave the country. Surprisingly, the same judge who took it easy on me at sentencing let me go to Taiwan. What a break!

When I arrived in Taiwan, Grand Master Lo welcomed me into his home, where I stayed for my trip. We had a two-hour private lesson every morning and a two-hour group class every evening. People flew from all over the world to study with Master Lo. At that point, I had been studying Wing Chun for about ten years, and there I was, practicing with great Wing Chun students from all over the world, some with a lot more experience than me. But when it came time to practice, I was able to handle them easily.

There were several times Grand Master Lo went out of his way to correct me in front of the other students, sometimes screaming at me,

"You're doing it all wrong!" I noticed that the Wing Chun I was doing was a little different than everyone else's. Then I started to wonder…what was I taught in the United States? Was it authentic? I was upset for a day or two, thinking I hadn't been taught the same authentic Wing Chun that Bruce Lee would've learned. Then one day as I was training on the wooden dummy, Master Lo walked up to me and yelled, "You're doing it all wrong, your teacher is stupid! This is not Wing Chun!"

Now that really pissed me off and offended me, but I kept calm and stayed respectful. That night I laid in bed and thought if my Wing Chun was so bad, why was I able to beat everyone there? Mr. Casey was the first person Grandmaster Lo ever gave a full teaching license. Mr. Casey had to be great at Wing Chun to receive such a high ranking. Then I remembered…Mr. Casey had a genius IQ with a photographic memory and had mastered all the different styles he had been taught. Mr. Casey's passion was the pursuit of realistic lethal combat—he was not interested in tradition, rules, or regulations.

Then it dawned on me. Mr. Casey had modified some of the traditional techniques taught in Wing Chun to make it far more efficient and effective than the one Bruce Lee learned from Yip Man. So, for the next couple of weeks I just did what I was told in class and analyzed what everyone else was doing. But the most important lesson I learned in Taiwan was that Mr. Casey was an absolute martial arts genius, and I was blessed to be able to be taught by his only senior student, Professor Cravens. My martial arts skills greatly improved after understanding the Kai Sai method.

On my return flight from Taiwan, my first connecting flight was in Hawaii. When the plane landed, I heard the pilot instructing everyone to stay in their seats. At first, I didn't think anything of it, but then two federal officers wearing navy blue wind breakers and U.S. Customs hats boarded the plane. One had a piece of paper in his hand and it was obvious they were looking for a particular seat. Since I was seated in an aisle, I was looking down the aisle to see who they are going to grab. It's not often that feds board a plane to remove someone. As they were getting closer to me, I got a little excited because I thought I was going to see some action. But then they stopped at my seat, looked down at me, and said, "Come with us." They took me off the plane first. As usual, they tried to play it cool and pretended they were nice guys and began asking me questions.

"What color is your suitcase?"

"Why do you want to know?"

Immediately their demeanor changed from nice guys to wanna-be tough guys.

"Because we're gonna search it."

"What the fuck for?"

"We have good information that you're smuggling heroin."

"You don't say…heroin, is it? Well, the only way there's going to be any such thing in my bag is if you put it there! And where's your warrant to search my bags, big fella?"

"We don't need a fucking warrant to search your bags when you're entering the country!"

"You're absolutely correct…good job on remembering the law. But the law also says I don't have to tell you shit. That should be on the first page of your Customs pocket manual. But since I have nothing to hide, I'll tell you exactly what it looks like. It's a blueish green bag with a hint of yellow and burgundy and pink and blue polka dots. Oh, and on the side is a big emblem that says, 'Go fuck yourself!' Now carry on, boys, there's a lot of bags under this plane."

"So you're a real smart ass?"

"Look, you and I both know you don't have any information about me smuggling heroin. But if there is any heroin under the plane, your partner here should be able to sniff it out in seconds. Have you seen the size of his fucking nose? He's gonna put the K9s out of a job."

While the rest of the passengers were all seated at the gate waiting to get back on the plane, they put me in a separate area and had two feds guarding me. There was a phone booth there that I used to call my dad and told him what was going on. He told me he would call Coast Guard John and to call back in ten minutes. When I called him back, he said, "Don't worry, it's just routine. Your name is on a list of people that have been flagged."

That was a huge relief, but for the next three hours all I got was dirty looks from the other passengers as the feds tried to find my luggage. After they found my luggage and found nothing suspicious, they put me back on the flight to Miami, but this time I was riding in the cockpit sitting next to a federal agent. It was better than first class and what a view! Nothing ever came of it, except that I knew I was still on their radar. And that was that!

19 | Up in Flames He Went

Hurricane Andrew hit Florida in 1992—and it was great for business. My painting business took off after Andrew. At the time, I was working with my brother Marc and my uncle Steve. I wasn't making as much money as I did selling coke, but I was making enough to be happy. Unfortunately, it wasn't meant to last. A contractor I had been doing work for screwed me out of a lot of money and I went bankrupt. Actually, he screwed a lot of people out of their money and then just skipped town. At least he was smart enough to leave town, but stupid enough to think he couldn't be found.

Now bankrupt, I had to revert back to my old ways to find this prick and collect my money. It took me a few years, but eventually I caught up to him and got back every penny, plus interest.

After this incident, I was sick of dealing with contractors and their bullshit. Still, I needed to work and spent six months looking for a job as a painter with a company other than my dad's. I didn't want to depend on him every time things didn't work out for me. But nobody would hire me because of my criminal history—I must have gone to over one hundred job interviews, and every single one said the same thing: "We don't hire felons." They looked down on me because I was so young and had already gone to prison.

I even applied for a job bagging groceries at three different supermarkets, and all three denied me. It got to the point to where I was denied food stamps because anyone convicted of a drug felony was not eligible even though fucking child molesters, murderers, and rapist were. Some fucking system we have. Then it finally sank in: Judge Coker was on the money when he said that he hated seeing a young man's life ruined.

So things were pretty desperate when one day my brother Marc and I were sitting on the couch, jobless and living with our mother. "Hey," he said, "why don't you go down and talk to the Cubans and get some coke? How much longer can we sit here on the couch staring at each other? I'll sell it and we'll whack it right down the middle. Don't get a huge amount. We'll keep it small."

I was hesitant because I had just gotten off probation, and a second offense of more than an ounce would get me at least ten years. But I agreed reluctantly, with the condition that he had to sell it, and we were back in business.

Immediately, the money started rolling in again. It was nowhere near as much as before, but it was plenty. Then Marc got a call from a very close friend, Butch, who said he had a guy he knew from New York who wanted a quarter-kilo and would pay top dollar. I didn't like the idea of selling such a large amount, especially to a friend of a friend. Marc reassured me he was only going to be dealing with Butch and if anything went south, Butch would take responsibility for it. My brother said they were going to be meeting this guy in the parking lot of Bennigan's restaurant in Hallandale.

I told my brother I had a real bad feeling about this and not to do it. But he insisted that he was just going to keep an eye on things. So I agreed but warned him, "If this guy shows up with anyone else, tell Butch to excuse himself from the table, go to the bathroom, and flush that shit down the toilet."

Marc reassured me he would make sure Butch knew what to do. They went to Bennigan's to meet this guy at 1:00 pm. I told Marc to call me no later than 1:30. So I sat at home waiting for my brother to call, all the while my gut telling me he's going down. One-thirty rolled around and I hadn't heard a word from him so I took the remainder of the coke we had stashed in the house and put it in a fake bird nest at the top of a giant oak tree in our back yard. I called his beeper several times and did not get any response, so I called Hallandale police station. When the dispatch officer answered, I said, "My brother was just arrested on the beach for fighting. Can you tell me if I can bail him out there, or do I need to wait until he gets sent down to the county jail?"

"What is your brother's name?"

"Marc Caucci."

"Stay on the line while I check."

"Thank you."

After a three-minute hold she returned and said, "We do have your brother in custody, but it's not for fighting."

"Really? What in the name of Jesus did he do?"

"He's been charged with trafficking cocaine. You'll have to bail him out of the main jail in Broward County."

"Oh my, that's terrible! Are you sure you've got the right person?"

"Yes, I'm sure."

It was only a matter of time until the cops got a warrant to search the house and kicked the door in. So I quickly propped my front door wide open so they wouldn't kick it in. I grabbed a can of Coke out of the fridge, put a lounge chair in the front yard, laid back, and waited for those fucking bozos to show up. A few minutes later, three unmarked police cars came flying around the corner and pulled up in front of my house. They quickly got out of their cars, drew their weapons, and aimed their guns at me.

"Hey, what took you guys so long? I've been out here for thirty minutes...how's my tan looking?"

"Put your fucking hands in the air and don't move!"

"Whaddya know? Hallandale's finest. How da fuck you expect me to put my hands in the air without moving?"

"Get your ass on the ground and lay on your stomach!"

"Fuuuuuck you, I ain't moving out of this chair. You're just looking for an excuse to shoot me. And if you do, it'll be with me lying right here in my front yard while all the neighbors watch. Why don't you fellas just go in the house and do your search, then get back to doing some real police work?"

"How'd you know we were coming?"

"Because the Hallandale Police Department's customer service is impeccable. All I had to do was call the front desk and they told me everything. I was very impressed."

Marc ended up getting busted for quarter kilo and ended up going to prison, so I had to get back into the drug business if I wanted to eat and keep a roof over my head. I still had most of my old contacts so it wasn't very difficult to get started. I started off slowly and sold only small quantities, but in a few months I was right back in it full-time. Between my connections with the Cubans and my friend Carlos Barco, I was selling hundreds of kilos. Carlos was one hell of a connection and could get thousands of kilos of cocaine into the country.

One day he told me he could put a couple hundred kilos on an American Airlines airplane, hiding the packages inside the food carts and nobody would touch them. He asked me if I knew anyone working at the airport. I reached out to Jerry Chilli.

Chilli was currently doing ten years for racketeering and extortion, so he had to call me from prison. I told him I needed to find someone who could give him a message in person. After a little bullshitting on the phone, he told me to go down to the Outrigger bar in Sunny Isles and talk to a guy who would relay the message. So I went down to the Outrigger and sent a message asking if Jerry had any friends who could help us retrieve drug packages from food carts after a plane landed at Miami International airport. Chilli sent a message back to meet with my old pal Steve Maruca. I called Steve and arranged a sit-down. After he realized how much money could be made, he said, "Okay, let me see what I can do." A couple of weeks went by before I got a call from Steve, saying, "Hey, kid, let's meet up at that place to discuss that thing."

"Okay, what time?"

"Lunch time."

Steve showed up with a young man who worked as a baggage handler. We had a brief conversation about the food carts, but the baggage guy suggested that my guys in Colombia should instead put the merchandise in Samsonite suitcases and he would get them off without a problem.

"Forget about it," I said. "You tellin' me you're just gonna walk on the plane, grab the coke, and badda bing just like that? Whaddya think I look like? A fucking baboon?"

"I don't mean any disrespect to you, but the truth is that nobody's paying attention out there. I've been working there for ten years. I'll get those bags off with my eyes closed."

I asked Steve to take a walk with me. "Steve, we're gonna pay $500 a kilo to get them off the plane. How much you gonna pay the kid?"

"For now, let's give him half."

"That sounds fair, but don't get greedy. And tell the old man not to either. We're gonna start with a small shipment of one hundred kilos...so it's $50,000 on the first run. And let's not tell the old man the details...the less he knows, the better off he is. He's already doin' a dime, and I don't think he'd want to know anyway."

"Sounds good, kid!"

After the meeting, I called Carlos and got all the details I needed. Our cost was $1,500 per kilo, plus $500 to get them off the plane, so Carlos had to come up with $200,000. Once the coke arrived in Miami, it would easily be sold for $15,000 a kilo. That would be a quick $1.3 million.

The operation went very smooth—it was so easy it was scary. Once the bags were unloaded from the plane, the baggage handler called me and told me to meet him outside the airport, near baggage claim. He pulled up in a golf cart with a few suitcases on the back. I got out, we shook hands, and he loaded my trunk as if everything was normal. I took the merchandise back to one of Carlos's apartments in Miami to do a quick count and discovered we were short two kilos. So I ran to a phone and called Carlos to let him know what had happened. He said, "We need to find out if this is on my end or on your end."

"I can't vouch for this kid 100 percent, but if you're gonna steal something, why just take the two? Why not just disappear with the whole load? That doesn't make any sense."

"That would put a target on his ass. I'm gonna round up a few people and start the process of elimination on my end. I'll call you when I know for sure who took it."

"Okay, talk to ya soon."

Things were done a lot differently in Columbia—and I mean a *lot* different. Carlos called the guys that worked for him and told them who to round up. They quickly tracked down six men, any one of whom could have taken it. Pablo, one of the six, was already on a hit list and was going to be executed anyway. Carlos was absolutely certain Pablo didn't take the missing two kilos because he had counted them after Pablo was gone—but the other five men didn't know this. After all six men were dragged into a barn in the middle of nowhere by twenty of Carlos's men with machine guns, Carlos told them what had happened. They all knew someone was going to die, and possibly their families as well, if someone didn't come clean.

They guys were all bound hand and foot with truck tires stacked over them until you could only see their heads. Carlos said, "Unless you tell me who took my merchandise, every one of you will die. I'm asking you now who took it."

He started with Pablo, who of course said he had nothing to do with it. Carlos knew he was innocent, but he instructed his men to pour gas over Pablo anyway (there was already a hit on Pablo, so they needed to get rid of him anyway). Pablo begged for his life and swore on the lives of his children that he was innocent, but Carlos ignored him. Instead he turned to one of his men and said, "Pablo looks a little cold. Do me a favor and warm his ass up." They lit the gas, and the other five men watched in terror as the skin melted off Pablo's face as he burned alive. The smell of burning flesh and rubber filled the air as black clouds of smoke drifted over them. Some of the men begged and pleaded with Carlos while the others prayed out loud in Spanish. Dying is one thing but being burned alive is another whole level.

"This is your last fucking chance. Who the fuck took my shit?" Carlos demanded.

Completely overcome with terror, nobody wanted to answer him.

"Okay motherfuckers, if that's how you wanna play…Hector, gas these motherfuckers up."

As Hector began to drench them in gasoline, they continued to beg for their lives and plead their innocence. Then Carlos said, "Gentleman, I'll make a deal with you, and this will be the last deal you'll ever get on this earth if I don't get the truth. Tell me which one of you took my merchandise, and instead of fire, I'll put a bullet in your head. But if I don't get the answer I want, you will all burn, and then I'll get all of your families, including your children, and burn them too."

That was one hell of a strategy to make someone talk. Either die by fire or by a bullet to the head. But more importantly, whoever came clean would be saving his family too.

Within a few seconds Carlos's cousin said, "It was me."

Carlos's heart sank. He didn't think it would be his cousin and had no intention of killing him. He was just there for show. Carlos slowly walked over to his cousin with tears in his eyes and his heart broken and said, "My own blood steals from me?"

"Please forgive me, primo."

"You've already stolen from me…so I'm not gonna lose another dime on your ass. You're not worth a bullet and a funeral."

Carlos turns his back and began to walk away.

"Thank you, Primo!" his cousin said. "I promise I will get your money back. Please forgive me."

Carlos turned around and looked at his cousin. "I said I wasn't gonna lose another dime on you. What I meant was I'm not spending a dime on a bullet or a funeral for your sorry ass." Carlos turned to Hector and said, "Put some fire on him. Primo, fire is free and this is your funeral."

"Noooo please!"

But up in flames he went. The screams of his burning cousin could be heard for miles, but Carlos had to make an example out of him or he would have been perceived as weak. In Columbia, if you were weak and didn't have the balls for the business, you wouldn't last long.

A couple hours later, Carlos called and told me he had fixed the problem. I could tell he had been crying. Then he said the lawyer had all the paperwork and it was already signed and notarized. This meant I could go pick up money because someone was taking the whole load. It wasn't like in the movies, where people meet in some secluded warehouse in the middle of nowhere and the buyers bring the money and the dealers bring the coke and everyone is carrying a machine gun. That's Hollywood bullshit. In this business, when you're dealing with millions of dollars and hundreds or thousands of kilos of cocaine, you had to trust the people you were dealing with. And you needed an insurance policy just in case someone did something stupid.

If the people we were dealing with wouldn't give us the money up front, or we didn't trust them enough to give them some product up front, then we wouldn't do business with them. There is an old rule: when you mix drugs and money at the same location, whoever brings the most guns goes home with all the drugs and the money. But if you just give them the product and trust them to come back with the money in a few days, they have no reason to rip you off or kill you on the spot. They can take your shit and leave town, but the cocaine circle was so tight that most people who tried that got caught and killed.

After Carlos gave me the green light, I took a ride to the buyer's house. When I pulled into the driveway, they opened the garage. Once inside, there was a quick handshake, then they put three suitcases full of money in my trunk and I headed back to the apartment. When I pulled up to valet, I got a dolly for the suitcases so I could wheel the money right through the lobby. I went into the condo and opened the suitcases. The money was in bundles of different denominations. Shit...this was going to take a very long time to count by hand. It was clearly all crack money. I called Carlos and told him "the paperwork is very unorganized, I gotta read through it thoroughly. It'll take me at least four hours to go over everything and put it in order. I hope there aren't any mistakes. Tell them next time to have everything put together neatly so I'm not here all day checking for errors."

After about four hours of counting, it was $ 2,000 short. So I made a quick call to Carlos and told him "the paperwork's not in order."

"What's missing?"

"Two important documents." This was code for $2,000.

Carlos made a call to the buyers, and without hesitation they said it was not a problem, they'll pay the difference. When you're dealing with that much money, nobody's gonna argue over $2,000. I grabbed the merchandise and drove to a restaurant in Kendall. I drove around back and knocked on the door. When the owner opened the door, he gave me a dolly to load the coke on. I wheeled the coke through the kitchen and into his office. He handed me an envelope with the missing $2,000 and the deal was done. I took $200,000 for me and $50,000 for my Italian friends, then dropped the rest of the money off at Carlos's fathers house.

The next day I met up with Steve Maruca and gave him their cut.

A few days later I got a call from Chilli. "Hey, kid, what's doing?"

"Not much. Just moving along."

"How'd everything turn out?"

"We had a nice meal. The food was great and everybody had full bellies."

"Good to hear that."

"Take care, my friend, I'll talk to you soon. Oh, and don't pick up the soap!"

"You little ball-breaking bastard. You're just like your father. When I get out of here, I'm gonna kick you right in the ass."

Carlos continued to do this for years and never got caught. He must have sent tens of thousands of kilos of cocaine through American Airlines and others. As for me, I had other things to do and didn't want to get nailed with an international trafficking charge and get life in prison. So I introduced Carlos to the kid at the airport, and Carlos got Fatman to pick it up, store it, and deliver it.

But since I helped get it off the ground, Carlos always gave me fist pick when the merchandise arrived. I usually paid about 10 percent less than everyone else. That may not sound like much of a discount, but when you're moving fifty kilos and saving $1,000 on each one, that's $50,000 in your pocket. Not too bad.

20 | There's a Blood Bath

As time went on and I got deeper into the drug trade, I was able to get hundreds of kilos of pure cocaine as soon as they arrive into the country. With that kind of volume, I was very careful who I did business with. Well, as careful as I could be, because in this business anyone could turn into a rat at any time.

Although my father was never into selling drugs, one day he called me out of the blue and said that he'd like to talk to me about the painting business in Miami—that was our code for the drug business. I met him at his house to see what he wanted. My dad told me that he knew a guy who wanted to buy fifty kilos of cocaine. Now that was a surprise and a concern, so I asked, "Who is this guy?"

"His name is Paul Sanzaro, they call him Sal. He owns Hemmingway's restaurant in Hollywood. He was a good friend of your grandfather and is connected with the DeCavalcante Family from Philadelphia. He's a real stand-up guy"

"He was friends with Grandpa Pasquale?"

"Yes, they were very close."

I figured he must be pretty fucking solid if he was friends with my granddad, but still, something was bothering me.

"Pop, something doesn't sound right. Nobody just asks if they can get fifty kilos right off the rip. It usually starts with a much smaller quantity, and once a level of trust is developed, you gradually work your way up to fifty. We gotta feel these guys out first. We need to make sure they have family members close by so we have some sort or leverage on them in case they are bad people. Look at it like this…if you had $750,000 to spend on cocaine, would you put the word out on the street through people you knew to find a connection? If the word gets out to the wrong people that someone has $750,000 cash and they are looking for fifty kilos, every fucking rodent in South Florida will show up claiming they can get it just so they can put a bullet in your fucking head and take your money."

"I never thought about it like that," he said.

"Something just doesn't add up."

"How 'bout we just meet up with him and listen to what he has to say? If something smells fishy, we walk away.

"If that's what ya wanna do…but we need to be very careful what we say. Once we get there, let me do the talking, and just in case they're cops, don't mention anything about drugs. Let's just refer to it as diamonds, and tell Sal to do the same."

"Sounds good."

So my dad made a call to Sal and set up a time to have sit-down at Sal's restaurant. When we arrived at Hemmingway's, the three of us sat in a corner booth. Sal was well dressed in a nice pin-striped Italian suit and was a little over sixty years old. His restaurant had been the classiest joint in South Florida at one time and it still looked great. After some bullshit-ting, Sal told me he knew a guy who was looking for fifty keys.

"Fifty keys? Are you sure you're talking to the right person, Sal? I know you're getting old, but I was told that we're here to talk about diamonds, so let's keep it that way. That kind of talk can get you locked up for twenty years so let's get our facts straight. The only reason I took this meeting is because you were a good friend of my grandfather's. I don't know who this other guy is, so make sure we're all on the same fucking page here."

It was obvious Sal just wanted to make some quick cash like my Dad, and although he seemed solid, he was also pretty old. I could tell he had never done a deal like this before.

"I'm sorry," Sal said. "I don't know what the fuck I was thinking… getting old sucks, kid. Let's talk about these diamonds."

"So how do ya know this guy?" I asked.

"He's my ex son-in-law."

"Okay, so let's just speak hypothetically here, complete bullshit. Let's just say, for example, a very large diamond deal like this were to take place, are you going to vouch for these people? No disrespect, but I don't know you and you don't know me. What guarantees are there? What if something goes wrong and all the money and diamonds are lost?"

"Lost how?"

"How? Where the fuck you been, Sal, living under a rock? A deal like this would require close to a million dollars. What if someone brings a gun? The party's over…either everyone dies, or you'll be lucky to be alive and you'll owe some very dangerous people a lot of money."

"Ah…don't worry about anything like that! I trust this guy with my life."

"That's good, because that's exactly what you are putting on the line here. If something goes wrong, these people will send some guys from their home country and burn you and anyone you love alive. They don't do business like us Italians. They are ruthless."

Sal looked at me in shock as my Dad chuckled nervously and said, "I need a fucking drink."

"Sal, I know you want to make a little money like everyone does, but are you willing to give up your restaurant and put your life on the line if something goes wrong?"

"Absolutely…if anything goes wrong on my end, I will sign it over immediately. And like I said, I trust this guy with my life. Let me give him a call so we can talk. He's just down the street."

Sal made the call, and fifteen minutes later two guys showed up. Sal introduced me to his ex-son-in-law Mario Adamo and another guy I wasn't expecting who went by the name of Alex. We walked up the stairs to the second floor, where we had complete privacy. We sat around a large table inside a private dining area. Both guys put their cell phones on the table. That was the first thing that caught my attention. Even back in the 1990s, cell phones could easily have recording devices in them.

Mario was very charismatic and outgoing, a real entertainer. But he seemed way too comfortable for a first meeting like this. And the whole idea of bringing another person to the meeting made me a little suspicious.

I started it off. "Hey, Sal, I thought I was only meeting one person, who's this other guy?"

"This is Alex, he's the money guy"

"I'm just the driver," Mario said.

"Okay, so what do ya fellows want?"

"I need fifty keys," Alex said right away. "Sal tells us you can get it."

"Fifty keys? Do I look like a fucking locksmith to you? I sell diamonds...you guys must have gotten your wires crossed! Gentlemen, have a nice day. We are done here."

I got up to leave and whispered in my dad's ear, "Let's get the fuck outta here."

But Sal jumped up right away and said, "Wait, hold on! Please don't go. Let me talk to my friends here. There's obviously a misunderstanding, we are all *friends* here."

"I think you and your two friends should go sit at another table and discuss this. Sal, I hope you're not losing your marbles in your old age. Fifty keys? You must have forgotten to take your medication today."

As they left the table, I could sense the tension in the air. It was obvious things were not going the way they intended. I looked over at my dad and said, "Pop, this is not a good start. Sal was supposed to talk to these guys about how to conduct themselves at this meeting, and the first thing out of his mouth is fifty keys."

"Maybe he forgot to tell them. Let's just hear what they have to say, then get the hell out of here. I need a fucking drink."

When Sal, Mario, and Alex returned to the table, Sal said, "Sorry for the confusion, gentlemen. Let's get back to business."

Mario jumped in and said, "Sal tells us you have a real solid connection with the Cubans in Miami and can easily get large quantiles of diamonds."

"I don't know about that, but I think I know someone who *might* know someone who can get what you're looking for."

Mario looked at Sal and said with a thick Italian accent, "What da fuck is going on here? You said you had a solid connection?"

Sal leaned across the table, grabbed me by the arm, and said, "Don't worry, these guys are good."

"Listen, gentlemen," I said, "let's just take it easy for a second and maybe order a couple of drinks, because things are starting off on a bad foot. I find it very unprofessional that you'd put the word out that you're looking to purchase such a large quantity of diamonds. To be honest, you sound like amateurs."

"Amateurs?!" Alex said, laughing, "I've been in this business for ten years."

"Oh really? Then why are you sitting here at a table with two guys you know nothing about, trying to organize such a large purchase? If you've really been in this business for ten years, you should have a shitload of connections by now."

"Why the fuck are *you* here?" he challenged.

"The only fucking reason I'm here is because Sal was a good friend of my grandfather's and is friends with my dad. I'm only here out of respect to them. Sal asked me to come hear you fucking clowns out so that's what I'm doing...hearing you out and nothing more!"

Sal stepped in, "Look, you're right, it was my idea. I'm good friends with your father, and I knew your Grandfather Pasquale very well. When you were just four or five years old, I met you more times than I can remember, and you were always hitting me up for a $20. Your grandfather used to take you everywhere with him. But that was twenty years ago. I trust these guys just like I trust your father. And now here we are. We're all just trying to make a little money. So let's all just calm down and get back to business."

I knew Sal wanted this meeting to be successful, so I went along with it.

"Alright. I'll hear you out."

After all that bullshit, I couldn't believe it when Alex said, "My main cocaine supplier cannot get large quantities all the time and his prices have gone way up."

I gave Sal a cold stare, then looked over at my father, who just shook his head. Then I turned to Alex and said, "Listen very fucking carefully, you moron. I don't know nothing about no cocaine, so for the third time let's get that shit straight! But since you like to play kindergarten games, let's just joke around here for a minute, nothing serious, just a bunch of hypotheticals and some questions to see how this fantasy of yours would play out in a perfect world if I could get you fifty perfectly cut diamonds."

"This is fucking ridiculous!" Mario interrupted.

"No," I said, "You two are ridiculous."

Alex's face turned beet red. "What the fuck is going on here with all this talk about diamonds? We're all solid guys here, let's just say it how it is. You bring the coke here, and we will bring the money. We can do the deal right here in the restaurant. Right, Sal?"

"Abso-fucking-lutely!" Sal agreed.

At this point, there was absolutely no doubt in my mind that Alex was a fed, so just to be safe I said it nice and clearly: "Open your fucking ears,

I don't sell coke and I don't want anything to do with a cocaine deal. And that whole fucking scenario you suggested sounded like some fuckin Walt Disney fantasy. Why would you bring…let's see, how much does a kilo go for, Alex?"

"Uh, roughly $15,000."

"And you want how many?"

"Fifty."

"How much money is that, Alex?"

"About $750,000."

"Three quarters of a million dollars. In cash. Here. And if I bring a gun, you die! Or vice versa. Or we both bring guns and there's a bloodbath. See, the whole scenario sounds ridiculous! Sounds like you two watched *Scarface* one too many times! I feel like I'm having a fucking sit-down with Moe, Larry, and Curly."

Mario slammed his hand on the table. "Nobody's ripping anyone off!"

Sal was looking very nervous by now. "Please, Anthony! I vouch for these guys…there's nothing to worry about. I trust these guys with my life, and I'll put my restaurant up as collateral."

"Well, gentleman," I said calmly, "I would never do something so stupid. I'd never be in the same room while an exchange that size is going on, especially with strangers. So, like I said, it's a complete fantasy and in the real world would never happen."

"But we are the ones taking the risk by bringing that much cash!" Alex said.

"Finally we agree on something, Alex, and that's a stupid fucking amateur move that makes me believe you're a cop."

"A cop? Are you out of your fucking mind?"

"You're either a fed or you got Down Syndrome. You might even be a fed *with* Down Syndrome. Either way, I'm not fucking with you. Pop, let's get the fuck outta here."

As we started to get out of our seats, Mario made another attempt. "Look, gentleman, this is about trust. We are all here because we trust each other, right?"

"Why should any of us trust one another? Because Sal made an intro? Right now, I don't trust any of you. If we were ever going to do business, this is how this fantasy would play out. I would give Sal two diamonds, at, let's say, noon, without any money exchanging hands. I would just give it to him out of trust. Then you would make arrangements with him to pick it up. At that point, you would give him the money for five diamonds, reciprocating the trust. I would then bring eight and so on until you get your fifty fantasy diamonds."

"That's a ridiculous idea," Alex said. "It's too risky, too much driving around."

"You three all trust each other with your lives, correct?"

They all said yes.

"Excellent. Then I have the perfect solution, you give your $750,000 to Sal, then Sal and I will make arrangements for your diamonds to be delivered. It's that easy. So whaddya think? Sounds flawless to me, if you all trust each other the way you say you do."

They were completely boxed in. Then Alex said, "We can't do that until we check the quality of the merchandise."

"Wait a minute…if this whole transaction is based on trust, then you have to trust Sal that you will get what you are looking for, and if something goes wrong, Sal said he would put his restaurant on the line. Gentlemen, I think we have solved the problem."

They looked defeated. Then Sal looked and said, "Anthony, please, these guys are good for it. Trust me, please!"

"No, Sal, trust me. I'm doing you a huge favor here."

Alex jumped out of his seat. "This will never work like this."

"I know it won't, that's what I've been saying from the beginning. I told you it was a fantasy."

"Fuck this shit!" Alex yelled, storming out of the room. Now it was just me, Sal, Mario, and my Dad. Sal and Mario tried to convince me to go ahead with the deal.

"No fucking way, I don't trust that guy, and I don't know you, Mario."

"I just did a fifteen-year prison sentence and didn't rat on nobody," he said. "You ask some of the people you know about me. My name will come back clean. Then once you do, give Sal a call and maybe we can have a better conversation next time."

"Okay, maybe we will."

After Mario left, I told my dad and Sal to watch out for those two guys because something wasn't right. The whole thing stunk. Sal ordered me a chicken parmesan sandwich and tried to smooth things over with me while my dad knocked down a couple martinis. After I left, my dad stayed behind with Sal and they tried to figure out a way for this to go down. They knew there was a lot of money to be made if these guys were legit. It could lead to hundreds of thousands or even millions of dollars.

But if the guys weren't legit, we would all either end up in jail for decades or at the bottom of a ditch.

21 | You'll Wish You Were Never Born

A few weeks passed and my father asked me to meet with him to talk. I met him at his favorite drinking spot, Joe Sonken's Gold Coast. When I walked in, he was in his usual corner seat at the bar drinking a Johnny Walker on the rocks. I took a seat next to him and gave him a kiss on the cheek. It was late in the afternoon so he was already three sheets to the wind. He put his arm around me and whispered in my ear, "I've been talking with Sal about trying to figure out a way that we can make this thing work."

"Pop, that's not a good idea. I want nothing to do with it. I have a real bad feeling about this thing."

"You don't have to...you stay out of it, and I will deal directly with Sal myself."

"If you wanna go through with it, that's fine with me, but if they aren't putting up the money first, the most they are getting out of me is one kilo."

"At least it's a start...how much we talking?"

"It'll run you $17,000, You put $1,500 on your end to it to make it $18,500."

"Sounds great, see how easy that was? Now let me buy you a Coke and I'll have a martini."

So my dad called Sal and they agreed to meet the next day at Hemmingway's at noon. My dad and I agreed to meet at the VFW Bar, which was directly next to Hemmingway's. Once I arrived at the VFW, I went in and took a seat at the bar next to him. He was probably on his second or third scotch by this time and was in a very good mood. He seemed very excited about making a quick $1,500. He also seemed very relaxed about the whole thing. I told him "that thing is in the trunk of my car in a bag" and handed him my keys so he could go and get it. When he came back inside the bar, I said, "Please don't say too much during the deal and do not mention me at all. Just let them look at it and get the cash. The less you say, the better off you are. You've never done business with these other guys so just be careful. When it's all over, give me a call and I'll meet you right back here at the bar."

"Sounds good. I'll see you in about twenty minutes then."

I gave him a kiss on the cheek and left. About five minutes later, he walked next door to Hemmingway's to meet Sal, Mario, and Alex. They looked at the merchandise and were very pleased with the quality. Alex handed him an envelope full of $100 bills so he did a quick count to make sure it wasn't light. Then Mario asked, "How are we going to move forward in getting a larger quantity?"

"Once this goes smoothly, I will talk to my son again."

"Do you think he'll come through?"

"I'm sure we'll figure something out that will make everyone happy."

"Look, we are serious about this and don't want to be wasting our time," Alex said. "Are you sure your son can get fifty keys?"

"Fuhgeddaboudit…he has a solid connection to some fucking Cubans and Columbians who bring in hundreds of kilos a month."

Alex's eyes lit up. "Really?"

"Yeah, he's known these people for about eight or nine years now and has been doing business with them since he was sixteen. They'll give him whatever he wants just on a handshake."

After their little meeting, my dad walked back to the VFW and called me. "Hey, come on by and let me buy you a drink."

"Yeah…how you feeling?"

"I'm feeling great!"

"Okay, I'll see you in ten minutes."

So I went back to the VFW, picked up the money, and went home. As I was driving home, I started to wonder if maybe these guys were for real. They had paid cash for one—but one and fifty are two different ballgames. Maybe they just bought the one to make us feel comfortable, before trying to rob us for the fifty. Maybe they're cops just trying to look legit. But then again, I had never heard of cops paying $18,500 cash and letting the money go. The whole scenario got me thinking.

After a couple of months of my dad negotiating the deals, I finally agreed to work directly with Sal and nobody else. Sal promised me Alex was no longer involved in any way, and my dad was able to confirm the story about Mario doing fifteen years and not ratting on anyone. So I went back to Hemmingway's and had a sit-down with Sal.

"This is how this thing is going down," I said. "I'm only dealing with you and nobody else. I don't want to see or talk to anyone but you. I'll give you seven kilos up front for $17,000 each. That is a total of $119,000. If anything goes wrong, it's your ass that's on the line. If you are lucky, I'll only take your restaurant. If you fuck this up or don't stick to your end of the deal, the Colombians will come for you. And remember what I said about the Colombians…you'll wish you were never born."

"Don't worry, don't worry, it's all under control."

A few weeks went by and I got a call from Fatman. He told me that, "A couple of Carlos's cousins are in town with a few of their friends. These girls are not as good-looking as the ones that were here a couple weeks ago, but if you want to take a couple of them out to South Beach and show them around, let me know. But they're not the best-looking girls I've seen, that's for sure." This meant Carlos had a few keys of coke on hand, but the quality was nothing like we were used to. The price to me was $12,000 a key. At the time, there was a dry spell so okay quality coke was better than no coke at all. I got a sample and gave it to Sal to see if his side was interested. They agreed that it wasn't the best quality but since there wasn't anything around, they decided to take it. I took a ride down to Miami and picked up the seven keys from Fatman. I made arrangements with Sal to meet at his house at 10 a.m. the next day. The next morning when I went to Sal's house to give him the merchandise, he said, "They're coming by to pick it up with the cash at noon."

"Okay, I'll be close by. Call me once you have the money."

I went down the street and waited in a low-key Cuban restaurant. I still didn't have a good feeling about the whole scenario. I'd been doing this long enough to know when things just seem right or add up, but on the other hand my Dad and Sal both vouched for this Mario guy, so he had to be okay. At 11:50, Sal called and said, "They will be here in ten minutes."

"Okay, cool."

At noon, Sal called back frantic and hyperventilating. "They ripped me off! Please come over quickly!"

I had to think fast. If it was a real rip-off, I could straighten it out my own way. If it was the feds making it look like a rip-off, my next moves would determine my fate.

I replied very calmly, "Rip-off? What are you talking about, Sal?"

He sounded like he was crying. "They ripped us off."

"Us? Sal, I gave you cash as a loan, and if you got ripped off that has nothing to do with me."

"Please please…come by, I don't know what to do."

"I'm all the way down in Miami. I'll have to call you later. And remember our agreement."

I had some very important decisions to make. This could be some kind of crazy FBI sting or was it just some old man getting ripped off because he wouldn't listen? If it was the feds, they'd be watching every move I made and listening to all my phone calls. They'd be watching to see who I contacted and any chain of events that resulted from it. From then on, I had to be extremely careful what I said to Sal because a simple threat on his life could get me an additional ten years. If this was the feds, I'd also have to make sure all my connections were protected so they didn't go down with me. At this point in time, I didn't know the story on how he got ripped off.

All I did know was that if I didn't get the money I was owed and find out exactly what had happened, the Colombians would expect me to kill Sal because in their eyes he either orchestrated the rip-off, was ripped off by the feds, was working with the feds, or was just an unlucky prick who legitimately got ripped off by some scumbags. If I couldn't prove it was a legitimate rip-off, they would expect me to kill him because he'd be a major liability and he was the only connection between me and whatever happened.

If it was the feds and Sal got arrested, he might cooperate to save his own ass, which would lead to my arrest. At that point, I would be the only connection to Carlos and the Columbians he worked with. If they thought for a second that I was going to cooperate, they would put a hit on me or my family. The bottom line was, it was either me or him who would get clipped. My long-standing relationship with Carlos wouldn't mean shit.

And if I was to run and they couldn't find me, they would just go after my family or loved ones. There was no getting away from this. They were very clever and always had a back-up plan in case something like this happened. This was the life I chose, and this was how they do business. No loose ends ever! I may have no choice but to whack out Sal, who was possibly just a naive old man trying to make some money. Although I felt very sorry for the old man, especially since he was such a close friend of my grandfather's, I gotta do what I gotta do. I had to protect my loved ones and the people I did business with. I really hoped it did not come down to that, but if it did…"Whaddya gonna do?"

I prayed it was a legitimate rip-off and that Sal would get a pass because he's just a naive old man. But the chances of that happening were slim.

With all of this in my head, I quickly stopped at a payphone to let Fatman know what went down and to pass the message to Carlos. I told Fatman, "The weather is very bad over here so I'm not headed to the beach." This meant something had gone wrong and to be very cautious. Then I said, "I'll call you later when the sun comes out," which meant I'd call him when I found out what had happened and knew it was safe. The last thing I was going to do was to try to hide the fact that the deal had gone bad. I needed to warn everyone involved so they could be prepared for the worst.

22 | Any Last Words Before You Blow His Head Off?

A couple of days later, Sal called and begged me to meet with him to discuss what had happened. I agreed to meet him at Hemmingway's. When I got there, I was shocked to see Mario there. Mario was acting extremely nervous as he began to tell the story on how the rip-off took place. "Anthony, please let me explain what happened before things get out of hand. See, I was supposed to follow Alex to Sal's house—"

"Stop right there, motherfucker! You guys said Alex was no longer a part of whatever the fuck you guys were doing! What kind of bullshit games are you playing...or are you two just a bunch of fucking clowns?"

"I know what I said, but the other buyer backed out at the last second and Sal had already given you the okay to move forward. I didn't want to screw things up and tell you the deal was off after you had already arranged everything, so I called Alex and he said he was in."

This pissed me off even more, but I was very cautious with what I said. I was beginning to have my doubts about Mario even though his name came back clean from the streets.

"The plan was for me to call Sal so he could come outside when we arrived," Mario said. "I was parked outside Sal's apartment, directly behind Alex. Sal was supposed to come out and get the money from Alex, then let Alex have a quick look at the merchandise. Once Alex gave it the all-clear, Sal was supposed to walk to my car and give it to me. Then I was supposed to follow

Alex. But instead, after Sal showed it to Alex, he handed Sal a bag and said, 'Here's the money.' Sal did a quick look inside and saw the money. Sal said he was going to give the merchandise to me, but at the last second Alex said, 'Just give it to me and tell Mario to follow me.' Once Sal gave Alex the merchandise, he took off. There was nothing inside the bag but a few hundred dollars. That motherfucker put $100 bills on the outside of each bundle and blank paper on the inside, with a couple rocks at the bottom. Anthony, I swear on my mother's life I had absolutely nothing to do with it. And now Alex has disappeared."

I was so angry I wanted to strangle them both with my bare hands, but Sal looked like he was going to drop dead of a heart attack at any moment. "So what you're telling me is that Alex ripped you off?"

"Yes, that's exactly what happened," Sal said.

"Well, that's very unfortunate for you, Sal, because you're the one on the hook for the money."

"Anthony, please hear me out," Mario said. "Sal and I are working on getting a shipment of heroin. We will pay you back with the money we make, plus interest."

"Sal," I said, "is this some sort of fucking joke? Am I in fuckin la-la land here? You've got to be the stupidest motherfucker I've ever met. I can't believe you were friends with my grandfather. What kind of moron would do business with this guy again? You just got ripped off, you dumb motherfucker! And I don't wanna know nothing about some fucking heroin deal, you fucking bozos."

"Anthony, please," Sal begged, "I have to! It's the only way I can pay you back."

"Ohhh no, motherfucker! Sal, look me in the eyes. Remember the deal we made?"

"Yeah, but give me some time please. I'm good for it!"

"Listen, Sal, the deal was that I give you $119,000 in cash. I told you over and over that I didn't want anything to do with these people. If you did some fucked up deal or something illegal and got ripped off, that's on you. You vouched for these two pricks with your life, and you agreed to pay me back with interest. And if something went wrong, you'd sign over the restaurant immediately. Listen carefully, Sal, that money came from some very serious Columbians down in Miami. They were reassured that you guaranteed it with your restaurant. Now the matter is out of my hands. They'll begin the collection process, and there is nothing I can do about it.

"Sal, you better stick to the deal and keep your word, because these people have a very special talent when it comes to collecting money."

I knew what I was saying could have been recorded, so I was careful not to say anything that would get me in trouble. When I was done, I ended the meeting abruptly and walked out of the restaurant, leaving them both clueless. Outside, I saw Mario's green BMW parked in front of the restaurant, so I wrote down his license plate number to see if I could find out where he lived or anything else about him. I drove to a payphone to call a girl I used to date named Tara. She was a really cool girl who had been on the path to become an FBI agent. Unfortunately, she didn't tell the truth during the preliminary interview when they asked her if she had ever been associated with anybody involved in criminal activity. She knew me very well and had seen a few illegal activities, so instead of becoming a fed she was training to become a police officer.

I gave Tara the license plate number, and in less than ten minutes she called me back with an address in Miami. I quickly wrote it down and headed to Miami to find this fucker's house. When I got to Mario's street, I drove up and down the street looking for this fuck's house, but the address didn't exist. I started thinking worst-case scenario: he was either a cop or a rat. I immediately called Tara back and asked, "Are you 100 percent positive on that thing you gave me?"

"Absolutely! Anthony, I double- and triple-checked it. What's the problem?"

"Aw nothing, I must be on the wrong street. I'll call you later, I gotta go."

I knew it was impossible to get a car registered to a fake address unless you knew a dirty state or government agent. Or you were a federal agent or informant. Fuck! Now I knew why my dad drank.

So I went home and recounted everything that had happened from start to finish. Then I started questioning myself. If they were feds, why not just arrest everyone? They could have grabbed all of us in one shot. Maybe they didn't arrest anyone because Sal was still in the middle of that heroin deal? Whatever the fuck was going on, I had to get ready for the worst possible outcome.

I let a few weeks go by and didn't make any contact with Sal. He called me a couple of times to give me updates on his stupid fucking heroin deal and to let me know when he should have the money. I told him it was out of my hands and that I was very surprised he hadn't gotten a visit from the Columbians yet. I said this to scare him, hoping he would pay up quickly before things went down the path of no return.

Sal had not been to his restaurant for weeks. He was hiding out in his house. I had to get him to sign that restaurant over to me quickly because my connections were expecting me to whack him very soon. So I called Carlos and asked if he knew a good attorney in town who could file some paperwork for me.

"What ya need done, kid?"

"I need someone local who's a professional at collecting money. I need to either collect the money, or have the restaurant signed over to me quickly, so I can close this deal once and for all. You follow me?"

Carlos understood that I needed someone local to scare the shit out of Sal so he would pay up or sign over the restaurant before he got whacked.

"Not a problem, kid. My cousin Edwin from Columbia just arrived in Miami. He'd be the perfect guy for the job, and he'd be glad to take care of it for you."

When I met up with Edwin, I gave him directions on how to carry out the job and the price for the work. I agreed to pay him $5,000 but emphasized that he had to convince Sal to sign over the restaurant. He pulled out a 9 mm handgun, smiled, and said in a thick Columbian accent, "No problem, my friend. I guarantee you he's gonna sign those papers, or I'll stick this gun up his ass and blow his brains out."

"I love that plan...now this is what you need to do. On Valentine's Day, I need you to get a dozen roses from a flower shop in Hollywood. The place is called Joey's Flowers..." This flower shop was owned by a Colombo Family capo named Joey "Flowers" Rotuno. He oversaw operations in South Florida. The Colombos had nothing to do with what was about to go down. I continued, "On Valentine's Day, I want you to go to Sal's apartment and knock on his door. You're gonna pretend you're a flower delivery man. Once that old fuck opens the door, you jam that gun in his face and take him to his bedroom. Make him lay face down on the bed and stick a pillow over his head, press the gun against the pillow, and ask him if he has any last words before you blow his head off. You have to convince him that you're gonna kill him. He'll either offer to pay the money or sign over the restaurant. If he refuses to pay up or sign over the restaurant, you stick that gun up his ass and pull the trigger. This way, a message will be sent to anyone trying to get in our way. If you have to kill him, I'll give you another $5,000. But don't kill him just so you can make an extra five grand. Once we collect or get the restaurant, I'll send $10,000 to Carlos to give to you."

"This sounds like fun. I always wanted to see what happens when you stick a gun up someone's ass and pull the trigger.

23 | Please Don't Kill Me

When Valentine's Day arrived, Edwin was full of enthusiasm and ready to go. He looked like a flower delivery man when he knocked on Sal's door.

"Who is it?" Sal said.

"I have a flower delivery for a Sal."

Sal opened the door, surprised, and said, "Flowers for me?"

"Yeah, and this too, motherfucker," Edwin said as he put the gun to Sal's head and forced him back into the house. Once Edwin was inside, he grabbed Sal by the hair and forced the gun into his mouth. Sal collapsed to the floor and attempted to protect himself by covering his face with his arms. Edwin stood over him and yelled, "Roll over!" Then he put the gun to the back of his head and said, "Crawl to your fucking room, you cockroach, or I'll blow your head off."

"Please...please don't kill me...I don't wanna die. I promise I'll have the money very soon."

"Your time's up, old man. You've had plenty of time to pay."

Edwin drove his knee into Sal's back, put duct tape over his mouth, grabbed him by the hair, and dragged him toward the bedroom. Sal began flailing his arms and legs, fighting for his life. As Edwin dragged him through the living room, Sal tried to grab anything he could get his hands on, trying to prevent the inevitable. Edwin shut the bedroom door, stood over Sal, and pulled a silencer out of his jacket pocket, then screwed it onto the barrel of the gun. Sal knew death was just seconds away.

"Get on your knees, you fucking puta," Edwin said.

Sal's face was beet red, with veins popping out of his forehead and tears running down his face. He had duct tape over his mouth so he couldn't speak, although he tried. As he got on his knees he tried to shield his head with his arms. Edwin pressed the gun against Sal's forehead and said, "Lay your fucking head on the bed...you don't want your brains all over the walls, do you? This way you only ruin a mattress, you piece of shit."

As Sal slowly crawled toward his bed, Edwin kept the pistol pressed against the back of his head. "Hurry up, you fuck, I don't have all day!"

When Sal finally made it to the bed, Edwin ripped the tape from his mouth.

"I'm begging you," Sal started, "please don't kill me, I don't want to die. God help me, please."

"Sorry, Sal, God's a little busy right now." Edwin cracked Sal in the back of the head with the butt of the gun, shoved his face into the mattress, grabbed a pillow, and put it over the back of his head. He pressed the gun firmly against the pillow and buried Sal's face into the mattress.

Sal began to suffocate, then he shit his pants and pissed all over himself. Death was one second away. Just before Sal passed out, Edwin removed the pillow and said in very calm and polite voice, "I have a great deal for you, my friend, it's one to die for."

As Sal tried to get some oxygen, he mumbled, "Anything, I'll do anything, just don't kill me."

"Sign over the restaurant tomorrow or I pull this trigger now...either way, we will be even."

"Okay, okay...tomorrow I'll sign it over, I promise."

Edwin grabbed Sal by the throat, dragged him into the kitchen, and duct taped him to a chair. He pulled out a .45 revolver, opened the cylinder, put one bullet in it, and gave it a quick spin then slammed it shut. "Now, since you like to gamble with other people's money and lives, let's play a little game of Russian roulette, you scumbag."

"What are you doing? I thought we had a deal...please...I'm begging you...I promise...I'll sign the restaurant over tomorrow."

Edwin pressed the gun against Sal's lips. "Open up, you piece of shit."

"No! No...please don't do this!"

Edwin grabbed Sal by the back of the neck and forced the barrel into his mouth, breaking a few teeth. "No need to be afraid, my dear friend. If it's meant to be, you will live. If not, your brains will come out of the back of your head. From what I understand, you vouched for those people with your life. That's a gamble, my friend, so let's start." Edwin began to count backward from five as Sal sobbed. "Four, three, two, one…"

Sal screamed as loud as he could with a gun in his mouth as Edwin pulled the trigger.

Click. No bullet.

Sal passed out. After a few minutes, Sal woke up to see Edwin standing there with a smile on his face. "You're one lucky old man," he said. Sal just sat there in his own shit and piss, whimpering.

Little did Sal know, there was no firing pin in the gun so there was no way it could have fired. After all, collecting money from a dead man is impossible.

"Well, Sal, looks like God wasn't so busy after all," Edwin said.

Sal began hyperventilating and crying again.

"Shut the fuck up, old man, or we'll try your luck again."

When Sal calmed down, Edwin asked very politely, "Hey, Sal, whatcha got in the fridge? I'm starving."

"Meat, cheese, bread, and a few other things."

"Okay, make me a sandwich with lots of meat, cheese, and a little mayo."

Edwin left with his sandwich. About thirty minutes later, I got a frantic call from Sal. "Please, Caucci! Please! Tell your guys that I'll sign over the restaurant tomorrow."

"What guys, Sal? What the fuck are you talking about?"

"The Columbians were here…they were going to kill me."

"Sal, I don't know nothing about it. Like I said, it is out of my hands."

"I promise I'll sign it over to you tomorrow."

"Okay…I'll pass on the message. I'll call you later and tell you where you can meet me."

"Okay, but I am going to the hospital now because I think I'm having a heart attack."

"Listen, you old fuck, if you die before you sign those papers, they'll come after your family. So make sure you don't die, you cocksucker."

24 | They Blow Up the Entire Fucking Courthouse

The next day I called Jared Anton, a very close family friend who also happened to be an attorney. He was an excellent attorney and always gave great legal advice, especially to wise guys. Everyone was always very careful on how they spoke to him because they did not want to jeopardize the oath he took when he became a lawyer. During conversations, Jared always used a lot of hypotheticals, maybes, and what ifs, just to cover everyone's ass. I told him I had a problem that I needed help with and as usual he said, "Sure, come on down to my office."

When I got there, I told him about the rip-off and what had happened. I told him how Sal guaranteed he would sign over the restaurant if anything went wrong. I also told him that Sal would be coming here tomorrow to sign the papers and asked if he would be able to have all the documents ready by then.

"Sure, not a problem," Jared replied. "You and Sal be here at four o'clock tomorrow and I'll take care of the rest."

"Ya know something, Jared, the Jews might have whacked out Jesus but I think he's gonna give you a pass."

"Fuck you, little prick. I'll see you tomorrow and tell your father I said hello."

"Will do."

The next day, Sal arrived with that piece of shit Mario Adamo. I wanted to shoot them both right there, but I had to keep my cool. Jared sat at the head of his very long table. I was seated on one side, and Sal and Mario were seated directly across from me. I started the meeting saying, "Sal, why the fuck did you bring this scumbag cock-sucker here with you? Hasn't he caused you enough headaches?"

"How the fuck were we supposed to know Alex was going to rip us off for the coke?" Mario jumped in.

"Coke? What fucking coke?" Then I spoke directly to Sal. "I hope to God you didn't do anything stupid with that money I gave you."

Sal just sat there, frozen, until Mario replied, "Come on with this bullshit. We all know what happened...I am just as pissed at that fucking son of a bitch Alex as you are. When I find him I'm gonna put a bullet in his head. We owe you for the seven kilos, and Sal is signing over his restaurant to you just like he promised, so let's just get this over with."

"Mario, listen very carefully, you fucking filthy sewer rat, I don't know you or anything about a fucking coke deal," I said, then I turned to Sal again and said, "You think very carefully about the next words that are about to come out of that shit-hole of yours. You came to me and asked me if you could borrow $119,000 in cash, isn't that right you decrepit old fuck?"

Sal sat in silence as his hands shook and his eyes darted back and forth between me and Mario. "Yeah, that's right, you gave me cash."

Mario slammed his hand on the table. "What the fuck is going on here? You think I'm a fucking cop?"

"You're a slimy fuckin' mullet, and if I were Sal I'd bury an ax in your fucking skull and put Alex's head in a vice and crank it till his eyes popped out. I told Sal from day one not to trust you or that fucking Alex, but you convinced this old man that you were a solid guy, and now look at him. He's losing his restaurant because you conned him into doing something stupid. But sooner or later, you and Alex will both get what's coming to you. Ask Sal...he knows how things work"

"Are you fucking threatening me, you little punk kid?"

I leaned back in my chair, put my feet on the table, folded my arms, and smiled. "Listen here, Mario the tough guy, why don't you go fuck your whore of a mother! Sal, didn't you tell me she gave you a blowjob for a pound of cheese once?"

The veins were popping out of Mario's forehead. "I'll fucking kill you, you little punk."

"Make your fucking move, tough guy, so I can stick YOUR head up Sal's ass."

Jared quickly jumped in. "Okay, okay, everyone just calm down for a second. Can we all agree there was a business transaction that took place but happened to go south, and Sal, prior to this transaction you agreed that if it fell through you would sign your restaurant over to Mr. Caucci? Would that be an accurate statement?"

"Yes."

"Okay, then it's simple. I have all the paperwork in place, just sign in a few places and the restaurant will belong to Mr. Caucci once I file the papers in the courts."

Sal pulled out a pen, signed all the paperwork, and he and Mario stormed out of the room. Jared and I stayed behind and shot the shit for a while before I left. Now all I had to do was wait for Jared to file the papers and the restaurant would be mine.

The next day, however, Jared got a visit from the Colombo Family capo Joey "Flowers" Rotuno. Flowers was the same guy who owed the flower shop where we bought the roses for Sal on Valentine's Day...what a fucking coincidence. Flowers was well known for his ability to collect gambling debts from people who were absolutely broke.

Flowers and a couple of his soldiers barged into Jared's office while Jared was in the middle of an important meeting with real clients, but Flowers told everyone to get the fuck out. Flowers and his goons surrounded Jared in his chair. "The word is that you're gonna be filing paperwork to transfer ownership of Hemmingway's to this Caucci kid?" Flowers said.

"As a matter of fact, that's what I'm going to be doing later today," Jared answered calmly.

"Not so fast, pal. You're doing no such thing, or you and this Caucci kid are gonna have some big problems."

"Really? And who the fuck are you?"

"So you're a wiseass attorney...ask around about Joe Flowers, then you'll smarten up."

Jared knew how this game worked—it wasn't the first time a wise guy had come into his office with some sort of beef.

"Sal doesn't own that restaurant anymore, We do! If you file that paperwork, you'll be taking it away from some friends of mine. You follow me, Mr. Lawyer? You tell that Caucci kid to give me a call...I wanna to talk to him right away!" Then he handed Jared a piece of paper with his number on it.

Jared looked at the paper and laughed. "Oh, don't you worry, Mr. Flowers, you won't have to wait very long at all to meet Caucci. After I tell him what you said, believe me he'll come looking for you. He is quite talented at finding people." Jared chuckled. Then, just as Flowers was about to leave, Jared said, "With all due respect, Mr. Flowers, if I were you, I would be the one asking around to see who you're dealing with. I've known this kid, as you like to call him, his whole life. He might be Italian, but he doesn't play by your rules. This I know for a fact."

"We'll just see about that."

"Unfortunately you will. Have a good day, Mr. Flowers, and if you ever need any legal advice please feel free to stop by."

"Go fuck yourself, you Jew bastard."

Jared called me immediately and asked, "Do you know a Joey Flowers?"

"Yeah, I've heard of him. Why?"

"Him and a couple of his men just came into my office and said not to file any paperwork against the restaurant because they own it, not Sal. And if I do, he said we will both have a big problem."

"Oh really? He said we'll have a big problem?"

"Yes, those were his exact words."

"Thank you, my friend, I'll take it from here. I know exactly how to find that motherfucker."

I knew Flowers was a Capo for Colombo Family. But I also knew this could be one of the oldest plays in the Mafia playbook. If they really did have a piece of the restaurant, all I had to do was call my friends in the Bonanno Family and let them straighten it out. They hated the Colombos anyway. If the Colombos were just trying to step in to protect Sal from losing his restaurant in exchange for becoming partners, it would be too big of a headache for them to fight for, especially once they heard drugs were involved.

So I made a few calls, got Flowers's phone number, and called him to arrange a meeting. We agreed to meet at Hemmingway's. When I walked in, he was sitting in a dark corner booth next to one of his goons, a big young guy. I took a seat at the table and said to Flowers, "Who da fuck's this guy?"

"He's with me."

I looked Flowers in the eyes, completely ignoring his goon. "Yeah? Well then tell him he can get da fuck out of here. I've come alone and don't need nobody to protect me. I heard you're supposed to be a tough guy. Wait till everyone finds out you need a babysitter at a sit-down. Either you stick him over in the corner somewhere or I'm leaving. I'll even order him a fucking ice cream."

The goon's jaw started to twitch as he tried to stare me down. I gave him a wink and blew him a kiss while Flowers told him to go sit at another table. "That's a good boy, do as you're told and get the fuck outta here," I said. Then I got up and sat right next to Flowers, so close he was uncomfortable. It was obvious things were not going as he planned.

"Do you know who I am?" Flowers asked, grabbing my arm.

I removed his hand from my arm and grabbed his. Then I said very calmly, "I sure do, Mr. Flowers, and some of my friends speak very highly of you. You are a well-respected, stand-up guy, and there is no arguing that. I've heard a lot of good things about you. But the real question is, do you know who I am? Have you done your homework?"

"That's funny," he said, chuckling. "Who the fuck do you think you are, kid?"

"I'm glad you think it's funny, Mr. Flowers. No disrespect, but I'm gonna tell you like it is. See, I'm the guy who doesn't give a rat's ass who you are. You obviously didn't bother to ask around about me, did you? So just for a brief moment, let's examine the situation you're in. Humor me for a second and try to look outside the bubble you're in. Here I am all alone. I didn't reach out to friends, of which I know quite a few, and ask them to come with me to have this sit-down with you, as protocol calls for. Mr. Flowers, you're a capo, and by your rules you shouldn't even be having this sit-down with me. You think your name and title is gonna scare me?"

Flowers knew he wasn't supposed to be sitting with me so I had him by the balls. "You must be curious why I didn't bring anyone with me. Your friends sent you here from New York, but I've lived here my whole life. So if you think I'm gonna walk away from this thing just because you're Joey Fucking Flowers, you need to come up with a better strategy."

"So you're a fucking tough guy?"

"Not at all, my friend. I am who I am and nothing more. So how you wanna handle this, Mr. Flowers?"

"Listen, kid, there's no way we're gonna let you take this restaurant. We have $100,000 invested in it, so it belongs to us. We already have plans to remodel it and turn it into a night club. When we open for business, stop by and I'll give you a couple free meals."

"A free meal? Now that sounds nice, but listen up, old man. I have $119,000 invested in this joint, and I'm taking it. And there's nothing you or your fucking friends can do about it. And when it's all said and done and you get put on the shelf, make sure you give me a call and I'll give you a job parking cars!"

"The fuck you are!"

"Who's gonna stop me? You? Your friends?"

"We got a lot of guys on our side, kid. I don't think you know what you're getting yourself into."

"Trust me, Mr. Flowers, I know you've got a lot of friends here in Hollywood and New York and you're all respected. But what you don't understand is that I've got friends down here too, but the kind of friends I'm talking about are completely different than yours. They're the Cartel type, you follow? And I've known these people a long time, and they make us Italians look like a bunch of fucking altar boys. Now listen to me and pay close attention. If my Columbian friends get involved, they will wipe you and your entire crew completely out, including your families. The Colombos will be extinct from South Florida. All I gotta do is make one phone call to Colombia and they'll send five button men on a cargo boat to Miami. They'll come down here and pick off every single one of you, including your wives, your kids, or anyone who gets in my fucking way. Then they get back on a boat and straight to Colombia, like they were never here. So tell me, how would you handle that situation, Mr. Flowers? Would you send a crew down to Colombia in the middle of the fucking jungle to retaliate? They wouldn't stand a fucking chance, and nobody would even have the balls to go. You think you got power? You don't know what real power is. You guys can barely control the streets without getting locked up for years. The Colombian cartel controls their entire fucking government. Let me tell you some minor differences between the Italians and the cartel. When one of us Italians get arrested, we keep our mouth shut, we don't cooperate, and we do our time, even if it's life. But if and when someone in the Colombian government has the balls to arrest a high-ranking cartel member, they never end up going to court to stand trial. They take the easy way out. They blow up the entire fucking courthouse and kill every cop, prosecutor, government official, and family member of everyone who is involved in the case. So, if you wanna go to war, I wish you the best of luck, but trust me, you want no part of them. You better think this one through before you stir this pot, Mr. Flowers."

He tried to play it cool, but it was obvious he was very concerned. His knee started bouncing up and down while he tapped his fingers on the table.

"Well, kid," he finally said, "it looks like we have a situation here."

"No, my friend, you have a situation here! If I were you, I would think long and hard about this one. Do you know anyone who has ever gone to war with the cartel and lived to talk about it?"

"Fuck the Colombian cartel," he finally said. "They ain't nothing but a bunch of Third World wet backs."

"Is that what you think? Just a bunch of Third World wet backs? You and your friends go by a code of honor with rules…no women, or children. They have one rule: kill everyone who gets in their way. Start with the women and children and make the men watch. They can get very creative."

As we finished our meeting, a new thought occurred to me. Maybe this was some fucked-up FBI sting after all. The Colombo Family just happened to be invested in the same restaurant that was used to facilitate a drug deal. The feds might just be letting this whole thing play out into one giant bloodbath between the Mafia and Colombian cartel, then they'd come and arrest anyone who survived. That would be one hell of a sting operation. But were the feds really that creative, and would they actually orchestrate a rip-off that could get people killed? This would be the first time I'd heard of that. It would be very unethical, but what did I know? There was always a first. The truth was, the feds didn't care if we lived or died. It was just another case to them.

25 | I'm Gonna Put A Bullet in His Fucking Head

Before I called Colombia, I wanted to see if I could handle this locally. It made more sense to me to have my Italian friends handle this.

Also, I had no idea what I was going to do with a restaurant. I'd have go through the hassle of selling it just to get my money back. Or maybe I could partner up with my Italian friends and make a killing. I really wasn't quite sure what the best move was.

After a few days went by, I decided to send a message to my old friend Jerry Chilli, who was still locked up in a federal prison in Miami. He wasn't too happy, as he had just found out he had been indicted for crimes that he was barely involved with because he was locked up when they went down. Apparently, Anthony "Natty" Passaro, a top crew member for Chilli in South Florida and a personal friend of mine, was indicted for re-coding credit cards and using them in various places. He would usually go to a business owner that was connected and had knowledge of the fraud and charge large amounts of money without receiving any services or merchandise. Bars and restaurants were great for this. Once the transaction went through and the money was deposited into the business owner's account, Natty would collect the earnings, then give the business owner a kickback. It was a beautiful non-violent crime that earned a lot of money. Natty had probably been the biggest earner for the Bonanno Family in South Florida for some time—he'd come up with some of the most elaborate and well thought-out scams I'd ever heard of. Because of this and his close connection to Chilli, nobody ever fucked with him. Besides, he usually had a pistol on him. He wasn't afraid to stand on his own and wouldn't hesitate to tell a made man in a different crew to go fuck themselves. He'd had numerous sit-downs because of this, but Chilli always bailed him out. Our personalities were quite the same in that regard, so we got along very well.

Getting a message to Chilli while he was behind bars wasn't going to be easy. They were listening to every phone call he made and watched his every move. He was the most powerful and feared capo in all South Florida. But I'd known Jerry from a very young age, and he was a good friend to me, my father, and my Aunt Roni.

Once he received my message, he sent one back with a time and day he was going to call me on a landline.

"This is the operator, we have a collect call from Jerry Chilli. Will you accept the call?"

"Yes."

"What's doin' kid?" came the familiar voice.

"Aw, you know…same old thing out here. How you doin'?"

"Ehhh. I could be better, more bullshit as usual. These cock-sucking feds never give up."

"What a fucking shame…bunch of motherless pricks."

"Whaddya gonna do kid?"

"What can ya do…Hey, I need to speak to someone about something." I was following an old protocol. Made men didn't have sit-downs with non-made men unless they were represented by another made man. This is why I went straight to the capo, so he could get someone to sit with me.

"I want you to go see the Beard," Chilli said. "I'll let him know you're gonna call."

"Thanks, pal, I hope to see you soon."

The following day, I called Tommy the Beard and we set a time to meet at Joe Sonken's restaurant. When Tommy drove up to the valet stand, I noticed another person in the car, but I couldn't recognize him as Tommy parked the car himself. When they got out of the car, I couldn't believe my eyes. It was my old friend, Steve Maruca! I hadn't seen him in years. He had to be almost sixty by then and was still tough as steel.

At that time I was twenty-three years old and had known Steve since I was about four years old. I walked over and gave them hugs and the traditional kiss of respect on the cheek. Then Steve said, "I hear you have a little problem, kid."

"It's a goddamn circus. Let's go in and have something to eat, I'll give you the whole run-down."

We sat in a booth near the bar; I was on one side, and Tommy and Steve were on the other. The first thing I said was, "Listen, gentleman, I gotta put everything on the table here before you get involved. This is drug money owed, and it's possible that the fucking feds are behind it, I just don't know. If it's the fucking feds, this could take us all down."

I went on, "Guys, it wouldn't surprise me if those cocksuckers are intentionally trying to get people killed just to make a case. I wouldn't put anything past those shit-eating parasites. They'll just cover it up with their fucking lies, like they always do."

Steve folded his arms and leaned back in his seat. He sat there for a minute or two, weighing their options, then said, "Okay, give me the run-down from beginning to end and don't leave out anything."

So I told them the entire story, and then told them about Joey Flowers and his friends claiming to have $100,000 invested in the restaurant and how they tried to stop me from taking it.

"So instead of me handling this with my Colombian friends and leaving bodies in the streets, I thought it'd be a better idea to call the old man," I finished.

Tommy looked at Steve and said, "Whaddya think?"

Steve sat for a minute and repeated the story under his breath, calculating each move, trying to figure out a solution. We all knew it was risky no matter how we looked at it. If it was the feds and Steve and Tommy got involved, it could bring down friends of theirs, including the Bonannos. Then they would have had to answer to the higher-ups in New York about why they got involved in a drug deal, and that could get them whacked. On the other side of the coin, if it was just the Colombos, they would enjoy collecting the money from them.

Steve snapped out of his state of thought and said, "Let me get this right…Sal got ripped off for seven kilos of coke, correct?"

"That's right."

"But what you're telling me now is that this has nothing to do with coke anymore. You just want us to collect the money, correct?"

"Exactly."

Steve raised his eyebrows, looked at Tommy, and said, "Money owed is money due." Tommy nodded in agreement.

"Okay, Steve, what's the plan?"

"It goes like this…Flowers claims they have $100,000 in the joint. If they do, I want solid proof! Not just a bunch of fucking papers with signatures on them. I'll bet my left nut those fucks don't have a dime in that joint. That crew doesn't have enough money to pay a fuckin' parking meter, and if they can't prove it, they can go fuck themselves. It's simple, kid, I'm gonna tell Flowers that they gotta come up with $120,000 cash or we're taking the fucking restaurant and there's nothing they can do about it. If the Colombos want to go to war, then I'll go in there like the Wild Wild West and shoot that fucking place up. Just like the good old days, hey Tommy?"

Tommy laughed, "Steve, you're one crazy son of a bitch."

"What, you think I'm joking?"

"Not at all, that's what's so funny…they got no idea what they've gotten themselves into."

It was obvious that Steve didn't like Flowers or the Colombo Family. There was probably still bad blood from an old beef and he had been waiting for a day like this to come.

"Just be careful, guys, this whole thing stinks. Tell the old man that once we get the restaurant, we'll go down the middle. We'll turn it into a night club on the weekends and a bar during the day, we'll make a killing. We can set up a couple of high-roller card games a few times a week and run book out of one of the offices. There's a beautiful lounge room on the second floor for meetings, and this place is the perfect place to clean money. All the cash that comes through the restaurant will look legit as long as we don't go overboard. You guys can have a real good thing here if it works out. We're sitting on a gold mine."

Then Tommy said, "Okay, kid, this sounds good. We'll stay in touch, and give your father our best."

"Will do, guys."

After a couple of months of sit-downs between the Bonannos and Colombos, things were not moving as quickly as I was hoping. Our last sit-down was me, Tommy the Beard, Steve Maruca, Joey Flowers, and Sal. Sal thought that he was protected by the Colombos and Flowers. But we all knew there was a good chance the Colombos hadn't put a dime into that restaurant and only went partners with Sal to stop me from taking it. So there I was, sitting at a table listening to a bunch of wise guys from the Bonannos and Colombos going back and forth on who owed who what. After ten mins of listening to horseshit and getting nowhere, I interrupted. "Gentleman, I don't have time for all this pussy-footing back and forth. It's been two months, and we haven't gotten anywhere. So this is what I'm going to do. I'm telling my attorney to file the papers Sal signed, naming me as the owner tomorrow."

Flowers said, "Hold on, kiddo, not so fast. It doesn't work like that."

"Maybe not in your world, Mr. Flowers, but this is how I do things. Sal already signed the restaurant over to me, so I'm gonna put a bullet in his fucking head and take him out of the picture. Then I'll own it outright with my friends here. And there's nothing you can do about that, is there?"

Steve and Tommy both started laughing because they knew I had Flowers by the balls. Then Steve said, "The kid's right...if Sal's dead and Caucci has the papers, the place belongs to us. Looks like you might want to get your money back from Sal before he gets whacked."

Sal looked terrified. He stared at Flowers like he was supposed to say something, but Flowers just sat there in silent defeat.

"Sal, you piece of shit," I said, "did you really think this guy and his friends could protect you? The only reason you're still breathing is because of me, not him. Gentlemen, our business here is done."

As Tommy, Steve, and I walked back to the car, Steve and Tommy started laughing. "Did you see the looks on their faces when you said you were gonna whack Sal and file the paperwork? I think Flowers shit himself. Well done, kid, the old man is gonna get a kick out of this."

"Fuhgeddaboudit. I learned from the best."

After our meeting, the papers were filed and the transfer of ownership began. Sal had completely disappeared—everyone was looking for him, including me. I had to find Sal so I could take him out of the picture once and for all.

26 | Go Suck on Some Dog Shit, You Lying Pigs

In the meantime, it was business as usual for me. I had my hands in almost everything: marijuana, counterfeit money, fake America Express travelers checks, credit card fraud, cloning cell phones, stolen electronics, insurance fraud, collecting money for people from scumbags who didn't want to pay…but cocaine remained my main source of income.

Over time, Fatman and I had become close friends; my girlfriend Noelvis and I often went on vacations with him and his wife. Since Noelvis was Cuban, she became very close with Fatman's wife, who was also Cuban. My personal life had become almost as complicated as business. I had two serious girlfriends, Noelvis and Smadar, and I had to constantly lie to them in order to keep them from finding out about each other. My criminal lifestyle had never bothered me—it was actually quite exciting—but lying to these two girls all the time did not make me feel very good inside. But…. whaddya gonna do? I was a selfish prick and didn't think about the consequences and the heartbreak it would cause.

Worse, Noelvis wasn't "that" kind of girl. I'd first started dating Noelvis when I was about twenty-one, give or take. Her parents were traditional Cubans, and from the beginning, they wouldn't let me take her anywhere alone. I was welcomed to come over, even sleep over on the sofa, but taking her out alone was out of the question. They lived in a small inexpensive house in Hialeah, very close to Miami, and her parents wanted to protect their daughter. They wanted to make sure that "only the man she married would have her." For me, it became very frustrating. Noelvis was in a bad position, but she respected her parents and did as they said. She never argued with them about their decisions but shed a lot of tears because she knew that the situation would eventually take a toll on our relationship and there was nothing she could do to change it.

I didn't give her parents much to complain about. I never flaunted my money with flashy cars, clothes, or other stuff. Instead, I was able to help my family out, enjoy the lifestyle I had become used to, and save a lot of money in case anything ever went south. I even bought her a car for her birthday. I knew that if I got caught by Hollywood police again, they were going to really fuck me good—they made that very clear the first time they arrested me and sent me to prison at a very young age. If they caught me a second time, they would give me at least twenty years. I had to come up with a backup plan, because I knew eventually I was going to get arrested again, and I was gonna be prepared.

I thought about it for a long time and came to the conclusion that If someone snitched on me and tried to get me sent back to prison, I would take their life. If someone tried to take my life, I was going to take theirs first—no witness, no case!

Unfortunately, I didn't have many options. I knew the Hollywood police were crooked, and I had absolutely no chance of getting a fair trial. So I had two choices, I could either go to some hell hole for twenty years (and that wouldn't be living) or I could beat the cops at their own game and make sure there was no trial.

Sometimes I wondered how my life would have turned out if the police and the state of Florida had given me a second chance when I was sixteen. I had turned my life around before I went to trial. They could have reduced my charges and kept me out of prison. I had my painting contractor's license and was working six days a week. The state had the power to help me or ruin my life. I wondered how many other sixteen-year-old kids got charged as adults for a nonviolent first time offense and how many got a slap on the wrist for the same exact offense. But here I was, a perfect example of what happens to kids when they get sent to prison young. Then again, maybe this was exactly how the system was designed...

One Friday evening I met my friend Jay Bass at a pool hall close to my house. Jay sold coke in the Davie area and needed to pick up a quarter key. He was about twenty-five years old and had a very young girlfriend, about eighteen and pregnant. After I gave him the coke, we hung out and bullshitted for a while.

"So you got your girl knocked up," I said. "Whaddya gonna do if you get busted?"

"I'll kill myself! I'm never going back to jail!" He had done a year on gun charges.

I thought, "If you don't have the balls to go to prison, you don't have the balls to kill yourself. He'll rat for sure, but he better not rat ME out! He wouldn't have to worry about killing himself, I'll gladly do it for him."

Later, Jay and I were having wings at Hooters in Hollywood and I couldn't stop thinking about what he had said about killing himself. I pulled him aside and said, "Listen, Jay, I know we're friends, but I just want to make something very clear. If you ever rat on me, I'm going to kill you."

"Anthony, come on! I would never rat on you. You are like a brother to me."

"Jay, I've heard that line a thousand times. Then once the handcuffs are slapped on, all that shit goes out the window. I just want to put all the cards on the table, understand?"

"Absolutely."

I saw Jay at least once a week for about another year and everything went smooth. One day, however, my buddy Lenny called and asked me if I could come to his house to talk, that it was very important. When I got there, he told me he had fifty kilos on hand and asked if I could move them. Lenny was a real cool guy, very mellow, down to earth, and solid. He knew I could get rid of them if the price was right. So I called Carlos in Columbia because he had sold out of everything from his last shipment and a lot of the dealers in Miami were looking for some merchandise. Carlos said he would take all fifty and told me to contact Fatman for the details.

I made arrangements to meet Lenny at his house the following day. When I got there, Lenny's girlfriend, who was the mother of his child, was there too. That made me feel very uncomfortable. I pulled Lenny aside and said, "What the fuck, Lenny? She shouldn't be here while we're doing business!"

"I know, I know…she's leaving now."

"This isn't cool, man, she's the mother of your child. You should have given me a heads-up."

"You know I don't work like this…she was just waiting for her friend Jodi to come pick her up, but she's late. I told her she needed to get the fuck out of here. Trust me, if I could throw her out I would, but she's my sons mother so my hands are tied."

"Fuckin' chicks are never on time…whaddya gonna do?"

As usual, the deal with Lenny went very smoothly and dat was dat, as they say.

About a week later, I was in Hollywood leaving a guy's house who owed me some money for fifty pounds of weed and was also good friends with Jay Bass. This guy lived in a residential neighborhood one block north of a busy road called Stirling Road. After I left his house, I drove a block and stopped at a stop sign. I was in my Toyota 4-Runner when a Hollywood police squad car got right behind me. I had a couple of ounces of coke down my pants and $30,000 in cash.

I waited for both east- and west-bound lanes to clear, put on my blinker, and proceeded to cross the road, then turned east on Sterling Road. When I looked in my rearview mirror, the cop was still at the stop sign, so I had a moment of relief.

It didn't last long. He put his lights on and got right behind me. I immediately had a bad feeling. I pulled into a Texaco gas station, put my truck in park, and rolled down my window. When the officer approached my car, he asked for license and registration so I gave it to him without hesitation. He returned to his car to run my plate and driver's license. When he returned, he gave me back my license and registration and said, "Everything checks out good, but would you please step out of the car?"

At this point, I knew something was about to go down. When your license and registration come back clean and a cop tells you everything checks out, there is no legal reason for him to ask you to step out of your vehicle. Unless, of course, they got you on something.

"Not a problem, officer," I said. My plan was to take off running until I was out of his sight, then get rid of the coke.

"Mr. Caucci, would you mind if I search your vehicle?" he asked.

"Not at all."

He had no backup in sight, so I was going to make my run for it as soon as he started to search my car. But then he caught me by surprise. "Would you mind sitting in the back of the squad car while I do the search? No handcuffs…just wait in the backseat while I search."

That put me in a bad position. If he had locked me in his car, I'd be screwed. "No problem, officer, take your time."

I casually walked back to the squad car with him. When he opened the door, I put one leg in the car and began to sit down. Then, just as he was about to shut the door, I took off as fast as I could. He wasn't expecting that, but he reacted very quickly and grabbed me around the waist. But all it took was a quick shake of my hips and he landed on his ass. As I was running down the street, five undercover cop cars came out of nowhere and blocked me from every direction. I ran directly toward one of the undercover cop cars, jumped onto the hood, and ran over the car—but I was blocked by a tall fence. I tried to jump the fence before they could get out of their cars and was halfway over it when three undercover cops grabbed me by my pants and slammed me to the ground face first.

Thankfully, I was able to reach into my pants and throw the coke over the fence when they grabbed me. After they pinned me to the ground, they yanked on my hair and pulled my head back, almost breaking my neck. As my mouth was open from the pain, one cop nearly emptied a can of pepper spray into my mouth and eyes. When he was done, they yanked me up by the handcuffs as fast as they could, dislocating one of my shoulders. They then threw me into the back of a police car and took me down to the Hollywood police station once again.

Inside the station, I remembered being sixteen and getting arrested for the first time. The place smelled and looked the same, and the cops haven't changed a bit. They started right away with their typical good cop/bad cop routine, and round and round we went.

When I finally got my one phone call, I called my girlfriend Smadar and thanked God when she answered the phone.

"Hey honey, listen carefully! I just got arrested...call my friend, he knows what to do."

She knew that meant to call my brother Marc. He was to get rid of any evidence and money before the cops had time to get a warrant. Smadar said she understood and would make the call. That's the kind of girl Smadar was. She was an American-born Israeli Jew and very streetwise. Smadar's father, Yigal Gretah, was good friends with Eli Tisona, a top Israeli organized crime figure in both South Florida and Israel. On top of that, Smadar's uncle Zev Gretah was married to the grand-daughter of Myer Lansky, the famous Jewish Mob boss who in the 1950s had strong ties with the Italian Mafia. She was a cool girl and learned some very important rules in my world very quickly. She knew how and when not to talk on the phone, understood codes, understood how to act around my associates, knew what to do if I got busted, and knew not to talk to the police EVER.

Unfortunately, the cops were listening to our conversation and called Smadar back right away. "We're in the process of preparing the paperwork for Anthony Caucci's bond, can you please give us his current address so he can make bail?" they asked. The address on my driver's license was my dad's house, and he lived in a different county. The cops wanted my real address, where my money was stashed. She thought about it for a second, and then said, "Whatever address he gives you is the correct address."

I needed to buy time so Marc could move the cash. Fortunately, the cocaine was stored in a warehouse registered in a fake name—I was sure they didn't know where it was. The cop told me I was being charged with trafficking cocaine and they had me on audio and video surveillance selling a couple of ounces of coke a month ago. At this point, I had two choices. I could cooperate with them and maybe stay out of jail, or I could man up and do the time. But that could mean twenty years in prison. No wife, no kids, no family. No life.

As I was sitting in the holding cell, one of the detectives opened the door and said, "Oh and by the way, you're being charged with assault on a police officer."

"Go suck on some dog shit, you lying pigs! I would never assault a police officer."

"Who do ya think they're gonna believe, you or us?"

"I hope your entire family dies of asshole cancer, you fuckwad."

The Hollywood police had not changed a bit…they were just different scumbag cops in the same station. They had fucked me when I was young, and they were going to do it again. After they let me think about my charges and the time I was facing, they came back to the cell for let's-make-a-deal time. "Listen, Caucci, just hear us out before your say no. We're not asking you to snitch on your friends. Just tell us where you keep your stash and we won't charge you with it as long as it is under 500 grams."

"That's half a fucking kilo!"

I knew they were lying, but I pretended I was buying it. So I sat there for a few minutes in deep thought. "Can you give me a couple of minutes to think about it?"

"Yeah, yeah, sure. Take a couple of minutes to think about it. Would you like something to eat or drink in the meantime?"

"No, thank you anyway, gentleman. Now what about the cash I had in my car? Did you put it with my property?"

"The arresting officer didn't mention any money in his report, and to be honest, it wouldn't look good for you if you went to trial. Can you imagine what the judge or jury would think if they thought you had let's say, hypothetically, thirty thousand in cash on you? You wouldn't have a chance of beating these charges."

This was the game. They lied to me, I lied to them…and in the end I was hoping my lies kept me from getting into more trouble. My plan was to get them to search my dad's house since he was visiting my Aunt Roni in Orlando. The only problem was, there was a gun in his house that belonged to Rabbit, a friend who lived in the apartment directly below his. If they had searched my dad's house and found a gun, they would have pinned it on me. That alone could get me twenty years.

I had to come up with some bullshit quickly. I needed to call my dad in Orlando and hoped he would understand my message without me having to say too much on the phone. So I waved the cops back over to my cell. "Gentleman, what if it's over 500 grams but less than a kilo? Does the offer still stand?"

"Less than a kilo? Hmm, that might be a little tough, to be honest, Caucci. But let me talk to the captain and tell him you are just trying to do the right thing. I can't promise, but I will give it a shot."

"All I ask is that at least you try. You never know…today might be my lucky day."

They returned with the biggest smiles on their faces. They looked so goddamned happy I thought they were gonna let me go home.

"The captain said we will not charge you as long as it's under a kilo."

"Hallelujah! We got ourselves a deal. Now let's shake hands like men."

"Okay, let's go do some good."

"I'm with you, but I need to speak to my dad first. If I let you search his house without his permission, he'll whack me out." So they handed me the phone so I could call my aunt's house. They hovered over me, listening to every word.

Aunt Roni picked up the phone. "Hello?"

"Hey, Roni! It's your favorite nephew. I need to speak to my dad. I'm in a little jam here."

"What's wrong?"

"I got pinched. I'm at the police station."

"Oohhh, you had me worried for a second. Let me get him…he's having a martini."

"Hey, kiddo, what's doin'" came my dad's voice a second later.

"I'm in a tight spot right now…I'm at the Hollywood police station."

"For what?" he asked.

"Same shit as last time, these pricks never give up. They want to search your house, but I wanted to run it by you first. They've promised me they will not charge me with anything they find as long as it's under a kilo."

"I don't give a shit…there's nothing in there anyway."

"Exactly…that's my point. But don't worry. Whatever they find, anything at all, it's on me. Plus, they gave me their word they won't charge me. They are not asking me to cooperate, they just want to get the drugs off the streets. These aren't your typical gun-carrying asshole beat cops. These guys have been around the block. Plus it makes them look good, ya know what I mean?"

"Oh, okay, just tell them not to make a fucking mess."

He obviously didn't remember about the gun so I gave it one last shot.

"Hey, Dad, by the way how is Rabbit feeling? Is his hand still fucked up?"

"His hand? What the fuck is wrong with his hand?"

I didn't reply, I just sat on the phone in silence, pretending I was listening to his side of the conversation while the cops breathed down my neck…

"Oh…that…yeah, he's doing fine. I'm going to give him a call right now. Call me back in five minutes. Tell the cops I'm consulting an attorney before I let them in."

"Okay."

When I hung up the phone, the cops were waiting eagerly for an answer. "What did he say? Is he going to let us search?"

"He said to call back in five minutes while he consults a family attorney."

"No fucking attorney in their right mind is going to give permission for us to search!"

"Why not? You said you're not gonna to charge me with anything so why wouldn't they?"

"Because they go by the book."

As they were leaving the room, I heard one of the detectives say, "Let's just charge him now and send him down to the county jail. This is just a fucking waste of time."

Exactly five minutes went by and they told me to call my dad back.

"Hey, Pop, what did the attorney say?"

"He said have at it, but don't make a fuckin' mess."

"Okay, Pop, I love you, talk to you later…"

"Well," the cop said, "what did the attorney say? Can we search?"

"The attorney said you can search the house."

You should have seen these idiots' faces light up, it was a beautiful moment. After their victory dance was over, they drove me to my dad's house. When we got there, they took my keys and tried to open the door, but couldn't get in. I only had the key to the bottom lock.

"What the fuck is this, you live here but can't get in?" they asked me.

"I only have the key to the bottom lock because my dad is always home to let me in, but since he's in Orlando, I'm spending the week at my girlfriend's house."

One of the detectives pulled a small leather case out of his pocket. It was full of tools for picking locks, and in less than a minute he had the door open. Once we got in the house, I went to the kitchen and made myself a bowl of Frosted Flakes while they began to search. I sat there watching these idiots search the entire house as if they were looking for a pot of gold at the end of a rainbow. I had to bite my lip to stop myself from laughing. It was incredibly entertaining watching these lying cockroaches crawling on their hands and knees while I was eating a bowl of cereal with handcuffs on.

27 | This Could Be My Last Day on Earth

As they searched my dad's house, I sat there trying to figure out who set me up and how I could take him out. Do I do it myself or fly some guys in from Colombia to do the work for me? I didn't have a clue who the rat was yet—it could have been any of my closest friends. Either way, they had to go.

After about twenty minutes of searching, they went into my little brother Sam's room and saw all his clothes and a New York Jets blanket on his child-size bed. Sam was about seven years old at the time and used to spend weekends with my father.

One of the genius detectives looked at me and said, "You don't fucking live here."

"Oh shit!" I said. "We're in the wrong house! Like you weren't going to charge me with a kilo of coke if you found one...Get da fuck outta here!"

"Okay, smart ass, we're taking you down to the county jail."

"Well now that sounds familiar...Hey, I got an idea. Why don't we stop at Winn Dixie on the way downtown? You can buy a pound of flour and add it to the coke so you can ramp up my charges like you did last time, you fucking termites."

When I finally arrived at the Broward County Jail, I was placed in a holding cell with a bunch of fucking crackheads. As I stood in the doorway watching the deputies process people on the computer, one of the deputy's eyes got real big and he said, "Holy shit! Someone's in some deep shit." He called the other deputies over to look. I could tell they were looking at serious charges on the computer. Then they started looking in my direction and it was obvious they were either talking about me or someone directly behind me. I did a quick look over my shoulder to see what type of people were in the cell with me, but all I saw were bums and crackheads. Then I thought about Hemmingway's. Although it had happened a long time ago, it had always been in the back of my mind.

"Oh shit!" I thought. "If I have a federal indictment against me, I'm screwed. There will be no chance of getting out to take care of the snitch. They got me right where they want me, and there's nothing I can do about it."

When I finally got called to the booking window, they told me my bail was $50,000 and I could make a phone call. Again, I called Smadar and she said the bondsman was on his way. For the next six hours I was extremely worried...something just wasn't right. I felt it in my bones. Then I heard the beautiful sound of, "Caucci, pack it up. You made bail."

At that moment, I knew I was in the clear with the Hemmingway's deal or they would have never let me out. But I needed to get the fuck out of there so I could get some sleep—I'd been up for twenty-four hours.

In the meantime, in the twelve hours since I'd been picked up, a brand-new case was brewing. But it wasn't against me—it was against my buddy Lenny. See, when they took me down to the police station, they confiscated my beeper and cell phone. While I was locked up, Cristy, a girl I had known for a very long time and who happened to be a very good friend, called me on my beeper because she wanted to get some coke for a party. The police called her back using my phone and Cristy said, "Who the fuck is this?"

"This is Franco," the cop said. "Anthony is in Orlando competing in a martial arts tournament. He gave me his phone so I can take care of things while he's away. Whatever you need I can bring it to you."

Cristy was pretty street-wise and knew I would never do some stupid shit like that. So she told him she'd call me in a couple of days when I got back. Unfortunately, Cristy had her friend Jodi with her that day, and Jodi was a real coke-head. She didn't care who she dealt with as long as she could score. She was the exact type of person I would NEVER deal with, especially because she had a newborn. Jodi also happened to be Lenny's girlfriend's best friend.

So this dumb bitch Jodi called the cop back and said she needed an ounce of coke for a wedding. They agreed to meet outside a McDonalds in

Hollywood. When she got there, the place was surrounded with under-cover cops, and the whole thing was being videotaped. She made another call to my phone and the cop answered, "Where are you?"

"I'm here at McDonald's parked in a blue Jeep."

"I see you…I'm over here in the red Mustang"

What happened next has to be in the top ten best junkie moves. Jodie got out of her car with her little nine-month-old baby girl in her arms. The cops arrested her for attempting to purchase cocaine with the intent to distribute. They slapped the cuffs on her and told her they were going to call the Department of Children and Families (DCF) and that she would never see her baby girl again.

They dragged her down to Hollywood police station and told her they wanted information on every dealer she knew and that she needed to get one of them to bring her some coke, then they'd consider dropping all charges. She told them the only person she ever went to was her best friend's boyfriend Lenny and that she wouldn't play ball.

"Okay," the cops said, "if that is how you want to play, then guess what? You'll never see your fucking child again!"

That completely cracked her, and she broke down hysterically. "What if I give you some information on Anthony and Lenny?"

"What kind of information?"

"A fifty-kilo deal they just did. Is that good enough?"

"Okay, we're listening."

"Lisa, Lenny's girlfriend, had to come to my house two days ago because she said Anthony and Lenny were in the middle of a fifty-kilo deal. So I had to go pick her up."

"Did she say anything about seeing the drugs?"

"Yes, she said there was fifty kilos wrapped in black duct tape."

"Does Lenny ever keep cocaine in his house?"

"Yes, sometimes."

The cops told her that if she cooperated, they'd drop all charges.

"We want you to call Lenny and tell him you are going to come by and that you need to pick up a little something. Once you do a buy from him at his house, we will be able to get a search warrant. After the bust, we'll tell Lenny that Anthony cooperated and that's why he got raided. We'll tell him that Anthony set him up and bought fifty kilos from him and that he is cooperating with us. We'll show Lenny Anthony's mugshot and arrest report and say we have Anthony in custody right now. This is a bulletproof plan...Lenny will definitely think Anthony set him up."

Jodi agreed to their plan and called Lenny, who told Jodi she could come right over. When she went inside, she made some small talk, then bought a few grams and said she had to leave. Once she left, she met with cops who were waiting down the street in a white, unmarked van. They had been listening to the whole conversation and even filmed her going in and out of Lenny's house. They immediately got a search warrant and kicked his door in.

Inside the house were Lenny, his girlfriend, and their five-year-old boy Tony. They grabbed little Tony and told Lenny, "You better cooperate now, or we're taking your kid to Department of Children and Families."

"For what?" he said. "You got nothing on me, motherfuckers."

"On yeah? We got fifty kilos wrapped in black duct tape from your friend Anthony Caucci, who has been working for us. You did that deal with him three days ago, so you better start talking or you're finished and we're taking your kid."

Lenny was pissed and believed every word the cops were telling him. However, he didn't talk or cooperate. They searched his house and found twenty-five pounds of weed and a half kilo (five hundred grams) of cocaine. He was arrested and taken to the county jail, where his bail was set at $250,000.

All this shit happened between the time I got arrested, got bailed out, and went home to go to sleep. After sleeping for almost twenty hours, I woke up and saw that my beeper was going crazy. I checked and saw that a good friend of mine named Joey Richard had been calling. Joey was real good friends with Lenny as well. I called him back to see what was up.

"Hey, Caucci, why the fuck did you snitch on Lenny?" he said.

"What the fuck are you talking about?" I said. "Snitch on Lenny? For what?"

"They just raided his house and said you snitched him out."

"Joey, you have both known me a long muthufuckin' time...you know in your bones I would never do that! And if I did, you think I'd answer the fucking phone? You call Lenny right now and tell him I will meet him anywhere he wants, even in the middle of the Everglades, and I will come alone."

We both knew the Everglades was the last place a rat would want to meet with the person they set up.

"Okay," Joey said, "I'll call Lenny now and tell him what you said."

About ten minutes later Lenny called and said, "Meet me off the dirt road west of I-75."

This was a very secluded place in the middle of nowhere. I knew that if Lenny brought a gun, I was dead. But if I didn't go, I would be tagged as a snitch and probably whacked anyway. I told him I would be there in thirty minutes. When I hung up, I thought, "This could be my last day on earth."

28 | "You're All Fucking Dead"

As planned, I met Lenny off a dirt road west of I-75. If he'd already made up his mind that I was the rat, I knew this would be a very short conversation. I saw him parked in his red Nissan Pathfinder with black tinted windows. I pulled up next to him; he rolled down the window and told me to get in. So I walked over and got in the passenger seat. The first thing I said was, "Lenny, if it was me who set you up, do you really think I'd be meeting you out here in the middle of nowhere?"

"Caucci, you got big balls, so anything is possible with you."

"Yeah, but I'm not a fucking idiot. Lenny, tell me exactly what happened."

"They raided my house and said you set me up with a controlled buy."

"Is that so?'

"That's what they said."

"Come on, Lenny, use your fucking head...you're smarter than that. What've you been charged with?"

"They got a half kilo of powder and about twenty-five pounds of weed."

"Well, if I set you up, why aren't you charged with the fifty we did the other day? Does that make any fucking sense to you?"

He hesitated for a second, then said, "Not really."

"Lenny, be honest with me, before they raided your house, who did you sell to out of your house?"

"I would never sell anything out of my house."

"Lenny, they can't get a search warrant without probable cause. You had to sell something to someone."

"Wait…I did sell an eight ball to Jodi."

"To Jodi? Have you lost your mind? I wouldn't piss on that bitch if she was on fire. She has a newborn baby, and all she does is put that shit up her nose." Then, out of nowhere, it all came together. "Hold on, Lenny, I think I know what happened. When we did that thing the other day, who picked up your girl?"

Lenny just sat silently; I could tell he was going over everything in his head. Then he started to shake his head as he put two and two together.

"Fucking Jodi that bitch."

"And who was the only other person in that house besides me and you who saw the bricks?"

"My stupid fucking chick."

"This isn't looking good, Lenny. Sounds like your chick might have had a few too many drinks that day and run her mouth to Jodi, but I think I can get to the bottom of this."

"How?"

"Give me a couple minutes…let me make a phone call."

So I called Cristy, the girl who was smart enough not to deal with a stranger who had my beeper and phone claiming to know me. Cristy answered the phone and said, "Hey, Anthony, what going on?"

"Listen, Cristy, I need you to tell me exactly what happened the day you called me and that dude called you back. Please don't leave anything out. This is very important."

"Some guy called me back claiming he was a friend of yours and that you were out of town competing in a martial arts tournament. I knew right away he was full of shit because I remember you telling me that you don't compete because there are too many rules. I told him that all I wanted to do was talk to you and then I hung up. But Jodi called the guy back and went to meet him. I told her it was a bad idea, but you know she'll do almost anything for a line."

"Have you heard from her since?"

"Not at all, and I've tried calling her a couple of times. I just figured she is recuperating from a few days of partying. Why? Is something wrong? Did something happen?"

"Yes, very wrong…don't talk to her until I see you and explain. Stay away from her and don't take her phone calls."

I gave the phone to Lenny and let Cristy tell him the story. As Lenny listened, his face turned beet red in anger but he remained calm. When he hung up, he pounded on his steering wheel and screamed, "I'm going to kill that fucking bitch!"

I had known Lenny for about ten years and had never seen that side of him. And thank God he had not decided I'd snitched on him before we met, or I would have been buried in a ditch somewhere off Alligator Alley.

When he calmed down, Lenny said, "Come on, follow me." So I got back in my truck to follow him. He took off down the dirt road, leaving a thick cloud of dust in the air. I assumed he was going to her house and I got a bad feeling. When he pulled into her driveway, he came to a screeching halt, got out of his truck, and slammed the door. I jumped out of my truck and grabbed him by the arm. "Lenny! Please don't do this here! They'll call the cops and your bond will be revoked for threatening an informant. It's better if she thinks she's in the clear. Let her think she pinned it on me and got away with it. Use your fucking head! Let things cool down, then take care of her. Right now, you have no motive to whack her because you're supposed to think I'm the rat."

He didn't give two shits what I was saying and wasn't thinking clearly. He banged and kicked on her front door as hard as he could. "Jodi, you fucking cunt, open the door!"

Jodi and her boyfriend were actually stupid enough to open up the door.

"You're all fucking dead, you scum bags," Lenny yelled.

Jodi's boyfriend, clearly terrified, pointed at me and said, "Caucci's an undercover cop!"

That had to be one of the stupidest things I'd ever heard come out of someone's mouth. An undercover cop? I just laughed and said, "You two morons obviously don't know how this thing works."

We ended up leaving after Lenny did some more yelling and threatening. The next morning the police came to his house and arrested him for tampering with the witness. When he got in front of the judge, his lawyer said, "Your Honor, the arresting officers told my client that Anthony Caucci was the informant. When my client went to the CI's house, he had absolutely no idea that indeed *she* was the informant. The arresting officers in this case acted recklessly by intentionally naming Anthony Caucci as an informant. This type of behavior from the arresting officers should be investigated. Giving the identity of an informant is illegal, and naming someone as an informant when they are not is even worse. This is how people get killed in these types of cases, Your Honor. The only logical reason we can assume that a young lady by the name of Jodi is the informant is because we are here today in front of Your Honor and the state wants to revoke my client's bond."

The judge let Lenny off with a warning, saying, "If you go near her again or threaten her in any way, I WILL revoke your bond!"

"Yes, Your Honor."

Since Lenny was Colombian and had some deep connections in Miami and Columbia, I knew Jodi wouldn't be around for long. He knew exactly what to do so he didn't go to jail.

Me, on the other hand...I wasn't sure who the informant was on my case, but I knew it was only a matter of time until my attorney found out. In the meantime, I had to start thinking about ways to getting rid of him. In a perfect world I could've made it look like he had just disappeared, leaving no trace of a body, like he skipped town. The only problem with that was getting rid of a body isn't a one-man job. The last thing I wanted to do was bring in someone else to help me, but I didn't have much of a choice. Either way, that piece of shit had to go. Not only did I get busted, Lenny busted too.

A few weeks went by while I tried to fly under the radar. Then, one night as I was pulling into my apartment complex in Dade County, just across the county line, I saw two men standing outside their car. They looked very familiar, but I couldn't figure out where I had seen them before, and something just didn't feel right. Instead of parking in my assigned spot, I drove a different direction. I was sure I knew these motherfuckers, but just couldn't make them out. Then a few seconds later, WHAM!, it hit me like a ton of bricks. It was those dirty, lying, motherless Hollywood narcotic cops who had arrested me a few weeks before. I had no idea why they were in Dade County and how they found my house. But I played it cool and drove right by them because I wasn't in my usual Four Runner. Thank God it worked. I drove within ten feet of them and was able to get away without them noticing me.

I checked into a cash-only hotel that didn't ask for ID. I sat on the small sofa, propped my feet up on a chair, and sat there in silence, trying to figure out what was going on. Were they going to arrest me again? Did they want to raid my house?

I noticed a mini bar in the corner that was filled with soda and booze. I'm wasn't a drinker, but that night seemed like a good time to give it a shot. So I open up a small bottle of Johnny Walker and, miraculously, halfway through it, things didn't seem so bad.

29 | A Hit Job

I knew the cops either had me under investigation or were planning to arrest me again, so I stayed at the hotel for a few days, hoping it would blow over. The next night I felt like I had to release some tension, so I went to my Chinese Boxing class in Pompano. While Professor Cravens was teaching, the school phone rang so I answered it, "Chinese Boxing Institute International."

"Yeah, um, I'm interested in taking some classes. Can you give me directions to your school?"

The voice on the other end sounded oddly familiar, so I stalled for a few seconds and asked him some questions. "Where are you coming from?"

"I'm coming northbound on I-95 from Miami."

"Okay, get off at the Copans Road and take a left..." I stopped talking suddenly when I realized something: it was those dirty cocksucking Hollywood police again. They were so dumb and arrogant they had actually called the school asking for directions. "Wait a minute...did you say you are coming from Miami?"

"Yeah."

"Sorry, take a right when you get off the exit, you'll be headed east toward the beach. When you get to Dixie Highway, you'll see us on the SE corner in the small plaza next to the convenience store. You can't miss it."

"Okay, I'll be there shortly."

"Awesome, I look forward to meeting you."

I hung up and wished these cops would get run over by a fucking Mack truck.

I knew I had about fifteen minutes to get out of there. As I quietly grabbed my things, Rick, a very close friend of mine, was watching me through the schools mirror so I waved him over. "I gotta get the fuck out of here, the pigs are on their way. I'll call you here in about fifteen minutes so make sure YOU answer the phone when it rings."

"You got it, brother, and be careful."

I parked my car across the street from the school where the cops couldn't possibly see me, but I was able to see them. I waited for about fifteen minutes, then called the school. Rick answered, "Chinese Boxing Institute International."

"Hey, Rick, it's me!"

"Hey, man, what the hell's going on?" he whispered.

"Ah, you know…Hollywood police are breaking my balls again."

"What for this time?"

"Who the fuck knows, but it's the second time this week these pricks tried to sneak up on me."

"How the hell are you always getting away?"

"Not sure, but I need a favor."

"Sure, what is it?"

"Casually walk out the front door and you'll see two dickhead cops sitting in a red Mustang."

"How ya know?"

"'Cause I'm looking right at the pricks."

"You're one crazy son of a bitch, Caucci."

"Politely tell them that they have a phone call."

"Hooold on…you want me to walk out there and tell the cops that someone is on the phone for them? I'm not too sure about this. I feel diarrhea coming on."

"Come on…have some fun once in a while."

"Aww, fuck it. Hold on…but if I get arrested…"

"Arrested for what? Telling someone they have a phone call?"

"I just want to put it on record that I think this is a bad idea."

Rick got nervous easily and always walked a straight path, but on that day he decide to have a little fun. Rick approached the car, leaned down, and said, "Excuse me, gentlemen, you have a telephone call."

"Where?" one of the cops asked.

"Inside the school."

"Can't be for us"

"I think I can pretty much guarantee it's for you two"

"What makes you so fuckin' sure?"

"Well, the guy on the phone asked me to go outside and tell the two dickhead cops sitting in a red Mustang that they have a phone call. I'm not trying to be disrespectful by calling you dickheads, but you're the only guys I see sitting in a red Mustang. But if you're not cops, then I guess the call's not for you."

They got out of their car and slammed the doors. They entered the school with their batons out and their radios turned up in an attempt to intimidate the students. Everyone stopped training for a few seconds and gave them a quick glance, then went right back to training.

One of the cops got on the phone and said, "Who is this?!"

"It's me, ya bum, the guy you're looking for."

"What makes you think we're looking for ya?"

"I got a phone call from one of your cop friends last night, he told me you'd be going to my house in North Miami and just called me to let me know you were coming to the school tonight. What took you so fucking long to get here?"

"Is that so? If you got someone on the inside, then why you got so many charges against you, smart ass?"

"Not for long…So what can I do for you ladies?"

"We have a warrant for your arrest, so you need to come down to the station immediately."

"I got a better idea…how about you bend over and have your partner shove that warrant up your ass? I'll give my attorney a call in the morning and get back to you. What type of bullshit charges you trying to pin on me this time?"

"Trafficking cocaine, baby…we got you, Caucci."

"Well, I guess I'll see you pricks tomorrow."

The next morning, I contacted my attorney and turned myself into the Hollywood police. While they were fingerprinting me, there was a strange feeling in the air. It was almost as if the fun on both sides was coming to an end. The game of cat-and-mouse was over for now, and for a few moments we all saw each other as men just doing their jobs. They were both aware of my arrest at the age of sixteen and agreed that I got fucked by the system. They also knew these new charges would put me away for a long time, and I think they felt a little empathy for me. Then one of them turned to me and said, "Your attorney will find out who the informant is very soon. If you go anywhere near him, we will have your bond revoked."

"Come on, guys, do you really think I'm stupid? I'm in enough trouble as it is."

"Okay, just warning you, if we get any hint of you going near him, you're done."

After some back and forth, they sent me downtown to the county jail, where I got booked and then bonded out immediately. After about a week, my attorney Eddie Kay called me with good news. "Hey, Caucci, we got the discovery from the state and know who the informant is. I'm going to give you his name and address so you can stay far away from him and his house."

"What's the cocksucker's name?"

"Jay Bass, he lives in Davie."

"That fuckin' sewer rat."

"If you go near him, they will revoke your bond, and it's very difficult to fight a case from the inside."

"Forget about it!"

Remember, this was the early '90s, so there was no Internet, Google, or Facebook. There was absolutely no easy way to find someone if they were really clever and wanted to hide. But I was determined to find this piece of shit and get rid of him. I decided to hire a private investigator who did a lot of work for the Mob and other organized crime syndicates. This guy was good! He was more valuable than any attorney. We had a quick sit-down at Denny's in Hallandale and I told him, "This is what I need! I want you to check his and his girlfriend's driver's license every day to see if either one of them get a ticket. I want every one of his and her's family's addresses, and check every phone number that appears on his phone bill going back one year and give me the corresponding address. His girlfriend had a baby not too long ago. I want her doctor's address and any other medical information you can get on either one of them. I want you look so far up his ass you can see the back of his teeth!"

He wrote everything down and said, "You got it, Caucci, I'll find the prick."

"Okay, so what do I owe you so we can get the ball rolling today."

"Two thousand for now, and then when we meet again, we will take it from there."

"Here is five thousand, I want you working for me around the clock until we find this prick. I don't care what it takes, are we clear?"

"Your case is my priority, Mr. Caucci. Your attorney told me your situation."

When we shook hands to leave, I looked him in the eye, squeezed his hand hard, and said, "I'm counting on you, don't let me down!" He had a startled look on his face, but he knew I meant business.

A few months went by, and that piece of shit wasn't anywhere to be found. He didn't show up to his mother's birthday, Christmas, or any of his or his girlfriend's relatives' houses on any holiday. He had vanished. He even moved out of his house and made sure nothing was in his name. I was sure he remembered our conversation about what would happen to him if he ever ratted on me. Then one morning I finally got a call from the private investigator.

"Hey, Caucci, your good friend Jay Bass got a speeding ticket and has a court date in two weeks."

"Great, let's meet later today to discuss this."

My heart started racing and my adrenaline kicked in. It was my turn...

When I met with the PI he handed me a piece of paper with the court date. It was a night court hearing, 6:30 p.m. at the Broward County Courthouse.

I quickly cloned a phone and called Carlos, who was in Columbia at the time. I gave him an update of the situation and told him I needed a clean-cut spotter, someone who understood and spoke good English. He said he had the perfect man for the job. A few days later, I picked up Hector, the guy Carlos recommended, from the Miami International Airport. On the drive back to my place, I told him what needed to be done. "All you have to do is sit in the back of the courtroom, and when the judge calls this cocksucker's name, get a good look at him, then step outside the courtroom and call me on my cell so you can tell me exactly what he's wearing. Then wait for him in the hallway, and follow him when he leaves. As soon as you get out of the elevator, call me and let me know which direction you're headed. Once I catch up with you, I'll take care of the rest, then I'll drop you off at the airport."

"No problem, my friend," he replied with a Colombian accent.

That night I barely got any sleep, tossing and turning as I thought about killing someone who used to be a friend. The pounding of my heart increased as every second passed. I had known Jay for a long time and knew he had just become a new father. I thought, "What are my options here? If he lives, he'll testify against me and put me away for at least twenty years. He'll be enjoying his family while I rot in a prison. My mother will have to come visit me behind bars until I'm in my forties and I'll break her heart again. I'll have no chance of living a normal life after prison. The chances of me getting married and having children of my own after doing a twenty-year stretch in prison are very slim. I'll have nothing when I get out and will probably end up right back in prison." Then I thought about an even worse-case scenario, "What if I get caught after I kill him? I could be sent to the electric chair, and my mother would be visiting me on death row. This is the most difficult decision I'll ever have to make...I told him to his face if he ever tried to put me in prison that I'd kill him. He knew the consequences but still took a gamble on his life. So I guess HE made the decision, not me. I'm just following through with a promise."

Hector and I arrived at the courthouse at 5 p.m. and parked in an alley behind an abandoned restaurant. I had a 9 mm with a silencer ready to go. I knew of a great place to sit outside the courthouse so I had a clear view of the front door. I had two cloned phones, one for me and one for Hector. Neither one had ever been used. I had left my personal phones at my house so the police couldn't track my location using the signal off the phone tower during the murder investigation. I was wearing a wig with curly blonde hair and a white Nike tracksuit on top of a black dress shirt with black slacks. They were total opposite colors, just in case someone got a glimpse of me. Hector was wearing an expensive suite and looked like an attorney; he blended in perfectly.

My plan was to wait for Hector's call so he could tell me which direction they were heading, then I could begin to follow Jay, and Hector would go back to his car. Once I was on Jay's tail, I was planning to walk up to his car and unload the magazine in his head, then casually walk back to my car. Nobody would see or hear anything. By the time the body was found I'd been long gone. Back in my car, I'd strip off my top layer of clothes, put them in a bag, and burn them later. As we drove away, I'd dismantle the gun, wipe it down with alcohol to remove fingerprints, file down the barrel so it couldn't be matched to ballistics, and dispose of the parts separately. No weapon, no witnesses, no crime. Hector would go straight back to Colombia, long before an investigation got rolling.

"Are you ready and do you understand what the plan is?" I asked Hector. Hector repeated the entire plan without missing a beat, down to the very last detail. I could tell he had done this plenty of times.

So that day, Hector went into the courthouse and sat in the back row and waited for Jay's name to be called. At 6 p.m., as soon as court was in session, Hector gave me a quick call to say he would call me back as soon as he heard Jay's name. I waited anxiously outside. A half hour went by and I still hadn't heard from Hector. I figured there were probably at least twenty people waiting to see the judge. If each person took five minutes, it would be up to one hour and forty minutes. I remained calm. Seven o'clock came around, and I still hadn't heard from Hector. As I waited, I imagined the look on Jay's face when I had the gun pointed at his head. He was pleading for his life with his hands stretched out to protect him from a bullet. Then he screamed, "I was never going to testify against you, I swear to God."

"I know you weren't."

I imagined his eyes filling with tears at his last minutes and the thoughts running through his head: "My child, my wife, God please help me! Please…!"

Thump, thump, thump…I imagined emptying the magazine in his head.

The phone rang and snapped me out of my daze. It was Hector…

30 | Nobody Ever Makes It to Testify

My hands shook as I answered the phone. "Did you see him?"

"No, my friend, he didn't show up. The judge called his name three times, and now the court room is empty."

"Motherrrrfucker."

This really put me in a pinch. I thought I had this guy and all my problems were going to be solved by the end of the day. Now I was back to square one, and I didn't know what my next move was going to be. As I was driving Hector back to the airport, he asked, "Whaddya gonna do now, my friend?"

"I'm not sure yet, but I'll figure something out."

"Why don't you just have your attorney call him in for a deposition? He'll have to show up. And if he doesn't, there is a very good chance the case will be thrown out. But If he does show up, he'll never make it home alive, I guarantee it. The next time I come, I'll bring some friends with me and we'll send this snitch to hell. In Colombia, nobody ever makes it to testify. This job is a piece of cake, my friend."

I couldn't believe my ears. This was a brilliant idea. It was obvious Hector knew our judicial system very well and had done this before. I felt relieved there was another plan in play.

Months went by as I wanted anxiously for my lawyer to give me a date he'd depose Jay. In the meantime, it was business as usual. One afternoon, my grandmother from my mother's side called me and said, "I have a nice chicken parmigiana sandwich ready for you."

That was the code for me to come pick up the phones she had cloned for me. At the time, I had a small electronic device called an ESN reader (electronic serial number) that I used to steal cell phone numbers. The FCC introduced the electronic serial number in the early 1980s as a unique identification number for all mobile devices. All I needed to do was park my truck near a busy intersection, and the ESN reader would intercept at least 100 telephone numbers, along with their corresponding ESN numbers, in about fifteen minutes. After I had gathered enough numbers, I would take them to my grandmother's house and she would program them into phones using special software and a computer. Each cloned line would last anywhere from two to six weeks.

Back in the early 1990s, cell phone companies charged around thirty cents a minute to talk, but that rate went up to about eighty cents a minute during peak hours. So the average person using a cell phone for only one hour a day would have at least a $500 phone bill. My phone bill was costing me between $2,000 to $3,000 a month. And for what, air time? It was a complete rip-off, so I decided to go into the cellular phone business myself, being the entrepreneur that I was. I had approximately two hundred customers paying $100 a month for unlimited minutes on their good old flip phones. I had a good friend of mine drive around all day, picking up and dropping off phones. I paid him $2,000 a week and kept the other $12,000, of which I gave my grandma a nice cut.

You're probably wondering why I would involve my grandmother in something like this. Well, one day my grandmother and I were bullshitting at the dinner table. I told her how phones were cloned and how much money some friends of mine in Miami were making. She said, "If you buy the equipment, I'll do the work." She was close to eighty years old, so she was bored and wanted something to do. We made a deal and agreed if the cops ever got involved, I was going to take the rap. It would have been a bullshit charge, and I wouldn't have been looking at much jail time anyway.

One day I went to my grandmother's apartment to pick up some phones, and when I got there my mother was visiting. My mother asked if I would take her to the Aventura Mall so she could do some Christmas shopping. I agreed to take her, but as soon as we left her apartment, my mother saw a car following us and said, "We're being tailed."

I told her to keep an eye on it. There was a Publix shopping plaza one block from my grandmother's apartment so I drove through it and then went back onto the main road, Hallandale Beach Boulevard, and saw the car was still following me. I headed east over the Intracoastal bridge, but as soon as I got to the bottom of the bridge, I pulled a U-turn and headed back west. The prick following me did the same. My mom shook her head and said, "Looks like you got some fleas."

"What a bunch of ball-breaking bastards."

At the next red light, I put my car in park, got out, and walked back to the car, about four cars behind me. As I walked up to his car, he looked straight ahead pretended not to see me. I walked up to the driver's side window and gently tapped on the glass with one knuckle. He looked up at me like a stunned mullet, then slowly rolled down his window. He was a very clean-cut guy, clean shaven, with straight brown hair parted to the side. He sat almost perfectly straight in his chair with his hands placed on the steering wheel at two and ten.

"Hey my friend, how you doin?" I said.

"Uh…fine."

"Look, I'm going to the Aventura Mall with my ma. Why don't you go park your car and come with me? I'll give you a ride."

"Uhh…what are you talking about?"

"Do I look like a fucking jerk-off? You've been on my ass for the last ten minutes. First from the house, then through Publix, over the fuckin' bridge and now here, in the middle of the goddamn street having a conversation like two old women."

Before he could say anything, the light turned green and cars began to honk. One guy yelled, "Get the fuck out of the road, assholes!" as he passed us by. I just stood there and stared at the driver, waiting for him to say something.

"I'm sorry…I was just looking for an address and got lost. I wasn't following you intentionally."

"You and I both know that's a load of shit. But now ya know where I'll be in case you wanna take a picture or somthin'."

Before I left, I walked to the back of his car to get a look at his license plate. When I got back into my truck, I said to my mom, "Write down this number down before I forget it." She scrambled through her purse and pulled out an eyeliner and a scrap piece of paper and quickly wrote it down. Then she asked, "Who do you think it is?"

"He looks like a fucking fed. Don't they have anything better to do?"

"Well, if you clean up your act, I'm sure they'll stop breaking your balls. I would've thought going to prison and living with the niggers would've straightened you out."

"Ehhhh...you're right, Ma, but how boring would life be? Plus, I couldn't get a job shoveling shit even if I wanted to."

My mom grabbed my hand and said, "Nobody said life was easy, son. One day you'll learn your lesson, and I hope it's not too late when you do."

I thought, "I've committed hundreds of crimes in just a few years, it could be anything."

I quickly went back to my mom's house and dropped her off, then went to a pay phone down the street outside a Big Daddy's liquor store. I called my ex-girlfriend Tara, who I was still seeing on the side on and off. After we broke up, we remained very good friends and stayed in contact. She was still training to be a cop. I asked her if she would run a license plate number for me, and as usual she didn't hesitate to say yes. About an hour later Tara called me back.

"Hey, T," she said, "I've look everywhere and even called a few friends, but that license plate number doesn't show up in anyone's system. It has to be a fed."

"Son of a bitch! Thanks for trying."

"Anytime."

"I'll talk to you soon."

"Okay, bye."

31 | 911-911

A few weeks later, I got a call from Fatman. "Hey, brother, you remember that hot Colombian chick Erica?"

"I sure do," I said, knowing that he was talking about Carlos and shipment of cocaine. "What's she been up to lately? Does she still have that asshole boyfriend?"

"No, she got rid of that dick, and she's coming into town with a bunch of her friends. It's someone's birthday or something." This meant Carlos was bringing in a new shipment.

"Now that sounds like fun!"

"Yeah, she's a wild one. She wants to know if you want to hang out with them and possibly go to a club on South Beach."

"Sounds good to me...how many girls are coming with her? I'll call the club we always go to and put them on the VIP list and reserve a couple of tables."

"It's her plus ten."

Now I knew how much cocaine was coming in, thanks to our code. Since her name began with the letter "e," which is the fifth letter in the alphabet, I knew the first number was a five. And since she had ten friends with her, the second number was ten. I multiplied the two numbers and knew Carlos was bringing in fifty kilos. It was all done over the phone without saying a single word about drugs. (For quantities over six hundred kilos, we would meet in person.)

"Sure, brother, I'm in for some fun," I said, meaning I'd take this shipment off his hands.

"They'll be in town in a few days, so I will call you when they check in to their hotel room."

"Okay, let me know when they get here so I can call the club and make reservations. Hey, how much are drinks going for in that club now?"

"Usually about $20 each, but since we go there all the time they'll run us around $13. That's if you don't go buying any of those fancy South Beach drinks." This meant our price was $13,000 per kilo.

We used codes because it was safe, but the feds were not stupid and were very good at cracking codes. But just in case a jury ever had to listen to any recordings, the feds would have to prove beyond a reasonable doubt that we were talking about cocaine. Nothing's bullet proof, especially when you're dealing with the government, but it was a little insurance policy.

"Okay, my friend, sounds good. I'll put it on my tab and pay the club at the end of the month." This meant the cocaine would be given on credit and I'd pay for it once it was sold.

"Sounds good, I'll call you in a couple days when she gets here."

That same night, my dad gave me a call—he was probably on his third martini. "Get your ass over here for dinner, I made a lasagna."

My dad's lasagna...fuhgeddaboudit!

"Okay, Pop, I'll be there around seven, and I'm gonna bring Boxer George with me."

"There's plenty of food...bring the whole fucking crew," he said in his happy all-day drinking voice.

Boxer George was a black American and one of my best friends. He mostly sold marijuana and was doing most of my running around while I was on bond for the two trafficking charges. If I got arrested one more time, the judge would have revoked my bond and I would sit in jail until my trial date—and that could take years. George also happened to be a very good boxer and almost went pro, but selling drugs guaranteed him a lot of money and fun with the ladies. That was no lifestyle for someone trying to become a professional boxer so, that went out the window.

So George and I went to my dad's apartment and had a nice Italian meal. My dad played his favorite Frank Sinatra album, "I Did It My Way" all night.

That was a night I will never forget. By this time, my dad was very sick—he had been diagnosed with cirrhosis of the liver, even though he seemed perfectly fine. All that drinking, from morning to evening, had finally caught up to him. When he was first diagnosed, the doctor said, "Mr. Caucci, If you quit drinking now, you'll be okay because we caught it early." But my dad loved to drink. It wasn't just the alcohol—it was part of life for him. He was in and out of bars and restaurants all day, every day doing business, having sit-downs, placing bets, collecting money, you name it. Everything was done from the bars, and if he couldn't drink while he was there he would have died in a week. So just a few weeks after he was let out of the hospital the first time, he started to drink again. His own father, my grandfather, drank on his death bed from cirrhosis, and I was almost certain my dad was gonna follow suit. Me, on the other hand, I hated alcohol.

After a great meal and a good time, George and I left my dad's around 10 p.m. But as we were walking to my truck, I noticed a red Jeep Cherokee with two men sitting in the front seat and their seats reclined all the way back. I could see them hiding and trying to look over the dashboard. Just a few months before, I had seen this same Jeep during a meeting with Sal's other "legitimate" partner in Hemmingway's Restaurant. At this meeting, Sal was trying to convince me not to take the restaurant because it wouldn't be fair to him. Well, that was a very fucking short meeting. But during this brief meeting, I noticed a man in the exact same color and model Jeep. At the time I thought he was just lying back and taking a nap or killing some time.

"This has to be the feds," I thought. A few weeks before, I had been followed leaving my mom's apartment and now they're outside my dad's apartment, which was only two blocks away. This was no coincidence. I pretended to scratch my nose and covered my mouth so they couldn't read my lips if they were filming us and said to George, "The fuckin feds are here watching us."

George played it real cool and casually replied while looking directly at the ground with his hand in his pockets, "Where they at?"

"They're in a red Jeep at the end of the parking lot right in the corner. Don't look over there yet, we don't wanna to let them know we're onto them."

"Okay."

"Let's pretend we're sparring, and when you circle around me, look over my left shoulder so you can see these scumbags."

George and I started slap-boxing in the parking lot. We looked like two friends just having fun. As we circled around each other, he got a clear line of sight. "Yeah, you're right, I see those dirty motherfuckers. Why you think they're here?"

"Who the fuck knows? Maybe because I caught those two state cases and that bitch Jodi told Hollywood PD about a fifty kilo deal I did with Lenny. I think it's mandatory for Hollywood to contact the feds on larger quantities. There're probably just fishing, because if they had something on me, I guarantee you we would never see them coming."

"Yeah, you're right about that, but let's get the fuck out of here anyway."

"Alright, I'll call you tomorrow and let you know what's up for the day."

The next day I got a call from Fatman to let me know that Erica and her friends were in town. I told him I would pick them up that evening around 5 p.m. (The best time to transport anything illegal is in rush hour traffic when the greatest number of cars are on the street because the chances of getting pulled over by the police are much lower.)

I went down to Fatman's house in Kendall at five o'clock and, as usual, his wife Mary answered the door. Not only was she attractive, she had a beautiful heart and was always very kind and respectful. She was a God-loving, church-going Christian, and Fatman was the first man she had ever been with.

I greeted her with a kiss on the cheek as she welcomed me into the house. When I entered, she yelled, "Papi, Anthony is here!" Fatman came out of his bedroom, all dressed up as usual. He was wearing his $25,000 Rolex, snake skin boots, and God knows what brand clothes. Not only did he like to have the most expensive of everything, he loved to flaunt it.

Me, on the other hand, was just the opposite. I was wearing a plain white V-neck T-shirt with a pair of Levi's and sneakers. We greeted each other with a big hug and shot the shit for a minute or two. Then he told me to follow him into his room so I could take look at the merchandise. I went in and, as usual, opened one of the kilos just to make sure the quality was good and that it was pure cocaine and not mixed with something fake. Pure cocaine looks like compressed, very shiny and flaky fish scales. The better-quality coke is pure white, while crappy coke has a yellowish tint. Just by looking at it, I could tell if it was any good. By the time the coke had reached the U.S., it had usually been through quite a few hands. All it took was one person who thought they could get away with stealing a kilo or two or adding some cut to the product and I'd be stuck with the shit. So everyone always checked the merchandise, no matter who you got it from.

"It looks very nice," I told Fatman.

Fatman said to his wife, "Go get two suitcases out of the closet and load it up in Anthony's truck."

Without hesitation and with a big smile on her face she did exactly what he had asked. I hated the way he talked to her like an employee and involved her in the business, but she was his wife and it wasn't my place to say anything. It was definitely not something I would expose my wife to, let alone ask her to pack the suitcases. She could have gotten a twenty-year sentence for conspiracy if we ever got caught. I had learned my lesson at the age of sixteen when I accidentally got my girlfriend arrested with me.

Once she was finished loading my truck and back in the house, Fatman said, "Hey brother, why don't you get your girlfriend Noelvis and come out dancing with us tonight? My wife wants me to take her to a salsa club. We'll get a table and a couple of bottles of champagne."

"Are you nuts? You know how protective Noelvis's parents are. I haven't been able to take her anywhere without her little sister tagging along. Her parents are old-school Cubans."

"You forget who I am brother? I'm the man that makes things happen. I'll have my wife talk to her parents…I guarantee you they'll let her go with us, and she won't be bringing her sister."

"Okay, I'll give it a shot."

So I called Noelvis and told her what Alex had said.

"Hay, Anthony!" she replied with her Cuban accent. "That would be wonderful, but my parents won't let me."

"Do me a favor and put your mom on the phone—Mary wants to talk to her. It's worth a shot."

"Uhh, Okay."

Mary got on the phone with Noelvis's mother, and they talked for about five minutes. I didn't have a clue what they were saying because they were talking Spanish about a million words a minute. But I could tell by the big smile on Alex's face and his arrogant look of "I told you so" that the conversation was going well. Once they hung up Mary said, "DONE! she can go."

"GET THE FUCK OUTTA HERE! I've been going out with this chick for months, for the SECOND time, and it only takes you a few minutes to get permission for her to go out alone with me?"

"I just reassured her parents that we will make sure she will be safe and we'll have her home by 3 a.m. I told them I won't let her out of my sight."

"Un-fuckin-believable...thank you, Mary."

So I left Alex's house with the fifty kilos and drove to an apartment Alex and I shared on Brickell Avenue, a very affluent neighborhood in Miami. The apartment was secure and was only used to store coke and count money. After I dropped it off, I went back to my apartment in North Miami Beach to get ready for a night out. I picked up Noelvis at her house and went back to Alex's house so we could all leave together. When we arrived at Fatman's mansion, there was a stretch limousine waiting in the driveway. Noelvis's eyes lit up with excitement, while I was in a state of disbelief. I had no clue how I was going to explain this. Noelvis had her suspicions about me being involved in the Mob and organized crime, but I always downplayed it. She had absolutely no idea I was involved in the drug trade.

Fatman, on the other hand, loved to show off. Not only did he buy very expensive things, he acted like he was some drug cartel kingpin like you'd see in the movies. The only reason I hung out with him and considered him a good friend and someone I could trust was because underneath all of his tough guy, look-at-me attitude, he had gone out of his way for me a few times and had never hesitated to help me if I needed it. I did the same for him. Also, his father had been sent twice to federal prison for ten years, and one of his brothers was doing a life sentence. Nobody in his family ever cooperated with the feds, so Fatman seemed like a pretty solid guy.

When we got into the limousine, out came the cameras. I didn't like getting my picture taken, especially with an associate. But we were out with our girls, so I obliged. I took a picture of Noelvis sitting next to Alex, and Alex took a picture of me with his wife Mary—but no pictures of me and Alex together were taken. As we were on our way to the club, Noelvis naively asked, "Alex, you have a beautiful house, what do you do for a living?"

Alex raised one eyebrow, and with a fake puzzled look on his face replied, "What do you think? I'm a drug smuggler just like your boyfriend."

There was nothing I could do but just cover my face with my hands to hide my expression. Noelvis sat silent for a moment, then said "Oh...I see."

After a few seconds, Alex said, "I'm just kidding...I have a car dealership and a flower shop on Marco Island." Noelvis knew he was full of shit, but she did a great job pretending to believe him because she could tell I was very uncomfortable. Instead, she spun the conversation back to normal. It was almost like second nature to her.

When the night ended, I dropped her off at 3 a.m. as promised and went back to the apartment on Brickell Avenue where the fifty kilos were stashed.

Leaving close to $1 million dollars of cocaine stashed in an apartment made me nervous, no matter how much security we had.

When I got back to the apartment, my cell phone rang. It was Claudia, a Colombian girl I was seeing on and off. We talked for about forty-five minutes before my battery died, so I called it a night. I took a quick shower, then jumped into bed. Then...just as I was about to fall asleep, my beeper went off. It was about 6: 30 a.m. When I looked at my beeper, it was my dad's home phone number followed by 911-911, which meant he had emergency.

My first thought was, "Oh shit, my dad must be going to the hospital again." He would never call me at 6:30 in the morning using a 911 code unless it was an absolute emergency.

I was in a real pinch, I couldn't use my cell phone because the battery had died, and I never used the phone in the apartment because it was too easy to trace the line back to this address. Then my beeper went off again: "911-911." I knew I wasn't supposed to use the landline, but my gut told me to make an exception if my dad was going to the hospital.

When my dad picked up the phone, he answered nervously "Hello?"

"Hey, Pop, what's going on? Are you okay?"

"Yeah, I'm fine, but the police are here and I'm getting arrested..."

32 | Please God, Don't Let There Be...

"Who's arresting you?" I asked my dad, my heart racing.

"It's just Hallandale police."

Since it was the local police and not the FBI, I felt better. I figured it was for something stupid he did, so no big deal. Then my dad said, "The cops want to speak to you."

"Sure, put those pricks on the phone."

"This is Officer Gonzales with the Hallandale Police Department...we have a warrant for your father's arrest and have to take him downtown."

"What's he being arrested for?"

"Not really sure, we're just here to pick him up. He'll find out once he's in front of the judge, then he'll get a bond and you'll be able to come pick him up."

"Okay, fair enough."

"We don't want to take him downtown and leave his house unoccupied. Do you think you could come down here and secure the house before we take him?"

"Is that necessary?"

"No, but If someone sees us taking him away, they might try to break in since they know the apartment is empty. Believe it or not, it's happened before, so better safe than sorry, don't you think?"

That sounded a little odd to me, but since it was the local police, I wasn't too concerned.

"I'm on a paint job in West Miami, and it's gonna take me at least an hour to get there, maybe more depending on traffic."

"Hmmmm…okay, we'll try to wait for you, so do your best to get here as fast as you can. Without speeding, of course. We've got to get him in front of the judge in a few hours or his bail hearing will be postponed. If that happens, he'll probably spend a few more days in jail before he gets back in front of a judge."

"Alright, I'm on my way. I'll get there as soon as I can."

I got in my Four Runner and headed north on I-95 toward Hallandale. As I was driving, my gut was telling me something just wasn't right. I'd never heard of a cop arresting someone and not knowing why. I decided to call the Hallandale police station to see if I could find out what the hell was going on.

Dispatch answered. "Hallandale police, is this an emergency?"

"No, not at all…I was hoping you could help me. My father just got arrested by the Hallandale police for an outstanding warrant. Could you please tell me what the warrant's for so I can get a lawyer to help him at his bond hearing?"

"Sure, no problem, let me check the warrant board. What's your father's name?"

"Anthony Caucci."

"Please spell the last name."

"CAUCCI."

"Okay. please hold…Sorry, we do not have any open warrants under that name."

"Well, that's strange. He just told me Hallandale was arresting him."

"Oh, it's probably the sheriff's office. We sometimes assist them when it comes to warrants. Call Broward Sheriff's Office and ask for the warrant division."

"Okay, thanks for your help."

Broward Sheriff's Office gave me the same answer: "We have no warrants for Anthony Caucci."

My heart fell out of my ass…I knew it was either the FBI, or he was being kidnapped by some people posing as police officers. I was still about thirty minutes away from his house and needed to get to a landline quickly. I was close to Noelvis's house, so I gave her a quick call. It was early in the morning, so she was very surprised to hear from me.

"Hey, it's me."

"Hay Anthony, is so early…"

"Listen, I was thinking of taking you to the beach today. But before I come and get you, could you go outside and check the weather? Make sure there's absolutely no clouds and it looks like it's gonna be a sunny day. You know I can't stand fucking cloudy days."

She sat silent for a second or two, and then realized what I had meant. She had been around me long enough to understand what I was saying.

"Sure thing, Anthony, give me a minute or two. I just got out of the shower."

She got in her car and drove around her neighborhood for a couple minutes while I waited on the phone. When she got back on the phone she said, "It's a beautiful day for the beach, Anthony. I'll get a beach bag ready."

"Okay, I'm on the way to your house now. Please keep your eyes open and let me know if you see any changes in the weather."

"Absolutely."

After we hung up, I called Smadar. When she answered, I said, "Listen carefully…I need you to get in your car right now and meet me at our gas station in Hialeah."

She knew exactly where I was talking about. The gas stations was one block From Noelvis's house. She could tell it was urgent and didn't ask any questions.

"Just wait for me there, and If I'm not there in exactly forty-five minutes, you leave." I hung up without giving her a chance to reply.

When I got within a block of Noelvis's house, I called her once more so she could give me the all-clear to come over. When I got there, I quickly told her what was going on and that I needed to use her phone. I called my attorney Eddie Kay, who was representing me on the two state trafficking charges. When he answered the phone, I gave him the entire rundown of what was happening and told him to look into it.

"Caucci, if it's the FBI and it's a sealed indictment, the district attorney won't tell me shit until everyone is arrested. They keep it sealed."

"Eddie, I pay you too much goddamn money for you not to try. Just do me this fucking favor and call the DA right now, or the next time I see you I'll put my foot so far up your ass I'll be wearing you as a boot."

"Okay, calm down, whatever you want. I'll give it a shot, but I'm telling you now this is a waste of time. Sealed means sealed! Call me back in ten minutes."

That ten minutes seemed like an eternity. Exactly ten minutes later, I called him back. He picked up the phone, and I could immediately tell by the sound of his voice it wasn't going to be good.

"I have some bad news for you, Caucci. I spoke to the district attorney, Kendall Coffey, and he just couldn't stop himself from gloating. You, your father, and five others are being charged with trafficking cocaine and conspiracy to possess with intent to distribute fifty kilos of cocaine, along with other crimes."

I felt like I had just been sentenced to death.

"As your attorney, I must tell you to turn yourself in," he continued. "But your father and I go back a long way, so as a friend I'm telling you to pretend I'm not your attorney."

I looked at Noelvis and said, "It's the feds! I've got to out of the country quickly. I'm in some deep shit."

Her eyes filled with tears, and she looked at me as if she would never see me again. I gave her a big hug and reassured her that everything was going to be alright as long as she listened to exactly what I was about to say. She quickly regained her composure as I sat her down at the kitchen table. Noelvis's sister translated for her parents while they gathered around the table. I held both her hands, looked her in the eyes, and said, "Noelvis, listen to me very carefully. The feds will be here very soon, and when they are here, they'll try all kinds of things to make you talk. As soon as they get here and ask you where I am, you tell them, 'Probably at that bitch Smadar's house. He's been cheating on me with her for a while. She lives somewhere in North Miami Beach off Miami Gardens Drive right behind a Walgreens pharmacy.'"

Noelvis pulled her hands away from mine. "No way, Anthony! I won't tell them anything. I will not talk to the feds. I will NEVER tell them anything about you."

I knew she meant well, but she didn't have a clue what I had in mind. I grabbed her hands again and said, "Noelvis, look me in the eyes. You gotta trust me on this one. The longer you talk to them, the longer they'll stay here, and that'll buy me some time. Trust me…they already know everything about you and Smadar, and they already know where she lives. So as soon as you lie to them, they'll think you're hiding something. We want them to think you're willing to cooperate. Be very sincere. Invite them into your house and act like you want a little revenge on me. Be as helpful as you possibly can while stalling them as long as possible. There's nothing you can say to them that will hurt me, Noelvis. This is why I have always kept my business far away from you. If you do this, you'll be helping me a lot."

"Okay, Anthony I will do my best."

"Once I leave the country, I promise to get in touch with you through Fatman."

When we were done, I gave her and her whole family a hug. Noelvis began to cry and said, "Please don't leave yet, just a couple more minutes." She wouldn't let me out of her arms. I looked over at her father and gave him a signal, letting him know I needed some help with her. He immediately came over and wrapped his arms around her and tried to comfort her so I could leave.

The clock was ticking...I had called my dad's house from a landline, so the feds would trace it back to the apartment on Brickell Avenue. When they did, they'd find fifty kilos of coke, and I'd be finished for good. I had a very difficult decision to make, very quickly. I could either leave town immediately and start to make plans to leave the country, or I could go back to the condo and try to retrieve the coke before the feds got there. If I got caught, I'd be facing a life sentence. I already had two state cases against me and one federal indictment for fifty kilos. If they caught me with another fifty kilos, I would be behind bars until I died, then come back and do another twenty years. But I knew the stand-up thing to do was try to beat the feds to the apartment and get the coke before they did. I couldn't leave close to a million dollars' worth of cocaine behind to get confiscated by the feds. Especially since it didn't belong to me.

My adrenaline was on overdrive, and I felt sick to my stomach. I went to the gas station where Smadar was waiting for me and told her what had happened. I asked Smadar to do the exact same thing I asked Noelvis to do. "Tell the feds I am probably at that bitch Noelvis's house in Miami. Some fucking Cuban chick he's been cheating on me with behind my back."

"Got it, done!"

"Do your best to make it look like you're cooperating with them...try to buy me some time."

"I will do my best."

"You know I have to leave the country...are you coming or staying behind?"

"Don't be ridiculous. Of course I'm coming with you."

"Okay, go home, and I'll get a message to you through Fatman. Act like everything's normal. Park my truck far away from your house and have someone pick you up to take you home."

I gave her a hug and a kiss and told her that I would see her soon. Then we switched cars because I knew they'd be looking for my Gold Toyota Four Runner. I knew that my freedom could end any second, so I had to think clearly and strategically. By this time, the feds were still waiting for me at my dad's house, and I assumed they didn't have a clue I was on to them. But it was only a matter of time, so I decided to call my dad's house to see if I could pull one over on feds. When I called, an agent answered the phone.

"Hello?"

"Hello, Officer, this is Caucci. I'm sorry...what's your name?"

"Officer Rodriguez"

"Officer Rodriguez, got it. Look, I'm on my way, and I'm moving as fast as I can. Please don't leave until I get there. My dad has some valuables in his apartment, and I don't want the house left unoccupied. There're a few slime balls in that building, and I'm sure they'll rob him if they see you take my dad away. But I'm still about thirty minutes out, the traffic's a bitch. Do you think you can wait for me? You'd really be helping me out here."

"Okay, but thirty minutes is as long as we can wait. We don't want to miss your dad's bond hearing."

"Ahhh, you guys are awesome. I'll be there in thirty minutes or less. See you soon."

I got back on I-95 and headed back south toward the condo. I had to drive very carefully—one mistake I'd be done. As I got closer to the condo, I started to think of where I was going to be in the next twenty-four hours. Would I be free, or would I be behind bars?

My phone rang. It was the feds, calling from my dad's house. Exactly thirty minutes had passed, and I was minutes away from the condo in Miami.

"Hello?"

"Hello, Anthony, this is Officer Rodriguez with the Hallandale police."

I thought, "I hope your mouth fills up with hemorrhoids, you lying prick." But out loud I said, "Hello, Officer Rodriguez. Sorry, the traffic is bumper to bumper, and I'm still twenty minutes away. My mother lives two minutes away. I just called her, and she said she's on the way to meet you so she can secure the house."

"What? We've been waiting here for over an hour. I wish you would have told us that a long time ago. What a waste of time."

"Thank you so much for your patience, Officer, but I did my very best to get there on time. You said you wanted to get my dad in front of the judge on time, so I thought this would better for all of us, don't you think? Anyway, what's the difference, my mother or me? We're just securing the house."

I hung up and drove the last few minutes to my condo. When I pulled into the circular driveway, I was driving Smadar's black Toyota Celica. I parked in front of the building at the valet stand, got out of the car as fast as I could, ran to the back of the car, opened the trunk, and took off running toward the building. The valet guy yelled, "Hey, I need your keys!"

"Sorry, but no time to park! I'm gonna miss my plane...I'll be back in five minutes!" I bolted through the doors and into the lobby. I got in the elevator, pressed the button for the eleventh floor, and prayed to God the feds weren't waiting to ambush me when the doors open. I did everything I could to stay as calm as possible as I watched the floors count up on the elevator control panel: eight...nine...ten...eleven.

DING!

When the elevator doors opened, nobody was there. I couldn't believe it. I ran as fast as I could to condo and said a quick prayer while my hands were shaking. "Please, God, don't let there be feds on the other side of this door."

I slowly put the key in, turned it ever so gently, and cracked the door open.

"Holy shit!"

33 | Orlando Police, Open the Door!

I couldn't believe it. The condo was empty. No feds.

I quickly grabbed the two suitcases full of coke and ran down the hallway to the closest fire exit. I kicked the door open and ran down eleven flights of stairs with 110 pounds of cocaine. By the time I got to the bottom of the stair well, I was completely exhausted and soaking wet with sweat. As I ran through the lobby toward my car, everyone was staring at me. It was obvious I had to either get somewhere real fast or I was in some deep shit.

I threw the suitcases in the trunk of the car and drove away at a normal speed. I couldn't believe I'd gotten away again. I wasn't sure how or why, but I did.

Then, when I was about one block away and when I thought I was in the clear, I saw an entourage of police cars with their lights flashing headed straight toward me. "Oh shit...I'm finished," I thought.

I tried to remain calm and kept driving toward them. As they got closer, I kept my eyes on the road and did my best to act like everything was normal. There were four Miami police cars escorting two black federal undercover cars. I approached a stop sign and came to a complete stop, then kept going toward them. When they drove by me, I was able to see "FBI" and "DEA" written in big gold letters on their hats.

After they passed me, I looked at my rearview mirror to see if they had recognized me. Immediately, every cop car put their brake lights on and stopped.

"Fuck, they saw me!"

But then they took off again…they had to stop at the fuckin stop sign. It was unbelievable. I literally drove right by them. I kept my eye on the rearview mirror and saw them pull into the condo valet.

Once again, I had gotten away by the hairs on my ass. That was the third time in less than twenty-four hours I had slipped through their fingers. I quickly pulled into a busy Publix parking lot because I figured being parked was safer than the streets. I got out of the car and walked to a pay phone so I could let Carlos know I had his fifty kilos on me. When he got on the phone, I said, "Hey, brother, no time to bullshit…the weather is very bad here. I need to see someone quickly so I can get you your things back."

He remained silent for a few seconds. He wasn't sure if I had already gotten busted and was trying to set him up. In that scenario, if someone got busted, they would usually snitch. But he also knew that I hadn't ratted when I'd gotten busted as a teenager. On top of that, he knew my family and some of my high-ranking Mob friends.

"Carlos, you have sixty seconds to make a decision or I'm leaving these things in the Dumpster behind Publix."

"Okay, kid, I'll call you back in two minutes, just sit tight."

He called me back right away and said, "Hey, kid, meet my cousin at the Miami Subs one block from where you are. He'll be there in twenty minutes."

"Which fucking cousin? You have about thirty of them."

"The one with the black hair and the white stripe down the middle. The Skunk."

"Okay, I'll be there, and sorry about the headache."

"No problem, you did the right thing, kid."

"I'll call you later from another pay phone."

"Okay, be careful and take care of yourself, my friend. If you need anything, you just call me okay?"

"Thank you. Talk to you soon."

I met the Skunk at the Miami Subs, gave him the two suitcases, and got the hell out of there. I destroyed my cell phone and threw it in a canal. I should've done it sooner but…whaddya gonna do? Thank God they didn't have GPS tracking on the phones back then.

I drove to the nearest sleazy sex motel on Southwest 8th street, also known as Calle Ocho or Little Havana. It was the perfect place to hide. They only took cash, never asked any questions, and I was able to park my car in a private area. Most people went to these motels to cheat on their spouses or spend a few hours with a prostitute. They were very discreet.

Once I got into my room, I jumped into the heart-shaped Jacuzzi surrounded by mirrors, turned on the TV, and tried to unwind. As I was watching TV, the local news came on. Rick Sanchez, a famous news anchor in Miami, was telling the story about Hemmingway's and how I was still wanted by the feds. They showed pictures of the restaurant and mentioned all the names in the indictment except Mario Adamo. So I knew he had to be the rat.

My picture was briefly shown on the television, but I wasn't too worried because those hotels were run by old-school Cubans and they're very tight-lipped. With all of the illegal activity that went on there, they'd never call the police.

After a couple hours in the hot bath, I was able to clear my mind and began to plan my exit strategy. Since there was no way in hell I was going to turn myself in, I knew I had to leave the country. I knew the feds would do everything in their power to get me to rat on my friends, including making up disgusting lies about me. That's what they do—they're one giant, corrupt organization that constantly broke the law and nobody ever got punished for it. Meanwhile, everyday Americans had to watch every single move they made. When was the last time anyone in our government was held accountable for breaking the law? They were the true untouchables and made the Mafia look like choir boys.

With two pending state trafficking charges, a new federal case, and my prior conviction, it would be strike three for me. I was looking at a life sentence. I needed a completely new identity and a fake passport to get out of the country, along with a driver's license, Social Security number, and birth certificate. I had to assume the identity of real person with a clean record. The last thing I needed was to get stopped by a cop for some bullshit traffic check and find out my fake identity had arrest warrants.

For the time being, however, all I had to do was lay low for a week or two until the shit blew over a little. I had to make sure that every single move I made was thought out way in advance. There were only a couple of people I could trust, but calling them could have cost me my freedom so I had to be extra cautious.

At that time in my life, Fatman and I had become very close friends. I didn't believe in some of the things he did—like flaunting his money and sleeping with people's wives and girlfriends—but we remained close friends. In the Italian code of honor, you never even look at another man's wife or ex-wife the wrong way, because that alone might get you clipped. But Fatman was Cuban and did not live by this code. He had his own code and did whatever the hell he wanted.

After sitting in that sleazy hotel for a few hours, my nerves calmed and I got hungry. Obviously there wasn't any room service, so I walked to a quiet Cuban cafe just a block away. After a quick meal in a corner booth, I walked to a pay phone just a few blocks away from the hotel to call Fatman and Carlos.

I could tell Fatman was relieved to hear my voice and obviously knew what had happened. I put on a slight hillbilly accent and changed my name to throw off the feds.

"Hey der, partner, what you up to?"

"Not much, just sitting here with my wife watching a movie. Trying to figure out the ending."

"That sounds mighty fun. Tell your pretty little lady that Dave says hello."

"I'll be sure to do that."

"Listen, I'm over here at that good old Espanola restaurant you took me to one time. Why don't you come on down here and let me buy you some grub? Then we can discuss our plans for our next fishing trip."

"Sounds good, I'll meet you there at six o'clock tonight my time." When he used "my time," it meant to add three hours. If he'd said "your time," it would have meant subtract three hours.

"Sounds mighty fine, see you at six, partner."

When nine o'clock came around, I waited across the street in a phone booth until he arrived. He sat at the bar so I could easily see him through the glass. I called the restaurant and asked to speak with the gentleman wearing the blue shirt who was sitting at the bar.

"Hello?"

"Hey, pal, I'm across the street looking right at you. Meet me at the gas station on the southwest corner, two blocks west. It's a Shell."

"Okay, I'll be there in five minutes."

When he arrived at the gas station, I could tell he was a little nervous. It was possible the feds were watching him too.

"Where to, kiddo?"

"I'm staying right down the street at one of those fuck motels."

"That's a great idea."

As we drove toward the hotel, I gave him the rundown. Most people wouldn't go near you when the feds were on you, but Fatman was solid. He knew me pretty well and was pretty sure I wouldn't talk if I got busted. There was a time when Fatman's dad was doing a ten-year sentence in Miami Federal Correctional Center at the same time Jerry Chilli, the Bonanno capo, was doing fifteen years in the same prison. I'd made the introduction and that was that. Everybody knew everybody, and nobody ratted. That's the way it was back then, at least for some people.

"I need to get the fuck out of the country quickly," I said.

"Yes, you do! I think you should go to Cuba. There is no extradition, and you'll live like a king with the money you have saved. I have a bunch of family over there."

"Sounds good to me, but I need a passport."

"Hmmm…Call Carlos in Columbia, he knows quite a few people in Immigration and Customs. He'll be able to get you a real passport right out of the immigration office. One you'll be able to travel on easily. Once it's ready, I'll pick it up for you."

"Okay, I'll give Carlos a call, but in the meantime, do me a favor and please go see Noelvis and Smadar and let them know I'm okay and will contact them soon. I'm sure the feds have already been to both of their houses by now and would love to hear what they had to say."

"You got it, I'll go see them, and I'll meet you back here at the hotel on Friday night at 8 p.m. If you get ahold of Carlos tonight, I should have your passport with me. But before we can do anything, we need to go get you a passport picture."

"Okay, let's do that now and get this ball rolling, and thank you for all your help, my friend. I owe you one,"

"My pleasure, and you owe me more than one."

We did everything we needed to do that night, and Fatman returned Friday night at 8 p.m. on the dot. He handed me an envelope with a brand-new US passport under the name Antonio Zambrana, along with all the other documents I needed to travel safely. Then he said, "This passport is so good, you come back into the United States and clear customs without a problem."

"That's great…but you're out of your fucking mind if you think I'm gonna put my balls on the line again. There's no way. I'm not taking that chance."

"Look, I got some bad news. I spoke to some people in Cuba, and Cuba's not a good idea right now. Castro is too unpredictable."

"So now what?"

"Mexico. It's close by, and getting you Mexican citizenship will be simple."

"Okay, Mexico it is, but in the meantime I'm going to Orlando for a few weeks before I leave. I'm gonna stay in Disney World. There are hundreds of thousands of people in Disney, so I'll blend the right the fuck in."

"That's a great idea! How you gonna get there?"

"Boxer George said he'll take me."

"Okay good…I saw Noelvis and Smadar. The feds went by both their houses. They went easy on Noelvis, but Smadar made them wait outside her house for an hour while she took a shower and got dressed."

"That's pretty fuckin' funny."

"They tried to scare her by saying if she doesn't tell them where you are, she will be charged with aiding and abetting. Then in the same sentence they said, 'We have evidence that can prove you know where he's hiding.' So Smadar said, 'If you have evidence that can prove I know where he is, then show it to me and I'll take you right to him, because that's news to me.' She really stuck it up their asses."

"Wow, that girl's got some balls."

"The heat's gonna be on her for a little while, so go to Orlando and give me a call when you get there."

Fatman handed me $20,000 in cash and said, "Here's a little gift from Carlos," then he gave me a big hug and said, "I'm gonna miss you and be careful, brother."

A few days later, Boxer George picked me up at the hotel and we headed for Disney World. He had two girls in the car with him—one of them was the Colombian girl named Claudia I was on the phone with just before my dad got arrested. As we drove, I took a good look at the scenery, as I knew my days in the good old US of A were numbered.

When we arrived in Orlando, we got a top-notch hotel room very close to Disney World. I wanted to be far away from any loudmouth scumbags who could cause trouble. It was pretty late when we arrived so we decided to stay in the room. We watched a little TV, ordered a pizza, and I decided to take a long, hot shower with the lights out so I could relax.

While I was in the shower thanking Jesus for the miracles he'd performed for me over the last week, George was having a little fun with the girls, just goofing around and being silly. He got the bright idea to start tickling one of them. She started laughing and screaming "Stop!" at the top of her lungs. She screamed so loud I had to get out of the shower and tell them to shut the fuck up.

"What the fuck are you doing, George? We're in a five-star hotel, and you're acting like a goddamn animal. People come here to relax with their kids, and it sounds like someone's getting raped. Cut the fucking shit!"

"My bad, Caucci, sorry."

I got back into the shower, but about fifteen minutes later I heard very loud pounding. I quickly grabbed my towel, wrapped it around my waist, and was getting ready to throw George a beating. I opened the bathroom door and saw George and the two girls sitting on the bed with terrified looks on their faces. Before I could get a word out, I heard the pounding again. It was coming from our room door.

BANG! BANG! BANG!

"Orlando police! Open the door!"

34 | Police with Machine Guns

"Oh shit, they found me," I thought.

I looked at everyone in the room and whispered, "Just relax and act normal." I opened the door with the towel around my waist and greeted the officers with big, welcoming smile. "Good evening, officers, what can I do for you?"

"We received a call about a girl screaming," one of the cops replied.

I rolled my eyes, shook my head, and pointed to George. "This fucking clown starts play-wrestling with the girls on the bed and then decides to tickle them. Common sense would've told him to stop once she started screaming, but look at that face. He don't look too bright, does he? He's been punched in the head one too many times and was about to get one more from me right before you guys knocked on the door."

"Oh, I see."

One of the officers asked the girls if everything was okay and they replied yes. Then they asked me and George for our drivers' licenses. George handed his over. But mine was still in the car with the luggage, so I told the officer that all I had was my passport.

"Okay, let me have your passport," he replied sternly.

I had a fake passport with someone else's name on it and hoped he wasn't going to ask for the matching address. I'd be screwed. I didn't have the time to memorize it. One of the cops took our IDs and went back to the squad car to check them out. While he was gone, two other police officers stood by the door waiting. I started up a conversation with the officers and tried to remain calm, but inside I was praying that I didn't hear something over the radio telling the offices to arrest me.

After about five minutes, the first officer returned with our IDs and said, "Now you guys make sure you keep the noise down and have a good night."

When they shut the door, I dived onto the bed with my face in the pillow, staring into darkness in disbelief. I had slipped through their hands again. Then it dawned on me…the passport was *really* legit.

I got back into the shower, shut the lights out, sat down, and thought about how many times I'd gotten away by the hair on my ass. First the Hollywood police were waiting for me in front of my apartment, then they came to the Kung Fu school, then the feds saw me and George leaving my dad's house just days before they raided his house and arrested him, then I escaped with the two suitcases full of coke leaving the condo, and now I had gotten away again. It was a fucking miracle. I got away five times. What are the chances that one man has this much luck, or was I being protected somehow?

I stayed in Disney World for a few weeks, then headed to Mexico. Before I left for Mexico, I called my friend Anthony "Natty" Passaro. He'd been indicted with Gerry Chilli for a credit card scam. I asked, "Hey, Nat, you know a guy by the name of Mario Adamo?"

"Mario Fucking Adamo! Forget about it…he's a fucking rat! Caucci, stay the fuck away from him. He's bad news and talks to bad people. That prick got busted in Italy but had so much dirt on friends of ours that the U.S. government stepped in and made a deal with the Italian government to release him. The feds gave him a special snitch visa so he could stay in the U.S. as an undercover informant. This cocksucker has been working for the feds for years and has put over one hundred friends of ours away from all different families. And on top of that, the cocksucker is getting paid hundreds of thousands of dollars to take people down."

"Okay, Natty, thanks for the info. That prick got me too! I'll talk to you soon, my friend."

"Take care, Caucci."

"You too, pal."

Getting into Mexico was a breeze. A couple weeks after I was in Mexico, Smadar got on a plane and met me in Cancun. We stayed there for about six months, but it got really boring, really fast. On top of that, there wasn't a way for me to make any money, and my savings was going quickly. Fatman came to visit me about once a month and brought my money a little bit at a time, but I knew I needed a better plan.

I decided to leave Mexico and head to a country on the other side of the world. Even though I wasn't in the United States, I was always looking over my shoulder because Mexico was loaded with federal agents. So I decided to go to Hong Kong. At the time, Hong Kong was occupied by England (and would be until 1997, when it would be returned to mainland China). Since Hong Kong was under British law, if anything went south for me at least I wouldn't be treated like a POW.

I took a flight from Mexico that didn't connect through the United States. Instead, I went via Canada, and it took me thirty-five hours to get to Hong Kong. When we arrived at the Hong Kong International Airport, it was much different than any other airport I had ever seen. There were police with machine guns and K-9s sniffing around everywhere. The Hong Kong police looked like they meant business.

Once I cleared customs, I headed to Tsim Sha Tsui, a district in Kowloon, Hong Kong. It was an awesome experience. There were food vendors all over the streets, the city was lit up by electric business signs, and the pungent smell of foreign food was everywhere. There were dead pigs, ducks, and chickens hanging in the windows, usually surrounded by flies. The pollution was thick, the sidewalks were uneven, and it was very crowded. We walked until we found a hotel that looked decent and wasn't too expensive.

Once we got settled in Hong Kong, we decided to take the train into mainland China. I was hoping I could find some good martial arts people. However, since we stayed close to the border, I didn't find any. The only interesting thing we saw on the mainland were the restaurants. Outside the restaurants were cages of live animals that were on the menu. This included cats, dogs, monkeys, rats, squirrels, and all kinds of animals that most people wouldn't eat. I stuck to fish just to be safe.

When we returned to Hong Kong, we decided to change hotels as the one we were in was very close to a construction site and bars, so the noise was too much. We moved to Wan Chai, a district on Hong Kong Island where the hotels were much cheaper. This area was not popular for tourists due to the heavy influence of the Triads (the Chinese Mob). There was a lot of prostitution, illegal gambling, and drugs in this area. But to me it all looked the same, so I didn't have a clue.

After about six months of living in Hong Kong, it got very old. The Hong Kong Chinese were very rude, and I was tired of the horrible smell coming from the tofu being cooked on the streets. Also, I couldn't find a way to make money. I only had enough money to last me a couple more years, so I needed to figure out my next move. I also knew Hong Kong would be handed back to mainland China soon.

One night, as Smadar and I were discussing what country we should go to next, we heard a heavy knock on the door.

BANG, BANG, BANG!

"Who is it?"

"Hong Kong Police!" a voice shouted through the door. "Open the door now!"

Smadar's eyes opened wide as she covered her mouth in disbelief.

"How the fuck did they find us?" I muttered.

She shook her head, completely dumbfounded. I gave her a reassuring look, but privately I thought my time was finally up. I opened the door to let them in and they pushed by me. While they were ransacking the room, the head officer asked for our passports and began to rudely interrogate me.

"Why are you staying in this hotel?" he demanded.

"Because it's cheap and comfortable. I was staying in Tsim cha Tsui, but it was too expensive."

After they tore the room apart, he handed us back our passports and apologized for the mess. Before they left, I asked, "What was that all about?"

"This hotel is known for drugs and prostitution," he said, pointing to Smadar, "so we thought she might have been a prostitute working for the Triads."

"She might as well be, she costs me a fortune."

The cops had a good laugh while Smadar gave me the finger. We shook hands and the police told us to be safe. I closed the door and sat for a moment and started to wonder if it was God getting me out of all these jams. If it was, I didn't know why, because I surely didn't deserve it.

I looked at Smadar and said, "I've got an excellent idea. I know where we're going next."

"Good, I hate this shithole."

"We're leaving the county tomorrow so pack your bags."

35 | Kidnapped, Tortured, and Killed

We were heading back to Taiwan. I had been there once before, at the age of twenty, just after I got out of prison. I had studied Wing Chun Kung Fu with Grand Master Lo Man Kam, the nephew of the late Grand Master Yip or Ip Man, Bruce Lee's teacher. Taiwan was a great place to hide and was not governed by mainland China. It was the Republic of China, which had a democratic government.

On my first trip to Taiwan, I had learned that many of the foreign students learning Wing Chun were also teaching English for a living while they stayed in Taiwan. They were making between $40 and $50 per hour just sitting in a coffee shop shooting the shit with a Taiwanese so they could practice their English. I was also hoping I would be able to establish some connections in the government through Mr. Casey's Martial Arts Instructors, who were still alive. I had studied with Grand Master Lo Man Kam, but one of Mr. Casey's other instructors was the famous Shen Mou Hui, chief instructor for the Taiwan Central Police. Mr. Shen taught Chin-Na (Joint Locking), and I was hoping I to somehow contact him.

Entering Taiwan was simple, but every time I had to go through immigration with that fake passport, it probably took a couple years off my life. When we arrived, we immediately got an apartment and settled in. I easily made a couple of Chinese friends and started teaching English. All I had to do was put an ad in the Chinese English newspaper, and I could teach as many hours as I wanted.

For her part, Smadar was quite pretty and had long, curly brown hair, something the Chinese rarely saw. So she signed up with a fashion modeling agency and made a lot of money. One day after she finished a photo shoot, her agent invited us, along with all the other models, to a party at a night club. As I was sitting at the table with Smadar, I couldn't help but notice two flamboyant gays staring and pointing at me while speaking in Chinese. I didn't have a clue what they were saying and honestly didn't give a shit. The people of Taiwan were great, and I knew they were harmless and didn't mean any disrespect. Then Smadar's agent walked over to me and asked in Chinglish if I had ever done any modeling.

"Not me, I'm not the modeling type."

He pointed at the two queers and said, "Those guys think your face will be a perfect match for a new beer campaign they are launching soon, here in Taiwan."

"What do you mean my face and what about beer?"

"They wanna put your face on a beer bottle."

"Why the hell do they want MY face on a beer bottle?"

"They said you've got the look they've been searching for."

"Oh really...and how much are they paying?"

"Five thousand U.S. dollars."

"Hmm. Not too bad. Do I have to smile?"

"No. No. No. Just the opposite, they want a blank stare with no emotion."

"Piece of cake!"

"Only half your face will be shown, and the other half will be a shadow."

It just sounded better and better. "Where's this beer going to be sold?"

"Only here in Taiwan."

"Okay, I'll give it a shot."

I got the details and went to my first modeling shoot in a huge warehouse packed with people. Most of them were flamboyant queers and wore very colorful silk scarves, dark oversized sunglasses, expensive suits, and walked with a limp wrist and a twist of the hips. But they were extremely friendly and had that "I don't give a fuck what you think of me" attitude, which I respected. When I arrived, I received a very warm welcome and even some applause. Most of the guests surrounded me and took a very close look at me, up and down like I was a piece of meat on sale.

"Oh, you so strong...American man," one said in Chinglish.

"Yeah, yeah, yeah...let's get this show on the road."

The director, who spoke perfect English, told me to go in the bathroom and take my clothes off. "Take my clothes off? What the fuck for? I thought this was a head shot?"

"Oh, must have been a misunderstanding, We need pictures for the newspaper promotions, and need full body shot."

"Okay, no problem."

I went to the bathroom, stripped down to my underwear, and did some pushups to get all pumped up. I was in great shape at the time; I was lean with a solid six-pack, so I didn't have any problem doing it. When I came out of the bathroom, they looked at me like they had never seen a man in his underwear before. As they were bickering, they keep pointing at my "schlong." I didn't have a clue what the hell they were saying, but I had a bad feeling. Then the director walked over and said, "Ohh wow, Mr. Anthony, you're in very good shape. But can you please take off your underwear too? We need a picture of you with nothing on."

"You're fucking with me, right? How the hell you gonna put that in the newspaper?"

"Oh, don't worry, it very easy…you just do some poses and we'll shoot at an angle so your big Italian part is not exposed."

"Poses? Do I look like someone who poses? I was told you needed me for a single head shot and I didn't have to smile."

He smiled, put his hands together, and bowed. "So sorry for the miscommunication."

The whole situation was kinda funny, and I would've walked out had it not been for Smadar's modeling agency making the connection. They would've lost face and been very embarrassed, which is one thing you never want to do to the Chinese. It would have cost Smadar her modeling contract, so I agreed.

My gut was telling me that these guys were having a lot of fun and using the photo shoot to get a peek at me naked, but I went back to the bathroom with the baby oil they gave me, got myself all oiled up, and did a couple more pushups. I couldn't believe I was doing this—none of my friends would believe it. I knew I'd remember this for the rest of my life.

When I was all pumped up (everywhere), I opened the door buck-ass naked and walked to the director and his crew and said, "I hope your lens is big enough." It was dead silent for a few seconds as everyone stared at me. Then they began to whisper amongst themselves and one of them loudly said, "Oh…you have so big one," then someone else said, "Itaran Stallion," and on and on it went.

After everything settled down, they took a few head shots of me and developed the one they wanted to use right on the spot. Then they took the picture, taped it to an empty bottle, and made a prototype bottle. The photographer said, "Take this bottle, balance it on the palm of your hand, and pose." So I took the bottle and performed a series of Shaolin Kung Fu stances. They loved it.

A few days later, my Chinese friend Jacky called me. "Tony! You not gonna believe this, you in the Chinese newspaper, the entire two page spread is for the beer advertisement!" So I ran down to the store and bought a paper. I couldn't believe my eyes. I had to admit they did a damn good job of making it look classy. Within a few weeks, almost everywhere I went, people recognized me from the beer bottle. People were constantly stopping and asking me to take pictures with them. I was starting to become somewhat of a celebrity, and for the first time in years I had a good feeling. I thought I could make some decent money modeling.

After that first photo shoot, I did a few TV commercials. It was quite funny, all I had to do was move my lips and say whatever I wanted about the product, and they would do a voiceover in Chinese. For the first time since I left Miami, I was finally making me decent money. Then one day I got a call from the agent who represented the beer company. They asked if I would attend a promotional party at one of Taiwan's biggest night-clubs because they were going to officially launch the beer. They offered me $5,000 just to show up and said the party would take place in about a month. That sounded great to me, so I agreed.

In the meantime, I needed to fix my visa because I was in Taiwan ille-gally. I had entered on a visitor's visa and was only allowed to stay for sixty days at a time. You could leave the country twice and get an additional sixty days each time, allowing you to stay for a maximum of a six months. After that, they wouldn't let you back in—and getting deported back to the U.S. was not an option.

So I contacted one of my martial arts instructors, Shen Mou Hui— who instructed the police—and told to him I accidentally overstayed my visa. He made a couple of phone calls and, badda bing, just like that he got it all cleared up. All I had to do was go down to the police station, sign some papers, leave the country for a few days, and then re-enter. My plan was to get a work visa through the modeling agency that connected me with the beer company once I re-entered.

I went back to Hong Kong for a few days and picked up my new visa at the Taiwan embassy. When I returned to Taiwan, and while I was going through immigration, things were taking a little longer than usual. During my two years on the run, I'd been through immigration in Mexico, Hong Kong, Thailand, Macau, China, and the Philippines, so I was pretty familiar with how long it took to clear immigration. As I was stood there patiently, trying not to look nervous, the lady at the immigration counter kept plugging away at her computer. After three or four minutes of her fucking around, I said to her impatiently, "Excuse me, but how much longer is this going to take?"

She immediately took a red pen and wrote something down and said, "Welcome back and enjoy your stay."

I knew something wasn't right. It took way too long and that red pen...what the hell was that all about? When I got home, I told Smadar what had happened at the airport.

"Ehh...you're just paranoid," she said.

But I was convinced something wasn't right.

That night, Smadar and I went out to celebrate me being legal in the country and all the good things that were happening. After dinner, we decided to head back to our apartment on our scooter, with me driving and Smadar on the back. On the way home, I was apparently in the wrong lane and a taxi driver literally tried to run us off the road. He rammed his car into our scooter, and we almost crashed.

When I got to the stop light, I kicked the side of his car and raised my middle finger in the international fuck-you sign. Then this prick tried to run us over. So with a wave of my hand I motioned him to follow me. I pulled into the parking lot of 7-11 and got off the scooter. He got out of his taxi quickly and started to make his way toward me. When we got face to face, we both were cursing at each other in different languages, but eventually I got tired and just give him the finger and began to walk away. As soon as I turned my back on him, the cocksucker punched me in the back of the head. I was so pissed off, I barely felt it. Without turning around to face him, I looked at Smadar and asked, "Did this motherfucker just punch me?" She nodded yes. I slowly turned around and looked at him for a second and thought, "If I punch this guy, I might kill him."

Instead, I thought I'd get creative so I kicked the fucker right upside his head. Not as hard as I could have, but hard enough to let him know not to fuck with me. It took him a second to figure out where he was and what had just happened, but then he ran back to his tax.

"Not so tough now, you slanty eyed chink!" I yelled.

I started to walk back toward Smadar, not realizing that he hadn't gotten in his taxi. Instead, he had opened the trunk and was getting something. Smadar yelled, "Hurry! Let's get the fuck out of here!"

I looked over my shoulder and saw the son of a bitch had pulled out a samurai sword and was coming back toward us. I jumped on the back of the scooter and yelled to Smadar, "Go go go!"

Her hands shook as she started the scooter back up. As we drove away, the taxi driver sprinted toward us, waving the sword. He was closing in on us, and I knew that with one swing of that sword I'd be fucked. The scooter finally started to gain some speed. He made one last attempt and threw the sword at me with all his strength, but thank God it fell short.

"We gotta get the fuck off the streets quickly or we're dead," I yelled.

There were two major taxi companies in Taiwan at the time, and both were run by the Taiwan Triads. One call on the radio from the taxi driver, and there would be a hundred taxis looking for us. We would've been kidnapped, tortured, and killed—and it wouldn't have even made the news.

Smadar quickly turned down an alley, parked the scooter in a crowd of other scooters, and we ran into a busy night market. After all, we all looked the same to them anyway. Go figure.

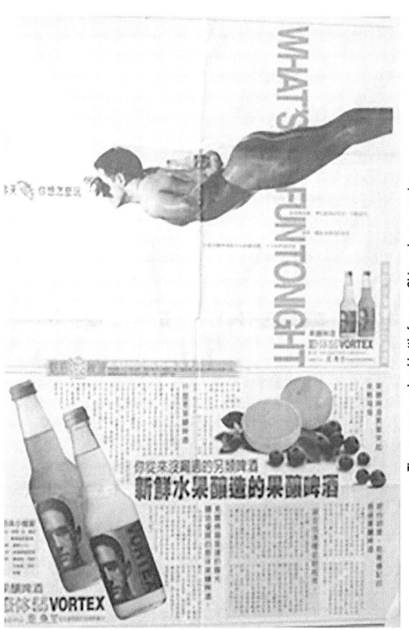

The newspaper ad and bottle from my Chinese beer campaign.

Mafia Made

36 | Two Police Officers Came Out of Nowhere

A few weeks later, it was time to go to the promotion party for the beer, which they were now calling Vortex. When we got there, the line was extremely long, and there was a shit-load of people inside. When we got to the front door, we were greeted like celebrities and got the full VIP treatment..

While Smadar and I were relaxing on a couch, drinking the grape-flavored Vortex beer, a girl named Rachel in the VIP area with us started up a conversation with Smadar. Rachel was dressed nicely and was quite pretty, but I think all the makeup she had on had a lot to do with that. She told us that she was also a model in Taiwan, but when she wanted to make a lot of money she went to Japan to strip. She said that on a bad night she would make $2,000 or $3,000, and she only had to take her top off. I wasn't sure if she was exaggerating, but she said there were only two strip clubs in all of Tokyo where only "foreign girls work" and that the Japanese love foreigners.

"You'd make a killing as a dancer," she told Smadar, "or if you don't want to dance, you could earn at least $1,000 a night as a hostess."

"A hostess?" Smadar replied.

"It's simple, all you gotta do is sit at the table and have some drinks and talk with the Japanese. And you don't even have to drink alcohol."

"Then why you here modeling if the money is so good in Japan?"

"Honestly, the drug scene is out of control in Tokyo. It's just like dancing in NY or Vegas. There are drugs everywhere, so I come to Taiwan when I need to dry out."

That caught my attention, so I asked Rachel, "What's the name of the club you worked at?"

"There are only two clubs, and only super-hot girls can work there. They're both in Roppongi. Seventh Heaven and Private Eye's. I work at Seventh Heaven, but Private Eye's is connected to a very popular hostess bar called One Eyed Jack."

"If I ever end up in Japan, I'll be sure to check it out," Smadar said.

After she named the clubs, I didn't think she was full of shit anymore. As the night went on, Smadar and I made some good contacts. I knew this was going to open a lot of doors for me. Drinking the grape-flavored beer with my face on the bottle, I thought, "How in God's name did I end up in this situation? I would have never thought in a million years I'd be sitting on the other side of the world, wanted by the FBI, drinking out of a beer bottle with my face on it. If my friends only knew..."

As for the beer, I wondered how much alcohol was actually in it because it tasted like Kool-Aid. The small print on the bottle was in Chinese, so that was no help. Then I got a shock of a lifetime. The only English on the bottle said: "FLORIDA DISTILLERS COMPANY, 222 Lake View Avenue, WEST PALM BEACH, Florida."

UUUHHH! What the fuck?! Not only was the beer bottled in the United States, it was bottled less than fifty miles from my house, where the FBI was looking for me. And just like that, it was all over. I leaned over to Smadar and whispered in her ear, "We have to get the fuck out of here right now."

"Why? What's wrong?"

I covered my mouth and said, "Read the bottle...closely."

Her eyes opened wide as she read the bottle, then we politely excused ourselves and went home.

"We got to get the fuck out of this country quickly," I said.

"Where we gonna go now?"

"How about Japan? All you have to do is sit at a table with a bunch of Japs, carry on a conversation, and get paid. It's a no-fucking-brainer. And to top it off, you don't even have to drink alcohol. Forget about it..."

She thought about it for thirty seconds, then started packing. My only concern was leaving the country. I remembered the immigration officer writing with her red pen the last time I entered. I had a feeling something wasn't right. So I came up with a plan just to be safe—and to make sure Smadar was safe too.

"Look, you stay behind until I arrive in Japan," I said. "If all goes smoothly, then you come. If it doesn't and I get caught, I don't want you with me. You could get charged with aiding and abetting. If I get caught, I want you to leave on your American passport and enter Israel with your Israeli passport. Once you're in Israel, throw away your American passport and get a new one at the embassy. Wait one month, then go back to Miami."

She looked at me like I had lost my mind, then rolled her eyes and said, "Okay, but I still think you're paranoid."

"I'm gonna buy a ticket to the United States, but will go via Japan for ten days. This way, if the Taiwanese grab me at immigration, it'll look like I'm going back to the United States. If they look through my passport, they'll see that I haven't been back to the United States for almost three years, and that might raise some questions."

"Anthony, I think you're going a little overboard with this!"

"How 'bout you just pack the fuckin' bags and let me think like a criminal, please? Or would you like to switch places with me, Ms. Fucking Smarty Pants?"

She gave me the middle finger, stuck her tongue out at me, and said, "Good, I'd rather be on a different plane than you anyway."

The next day I got my ticket, from Taiwan to Japan to the U.S. When It came time to leave, the closer I got to the airport, the faster my heart started to beat. I knew it could all be over in a matter of minutes. I gave Smadar a big hug and told her to say a prayer for me, but to please include Jesus just in case God was still pissed off at you Jews. That made her laugh. At the airport, I made sure she was far away from me before I went through immigration. I looked over my shoulder and saw her on the other side of a column, trying not to be noticed. She blew me a kiss, and I gave her a wink.

When I approach immigration, I remained calm and handed my passport to the guy behind the counter. He placed it down in front of him and began typing on his computer. Then he grabbed my passport, raised it in the air, and waved it back and forth like a flag. Two police officers came out of nowhere and grabbed me, one on each arm, and began to escort me down a long hallway. I discreetly looked over my shoulder to see if Smadar was okay, and there she was with same wide-eyed look on her face and her hand covering her mouth.

37 | A Story You'll Never Believe...

The two cops escorted me into a small room filled with police officers. Two carried machine guns, and another had a very nasty barking K-9 on a leash. There was a lot of commotion, but everyone was speaking Chinese so I was in the dark. As they were yelling back and forth, I just stood there very patiently trying not to look worried. They gave me a thorough pat-down, then took my bag and emptied it on a table. They examined my passport under a florescent light. I assumed they were trying to figure out if it was fake. Then they tried peel away the laminated portion that covered my picture. As they were literally picking apart my passport, I decided to jump in and say something. I thought that if I just stood there and let them do whatever they wanted, I would look guilty. "What the fuck are you doing?" I said to the nearest police officer. "You're gonna ruin my passport! Your tampering with property that belongs to the United States government! So quit fucking with it, or I won't be able to travel on it."

He slammed it on the table and said, "Why have you stayed here so long without going back to the U.S.?"

I put my hands on his desk, leaned toward him, looked him dead in his eyes, and said "You listen to me very fucking carefully...I'm an American citizen and YOU have no right treating me like I'm some washed up refuge from mainland China! I had no intentions of staying here in this shit-hole country for such a long time, but unfortunately a few things happened that were out of my control."

"Explain yourself!"

"At first I was just on vacation. I went sight-seeing and studied a little kung fu. But then I ran out of money and overstayed my visa. But while I was here illegally, I fell in love with a Chinese girl named Mei Ling"—I got that name from a Bruce Lee movie, It just popped into my head—"and I decided to fix my visa so I could be here legally because we talked about getting married. So I had a friend of mine take me down to the police station and help me fix my visa status. I left the country, went to Hong Kong, and came back on a new visa. When I returned, Mei Ling left me and stole all my money. She scammed me from the very beginning. Then I had to call my parents so they could send me some money so I could leave the country and go home."

"How did you get another visa after overstaying for such a long time? This is not possible! You're lying!" he shouted and slammed his fist on the desk.

I yelled right back at his ass: "I'll say it one last time just in case you're a little slow. I had a friend take me to the police station and he worked out all the details. I don't know how he did it, but he did it quite easily."

"No way! Impossible! I don't believe you! What are you doing in Taiwan and what country are you from?"

I threw my hands in the air as if to surrender, lowered my head in defeat, and said "Okay, okay, I give up, you caught me."

He leaned back in his chair, folded his arms, and looked at the other officers as if he was saying, "See, that's how it's done."

They all remained silent and waited for me to speak.

"The truth is, I'm from Africa...I'm a white Negro. It's a very rare condition...there's only one in every ten million."

"You think this is joke? You will sit in Taiwan prison for long time until we find out where you're from. And we can be very slow in this shit-hole country, Mr. Antonio."

"Tell me, Mr. Chinaman, where the fuck do you think I'm from?"

"I don't know, but I'm going to find out!"

The situation didn't look good, and I figured I was finished. All they had to do was call Interpol or the U.S. Consulate and badda bing—DONE! My heart was pounding and my adrenaline was maxed out, but I was doing everything I could not to shake or look nervous in any way. I said a quick prayer in my head: "Jesus, I know you're busy, but I could really use another miracle here."

Then the strangest thing happened: immediately, the perfect strategy was planted in my head. I was going to call their bluff. I pretended to be even angrier and yelled to the room full of police officers, "If I'm under arrest, I demand to speak to someone from the U.S. embassy right now! Or put me on the next plane back to the United States! I already have a fucking ticket paid for."

Now that got their attention. Suddenly his demeanor changed, and he began to speak to me in a calmer tone.

"Why are you going to Japan for ten days and not back to U.S. now? It's been two years since you have gone back to U.S.A."

"You are correct, but I have been to Hong Kong, China, Philippines, Thailand, Macau, and Taiwan. So before I go back home, I wanted to see Japan. Look in my bag over there on the table. In the front zipper you'll see that I have plenty of money. Like I said before, my parents had to send it to me."

With a nod, he commanded the other officers to search my bag. As they were going through my fanny pack and pouring all my shit on the table, a business card fell out. I had no idea it was in there and didn't know who it belonged too. The card was white with blue Chinese writing on it, and in the center of the card was the Taiwan National Police Logo. Their eyes opened so wide the fucking slants disappeared. As they passed the card around, I could hear them whispering the name, "Shen Mou-hui... Shen Mou-Hui."

The atmosphere in the room changed. They seemed to be a little nervous.

"Please tell me, where did you get this card from, Mr. Anthony?"

"I got it from Mr. Shen. He's one of my kung fu teachers. He teaches me Chin-Na."

They were completely shocked and embarrassed. "He is our teacher too. He teaches all of us every few months."

"Mr. Shen was the one who took me to the police station to help straighten out my visa," I said.

"Now it all makes sense...Please forgive us...We thought you were somebody else."

"Who in the world did you think I was?"

"There are a few Americans here in Taiwan who are fugitives and teach English for a living."

"No way…fugitive…here in Taiwan? Why would anyone want to come here as a fugitive?"

"Many Americans come here when they are running from police."

"Well, that's not very smart. Taiwan and America are good allies. They should go to China if they really want to hide."

"We arrested a man who was wanted for murder in the U.S.A. He was teaching English in kindergarten."

"Are you serious? Well, thank God you got him."

The tension in the air was gone. The lead officer asked, "Do you mind if I call Mr. Shen to verify your story?"

"Please go ahead. That's a great idea. Tell him I said hello."

As one of the officers was on the phone, I asked the others to show me some of the Chin-Na techniques they had learned from Mr. Shen. Their faces turn red with embarrassment and they couldn't even look me in the eyes. I knew they were probably not very skillful, but I was just trying to get them to see me as fellow student and not someone being detained.

"Come on guys, show me something."

"Don't remember much, only practice a couple of times a year."

"Okay, then give me your hand, I promise I won't hurt you. Plus you all have guns and a dog."

Hesitantly, one put his hand out. I gently showed him some basic joint locks, and then let him do some on me. I couldn't believe was happening…fifteen minutes earlier, I was doomed and now I was practicing kung fu with the police.

When the officer hung up with Master Shen, he gave the thumbs up and said, "Everything is A-okay! You are free to go, but you need to hurry, your plane is leaving soon and you haven't cleared customs yet, so we must go now."

They quickly photocopied my passport and asked me to place my thumb on a scanner so they could take my fingerprint. "This is just procedure, must do," one said. Then they gave me a ride on their golf cart and rushed me through customs and immigration. They radioed the plane and told them to wait for me and escorted me all the way to the front door of the plane. They shook my hand, apologized, and bowed a number of times.

When I was on the airplane, all I could think of was them taking my fingerprints and copying my passport. It was a four-hour flight to Japan, which gave them plenty of time to check me out. So once again, I was a nervous wreck.

I had no idea what had happened to Smadar—I figured she probably thought I was finished and was crying at the house. I felt terrible for all I had put her through. As I sat on the plane, I wondered, "How do I keep getting away like this? It just doesn't make sense. Once or twice I'll call luck, but this is about the seventh time I've slipped through the fingers of the law." I didn't deserve to be spared, but I wasn't complaining. I couldn't help to wonder what supernatural power was helping me.

The next four hours before we landed were torture. I didn't think there was any way in the world I could get away with it any longer. I knew my time was up, and the feds would be waiting for me in Japan. So even though I hated alcohol, I decided to have a few glasses of red wine so when the show ended, at least I'd be feeling good.

As the plane landed, my heart rate began to increase. I convinced myself it was finally over and was ready to deal with the consequences. They had taken my fingerprints and photocopied my passport. I was sure they had also made a phone call to the U.S. Embassy just to make sure I wasn't who they thought I was. And if they called the embassy, all they had to do was inform the Japanese authorities that my name was really Anthony Caucci and that I was on the run from the FBI, DEA, Secret Service and a number of other law enforcement agencies and I was fucked...

When the plane landed, I decided to stay in my seat until everyone got off so I could enjoy every last minute of freedom. If they wanted me, they were going to have to come and get me. After the plane was completely empty, I looked down the aisle, waiting for the police to storm the plane. A stewardess came up from behind and said, "Sir, time to get off the plane."

"Oh, I'm sorry, I was just feeling a little nauseous from flying. Now that we have landed, I'm feeling much better."

My mind was racing. "No police? Impossible!" I figured they were hiding behind the corner and were going to tackle me as soon as I got off the plane.

I braced myself as I exited the plane into the tunnel. But nobody was there.

"This can't be!" I thought. "I'm the last passenger off the plane and all the other passengers are out of sight."

I walked down a very long corridor and turned the corner and... "FUUUUCK ME. I KNEW IT!"

Four Japanese police officers were standing thirty feet in front of me. I casually ignored them and kept on walking—right until I realized they were holding a poster sign with my fake name on it: "ANTHONY ZAMBRANA."

I didn't know what to do except remain calm and keep walking. When I got closer, one of them said, "Zambrana-san?" and did a small bow.

"Well," I thought, "I'm the last one off the plane and they do have a sign with my name on it. There's no way in hell I'll get past customs," so out loud I said, "Yes, that's me, what can I do for you?"

"Please follow us."

I wasn't in handcuffs, and they didn't seemed too concerned. They moved very fast through the crowds. Again my heart was pounding, and I had no clue what was going on, but I was preparing for an ambush. They took me to a counter in front of a very stern Japanese woman and spoke quickly in Japanese. The only thing I understood was my name. Finally, she looked at me and said, "Zambrana-san?"

"Yes, that's me. What can I do for you?"

"Please give me your passport, there's something urgent that was sent to the airport."

I knew my freedom would be gone in a matter of minutes. She quickly grabbed my passport and started plugging away at the computer. Behind her, an electronic printer started printing something out. I figured it was an arrest warrant. I still was surrounded by cops and hadn't cleared customs yet. There was nowhere for me to go.

When the printer stopped, she ripped the paper out and handed it to me.

I read it: "This is Smadar, please call me once you have arrived safely, I am worried about you."

Get the fuck outta here!

I looked at the officers, rolled my eyes, and said, "Women, you know?"

They bowed, said thank-you, and apologized for the inconvenience. Inside, I was in shock, but I still had to clear customs so had to stay calm. The line was huge, and I was afraid my nerves couldn't stand one more second. I got the attention of one of the police officers and pointed to the line at immigration and pointed to my watch. I said, "Long line. I'm going to be late for meeting…can you help me?"

He gave a quick nod, escorted me to the front of the line, and stood right next to me while I handed my passport to the immigration officer. The immigration officer put my information in the system, and in less than fifteen seconds he said, "Welcome to Japan."

The police officer bowed again and said, "Have a good day."

I could not believe it. I was in Japan, a free man. Once again I had been spared from being locked up for a very, very long time. I recounted all the times I had escaped arrest by the hairs on my ass and decided right there on the spot that this was the last airport I would ever go through. The next time I went through an airport, I was going to have to be in handcuffs.

Epilogue: Back in Business

Walking out of the airport, I couldn't believe I was once again a free man. But here I was, walking to the baggage claim, cutting through crowds of Japanese who all seemed to be walking very quickly but never cutting around each other. I followed arrows on the floor, letting me know which way to walk. It was a little strange for me because they walked on the opposites side.

Once I got my bag, I grabbed a taxi and headed for Roppongi. When the taxi driver opened the door, I noticed the price on the meter was 700 yen. I did some quick math and realized it cost $7 just to get in the taxi. Driving to Roppongi, I realized I was probably going to be stuck in another Asian hellhole for "the rest of my life." It beats the fuck out of life in a federal prison.

When I finally arrived at Hotel Ibis, I paid the grumpy prick of a driver, got out, and took a look around. I couldn't believe it. The bright lights of Roppongi glowed for miles in all directions. The streets were clean, and everything was lit with neon signs. The girls on the street were beautiful...and I don't just mean pretty, I mean really fucking beautiful and sexy and from all over the world (that girl Rachel in Taiwan was not bullshitting). There was club after club, with signs showing half-naked women...AND THE MUSIC?! Fuggetabouit! I hadn't heard techno like that in a long time.

I also saw what looked like drug deals going down in plain site on the corner and in alleyways, but I didn't think there was any way people would be so stupid. The streets were packed with guys scouting models and hostesses to work in their club, along with banging hot chicks in high heels and sexy dresses handing out flyers to people passing by.

People were laughing loudly...it looked like something out of a fucking movie. Roppongi was definitely not your typical Asian city, with fried insects, duck heads on sticks, and nasty smelling piles of garbage on the streets. It made Miami look like Disney World. I couldn't wait figure out how things worked. So I checked in to my hotel, had a quick shower, and walked outside. I walked behind a large group of well dressed, dark-suited, middle-aged businessmen. They drew all the attention, which allowed me to walk without being harassed by the scouts.

As I took the place in, I couldn't help smiling. It was electric crazy—everyone was there to party and make money. A guy got into my face. He was trying to get people to come into a hostess club called Casablanca. He was really in my face, but at the same time he was very polite and charismatic. He spoke very good English with a thick Nigerian accent. So I finally gave in.

"Okay, okay, stop with the bullshit. What's the deal?"

"Come into my club, we have the most beautiful girls in all of Japan."

"What's the cover charge?"

"Usually is 10,000 yen but I'll get you in for 7,000 because I like you."

"Wait...get da fuckouddahere. That's about $70. Those girls got platinum pussies or something?"

I started to walk away when I heard a girl laughing. I stopped, turned around, and saw a beautiful girl with long, wavy, jet-black hair and a body that looked like it was hand-crafted by God. She was talking to the Nigerian. I just stood there for a moment, staring at her as she sipped on an ice coffee while she leaned up against a wall. For a moment, everything around me seemed to go silent. Then she clapped her hands and snapped her fingers toward me and yelled, "Oy...you okay?"

I quickly snapped out of it and looked around to see if see was talking to me.

"You talking to me?"

"No, I'm talking to the fucking wombat on your shoulder."

For the first time in my life, I didn't know what to say. She had an unfamiliar but very sexy accent; she was a cocky but also looked like she was just having some fun. Then the Nigerian ran back over to me and said, "That's the type of girls that work in my club, come on in."

"She's hot, that's for sure, but I ain't paying $70 just to get in a club. Ain't no fucking way."

Then she yelled again, "Oy!" and waved me over.

So I played it cool and walked over to her. "What's up?"

"What's up with you? Why don't you go in the club?"

"I've never paid to get into a club."

"Oh really…who the fuck are you?"

"My name is Tony…and yours?"

"Rebecca."

"What's that accent you got?"

"I'm Australian. And I'm guessing you're A-MER-I-CAN."

"Why d'ya say that?"

"Because you guys don't know how to speak proper English."

"Well, I can barely understand half the shit you say."

"Didn't you go to school?"

"Well, Rebecca, it was nice to meet you. I like your style, but I gotta go now."

"You have to be somewhere, mate?"

"No, but I'm not paying to get into a club."

"Okay, that's fine." She grabbed my hand and walked me right in. When we passed the cashier, she said, "He's with me, put it down as a dohan."

She walked me over to a booth and we took a seat. There were about fifty beautiful girls in the club sitting at tables, drinking and talking with Japanese men. I checked out every single one of them, but Rebecca was the by far best looking one there. The waitress came over so I asked for a coke. Rebecca looked at me, leaned over, and whispered in my ear, "Pussy." Then she turned to the waitress and said, "He'll have a Chivas on the rocks, and I'll take a cranberry juice."

I immediately thought she was trying to get me drunk and run up a huge tab. But another part of me had a good feeling about her, and she seemed genuine. As the night went on, something happened to me. For the first time in my life, I was actually having a great time just sitting at a table drinking and talking with a girl. It was a great and sad feeling at the same time. Smadar was on her way from Taiwan, and there was no way I was going to make a move on Rebecca. I wanted to see her again, but I knew if I did I would fall for her. She was just too cool and fun.

As the night went on, she told me all about Japan and the club scene. I asked her how difficult it was to buy weed in Japan, just to feel her out. I knew she probably had all the answers to my questions, but I didn't want her to think I was some kind of junkie so I eased my way into it. She looked at me and said, "This is one big party town. There are more drugs in Roppongi than I have ever seen in my life. Most of the expats, strippers, and hostesses in this club are on coke every day, except for me. I don't touch the shit."

"Good for you, neither do I. It is fucking poison and will ruin your life."

But this was very interesting to me, and I immediately started wondering how difficult it would be to get coke into the country and how I could make connections.

"I have a friend coming into town tomorrow from Miami and likes to party a little. How much is a gram of coke?"

"It's fucking cheap here…only 15,000 yen."

"That's $150 per gram!"

"I told you it was cheap."

"Cheap?! In Miami it's $50 a gram."

"Are you kidding? It's $300 a gram in Australia and I heard it's garbage. You see those two guys sitting over there?" She pointed discretely. "They sell all the drugs in Roppongi. They are the only two in the city you can get anything from. They have this place locked down. The tall guy's name is Kami. He's Iranian. And the short, fat one with the long, curly hair is Ossy. He's Israeli."

"Wait…you're telling me a Jew and a camel jockey are running this whole town? They are supposed to hate each other." I couldn't believe what I was hearing. These two idiots were both dressed in black, with gold on their wrists, fingers, and necks. One of them had a diamond in his tooth. They were also fucking loud—I could hear everything they were saying even in a busy club. Kami, the tall one, was quoting scenes from the movie *Scarface*. I have to admit he sounded just like Al Pacino: "Ju wanna fuck wit' me, I kill evey last one of you cock-a-roaches."

"Why would anyone selling drugs want to attract so much attention to themselves?" I wondered. "He wouldn't last two minutes in Miami."

As the night went on, I kept thinking about my old days back in Miami, and I started having feelings for this girl I had just met only a few hours ago. It was getting late—I'd had too much to drink and I was afraid the bill was going to be outrageous. So I told Rebecca to ask for the bill. When the bill came, it was $500 just to sit down for a few hours to talk to a beautiful girl and have some drinks. What a fucking rip-off. But I knew I would get the money back as soon as Smadar started working, so I wasn't too pissed off. When I went to pay the bill, Rebecca said, "Wait," and opened her little purse and pulled out a wad of cash.

"It's on me."

"I can't let you pay the bill...get da fuck outta here."

"Really, it's okay. You're new here...I understand how it is. I felt the same way when I first arrived. But honestly, it was nice talking to you. I am so sick of sitting down night after night talking to these fucking perverted Japanese men. Five hundred dollars for three hours of sanity is well worth it. Besides, I have a regular that'll be coming in soon, and he's usually good for at least $3,000. So he's really the one paying the bill. The money here is crazy. It just comes and goes for most people, but I have plenty put away so don't worry about it."

"That's a first for me, Rebecca. Will you be here tomorrow?"

"Nope, I leave for Australia tomorrow night. I'll be back in a few months."

Hearing her say that hurt me and was a relief at the same time. Smadar was going to arrive the next day. And the last thing I needed was Rebecca on my mind.

When I got back to my hotel room, I laid down in the bed and thought about the entire night. I knew this was the place for me...then I started thinking about what Rebecca had told me about the price of coke and the two idiots who controlled the whole town. I sat up, grabbed the hotel telephone, and called Carlos.

"Hey, brother, it's me," I said when he answered.

"Holy shit, kid, where you at?"

"I'm in Japan, baby."

"No fucking way."

"Oh yeah, and you're not gonna believe what I just heard."

"What's that?"

"A hundred fifty a gram."

"Are you serious?"

"Have I ever bullshitted you, Carlos?"

"Not that I remember."

"You wanna do something?"

"At that price, damn right I wanna do something. Call me back tomorrow and I'll let you know how I will get it in. I have to make some calls."

"Okay, brother, let's get back to it."

I hung up the phone and thought: "I'm back in business."

Coming Soon!

Dying to know what happened next? Check in with us at www.anthony-caucci.com or our Amazon Author Central page (https://www.amazon.com/Anthony-Caucci/e/B0876F9ZWP) for updates on the anticipated release date of Book 2.

CPSIA information can be obtained
at www.ICGtesting.com
Printed in the USA
BVHW092119220122
626871BV00006B/403/J